THE TRANSFORMATIVE YEARS AT KANSAS STATE:

THE YEARS OF PRESIDENT JON WEFALD FROM 1986 TO 2009

Jon Wefald

Ag Press Publishing
Manhattan, Kansas

For Information:

AG Press
1531 Yuma
Manhattan, Kansas 66502
1.785.539.7558

Printed in the United States of America on acid-free paper.

ISBN 0-9894429-8-5

Cover Design and layout: Christine Goodmiller
Cover and Inside Photo Credits: Charlie Thomas
K-State Photographic Services

This book is dedicated to my dear wife, Ruth Ann Wefald, who has played an extraordinary role in any success I had in my years at K-State and to my two outstanding sons, Skipp and Andrew and their families.

Contents

Acknowledgments

In the early spring of 2010, I met with President Kirk Schulz about writing a book on the history of Kansas State—with a major emphasis on my years as president from 1986 to 2009. President Schulz was very supportive of my project to write a history of our school. There had been no history of Kansas State since 1975. I also want to thank him for providing a research assistant for the first two years of the project.

I want to thank so much three people who helped make the publication of my new book possible. I want to thank Paul Edgerley, a senior advisor for Bain Capital in Boston, Massachusetts, Mike Goss, the CFO for Sotheby's in New York City, and Terry Matlack, the managing director of Tortoise Capital Advisors in Leawood, Kansas. All three business leaders are K-Staters and I will always be grateful for their support.

For the first two years, I did considerable research and reading about the history of Kansas State—including my 23 years. My research assistant was David Vail, who was a doctoral candidate in history at the time and who now has his Ph.D. David analyzed a multitude of research and historical materials, including area newspapers, in the Hale Library Archives. I also want to thank Anthony Crawford, an associate professor in the Hale Library, for his help in the library archives.

I started writing the first draft in 2010 and 2011. The first draft took over a year and it was over 700 pages. Over the next four years, I sharply edited my manuscript at least ten different times. I had excellent help from a number of people in reading several of my earlier drafts.

I want to thank my readers for providing excellent suggestions and criticisms. Most of my readers were people who worked with me over 23 years. They include Provost Jim Coffman, Vice President for Administration Tom Rawson, Associate Vice Provost for Information Technology Beth Unger, Chief of Staff Charles Reagan, Dean of Education Mike Holen, Associate Athletic Director Jim Epps, Professor of Psychology Jerry Frieman, and Professor of Education Bob Shoop—along with people like the former Chancellor of KU, Gene Budig, and four former members of the Board of Regents, Nelson Galle and Jerry Boettcher from Manhattan, and Clay Blair from Olathe and Dick Bond from Overland Park.

I also want to thank Charles Thomas, the Senior Associate Athletic Director for Facilities, and the author of a great photography book on Kansas State entitled A SPOT THAT I LOVE FULL WELL published in 2008. I also want to thank the Kansas State University Office of Photographic Services and its Director, Tommy Theis. Charles Thomas and Tommy Theis both provided me with extraordinary and beautiful photos of new buildings, new entrance gates, new athletic facilities, Landon Lecture speakers, and photos of the devastating June 11, 2008 F-2 tornado that hit our campus.

I am very thankful for the excellent work of three leaders at Ag Press in Manhattan, Kansas. Tom Carlin, President, Christine Goodmiller, the Graphic Artist, and Kevin Macy, the Proofreader, all provided outstanding advice and leadership in the production of my new book.

I want to thank several of my assistants in the president's office over the years. Dana Hastings worked as my administrative assistant from 1993 to 2009. Dana was committed to excellence in every way. Michelle Broccolo was an outstanding events coordinator and administrative assistant for Chuck Reagan.

Finally, I want to thank Monica Strathman, the Business Manager for Leadership Studies, and Dorothy Smith, Administrative Assistant in Leadership Studies, for providing invaluable assistance and help on my various drafts in the past several years. I also want to thank Charles Appelseth, Information Technology Consultant, in the Hale Library for helping me make sure my computer always worked well.

Preface

Preface

WHY I BECAME INTERESTED IN APPLYING FOR THE JOB OF KANSAS STATE UNIVERSITY PRESIDENT IN 1986

On June 25, 1985, Kansas State President Duane Acker announced that he would be retiring on June 30, 1986. Ruth Ann and I and our two sons, Skipp and Andy, were living in North Oaks, Minnesota. I was the Chancellor of the Minnesota State University System. It included seven state universities with an enrollment of over 50,000 students. I liked the job.

Our family loved Minnesota. I had not considered leaving the state. After receiving a Ph.D from the University of Michigan in 1965, I was appointed an Assistant Professor of History at Gustavus Adolphus College. It was a good Swedish Lutheran college in the small town of St. Peter, Minnesota.

After five years at Gustavus Adolphus, the new Governor, Wendell Anderson, appointed me the Commissioner of Agriculture for Minnesota in December of 1970. I had run for statewide office in 1970 for the position of state auditor. I also lost a race for Congress in the 2nd Congressional District in 1968.

My interest in politics can be traced to my grandfather, Knud Wefald, who was one of the founders of the Minnesota Farmer-Labor Party in 1922 and a member of Congress in the 7th district from 1923 to 1927. After losing those two contests in 1968 and 1970, I never thought about running for a political office ever again.

Meanwhile, I learned a lot about Minnesota and American politics in running for office twice and, more important, I learned a great deal about working with an incredible variety of people in a multitude of occupations. Indeed, I learned so much about people and their attitudes in those two campaigns that they represent for me the equivalent of a MA degree in human relations—experiences that would help me down the road no matter what I ended up doing.

Led by the former Vice President, Hubert Humphrey, for the U.S. Senate seat, and Wendell Anderson for Governor, my assigned role for the Democratic Farmer-Labor statewide ticket in 1970 was to speak out for the state's farmers.

With all of that in mind, Anderson believed I would make a good Commissioner of Agriculture. The factor of "good luck" was the major reason I was selected. I was in the right place at the right time. Wendy Anderson was a risk taker. He became one of the state's greatest Governors.

When I came to St. Paul in early January of 1971, I discovered the Department of Agriculture was a major cabinet agency with over 400 state employees. For the first time, I learned about good leadership practices. As a Gustavus Adolphus history professor, I had not even supervised a secretary. As the new commissioner at age 32, I had no choice: I had to rely on the agency's veteran staff.

I soon learned if I trusted these department heads, they would do an even better job. *Because I had no choice, I adopted the practice of delegation of authority and empowerment. This theory of management guided me for the rest of my career.* From 1971 to 1977, I found that the strategy of empowerment worked very well.

Early in 1977, I read that Southwest State University in Marshall, Minnesota was in desperate need of a new president. Because I had never been an academic department head, a dean, or a provost, I doubted whether I would be competitive. And I recognized that Southwest faced daunting challenges.

Founded in 1966, the Southwest State faculty and administration soon became embroiled in many serious academic and political disagreements. The enrollment fell badly after 1971. A number of faculty and staff members were retrenched. From 1970 to 1976, the infighting between the administration and the faculty increasingly divided the school and the community.

The Vietnam War, moreover, exacerbated the divisions between the school's administration and its faculty. The divide became so bad that a number of prominent state legislators issued dire warnings in 1975 and 1976 that they might very well shut the school down.

Not just anyone would take on this job. Many city leaders and faculty members believed that Southwest needed a skilled administrator and a unique political leader with academic credentials. A history professor, David Nass, called me to say no one could save his school. His message was blunt: Forget it Jon—even you cannot turn Southwest State around.

I thought I could. I believed I could regain the support of the people in southwestern Minnesota. I knew the job would be a high risk/high reward opportunity. I got the job mainly because I was confident that I could turn the university around.

When I became the president, I knew that a number of legislators still wanted to close it down. It faced stiff challenges, maybe even impossible ones. There were few people in Marshall or on campus that exuded optimism about the school's future. It had lost the support of many citizens in the southwestern part of the state.

By July and August of 1977, I had not come up with any solutions for the enrollment decline. I was worried. Moreover, as I looked around the campus, I saw that regional offices from a number of state agencies were occupying a vast amount of the vacant space in two buildings. That spoke volumes about the school's future.

Two presidents had failed to halt the enrollment decline. Sometimes, one event can get your attention. I had received an invitation in early September from the Ivanhoe High School Superintendent to give a pep talk to their students. It was a town 20 miles west of Marshall. In driving back, it hit me. I had just talked to the entire Ivanhoe High School student body.

In an a-ha moment, I came up with a high-risk game plan to solve the enrollment crisis. I decided to speak to high school students in every town on every highway leading out of Marshall in every direction for up to 90 miles. There were over 95 high schools in that region of the state. I would have to do it myself. I would have to personally call every school superintendent.

The game plan involved a bit of chutzpah. I would personally call the high school superintendents of those high schools. I would ask each superintendent if they would like me to stop by and give a talk to their high school students on the values of higher education. I soon found out their answer.

Every superintendent was positive. Indeed, every one said that I could have a full 50-minute period to talk about the importance of post-secondary education for their students. In the next 7 months, virtually every high school leader told me that no college president had ever called to talk to their students.

Between September of 1977 and March of 1978, I gave talks in 94 high schools all over southwestern and western Minnesota. I doubt that any university president has ever done anything like this. It was a high-risk strategy—because I would be off campus in my first year for about two-thirds of the time.

In those seven months, I talked to thousands of high school students in that region of the state. During that same period, I also gave speeches to well over 90 civic groups in the region at a noon lunch or at a dinner.

The enrollment of new freshmen at Southwest State went up by over 30 per cent in the fall of 1978. I learned a great deal from my unorthodox strategy. For any future job, I learned I might have to take calculated risks or take a road that was seldom traveled.

Today, Southwest State is recognized as an excellent regional university in Minnesota. In May of 2007, I was invited by the president to give the commencement talk and receive an honorary doctorate at the school's graduation.

The day before, a former editor for the MARSHALL INDEPENDENT, and now the SMSU Director of Communications, Jim Tate, wrote in the Marshall paper about my years as the school's president: "Mention the name Jon Wefald around campus and things stop.

There's a hushed reverence when people talk about the man: Jon Wefald. The guy who saved Southwest Minnesota State University."[1]

In 1982, the Minnesota State University System was looking for a new Chancellor. It included seven state universities—Mankato State, St. Cloud State, Moorhead State, Winona State, Bemidji State, Metropolitan State, and Southwest State. I thought there was no way a president from the smallest state university in the system would have a chance. I applied anyway.

After five years at Southwest State, I had a deep appreciation of the challenges facing the state university system. I was selected for the job unanimously. It was one of the two most important public higher education jobs in the state of Minnesota. We moved from Marshall to North Oaks. I was a happy camper. It was the best job I ever had.

I was thinking how lucky I was. I had been a C student in Minot High School in Minot, North Dakota. My 12th grade English teacher, Ann Ackerman, had looked me in the eye and declared that I should never go on to college. She said I was not smart enough. Several of my high school teachers tried to convince me to become a clerk in one of the town's department stores.

It was now 1982. I had received a Ph.D in history from the University of Michigan; I had been a good professor of history at Gustavus Adolphus College for five years. I had successfully managed the Minnesota Department of Agriculture for six and one-half years. And I had turned around the fortunes of Southwest Minnesota State University in five years.

Now I was the Chancellor of Minnesota's State University System of 50,000 students. My main job was to represent the 7 universities in the state legislature. I was on a first name basis with Governor Rudy Perpich, his Chief of Staff, Terry Montgomery, and most of the state's key state legislative leaders. I met with them quite often.

I had to pinch myself. I had gotten to know quite well the other six state university presidents. I never considered a policy of micromanagement of the seven state universities. Rather, I continued my policy of delegating authority to all seven CEOs. The nine members of the Minnesota State University Board were exceptional. Indeed, it was a great Board that absolutely practiced empowerment.

The three words—Kansas State University—had never entered my mind. In the fall of 1985, Dr. Jerry Frieman, an associate professor in the department of psychology at K-State, was selected as the Chair of the Kansas State Presidential Search Committee.

The Kansas Board of Regents had appointed a large search committee. Frieman sent me a letter in the fall of 1985 asking me if I had any interest. I had none.

In December of 1985, Frieman called me. He convinced me to reconsider. Frieman frankly explained the challenges facing the new K-State President: it suffered from a poor image; it was often called the "cow college;" its enrollment was declining; it had poor relations with the governor and state legislators; and it had a horrible football program. Those were just a few of his comments.

Most presidents might have been turned off by this kind of bluntness. I was just the opposite. His conversation reminded me almost exactly of what I was told about Southwest State in 1977. Few wanted that job either. Whenever anyone told me a job was impossible, I brushed it off. Rather, I thought that K-State might be another "high risk/high reward" kind of position.

I even came to believe I had the perfect credentials for Kansas State—a Ph.D in the liberal arts from Michigan and six years experience as Minnesota's Commissioner of Agriculture. I told Ruth Ann I could do the job. From 1980 to 1986, I knew that K-State's enrollment had plummeted. It reminded me of Southwest State.

Unlike Southwest, however, K-State was a statewide land grant university. It had agricultural offices in every county. It had thousands of alums prepared to lift every stone to advance the school. I knew that I could meet this enrollment challenge head-on. I had been there and done that.

I could argue the jobs I had after 1971 would help me to do the job of K-State President. I had taken a sleepy Department of Agriculture in Minnesota in 1971 and made it into a major state department.

I had transformed the image and standing of Southwest State from 1977 to 1982. I had been a good chancellor of seven state universities in Minnesota with 50,000 students from 1982 to 1986.

The search committee invited me to an airport interview in Kansas City. I met with three of the committee's members on Tuesday, January 21, 1986. The first interview went well. A month later, I was one of nine individuals selected for a second interview on Monday, February 24 at the Hyatt Regency in Kansas City. My wife, Ruth Ann, was with me for that interview.

In March of 1986, the Kansas Board of Regents narrowed the search to three candidates. In addition to me, the other two finalists were Charles Sidman, the Dean of the College of Arts and Sciences at the University of Florida, and John Campbell, the Dean of Agriculture at the University of Illinois.

In his book entitled THE OUTLIERS: THE STORY OF SUCCESS, Malcom Gladwell quotes a neurologist by the name of Daniel Levitin on success. Levitin said that researchers came to believe that the "magical" number for becoming an expert at anything is to practice for 10,000 hours.[2]

Gladwell used the example of the famous British singing foursome, the Beatles. Before they appeared on the Ed Sullivan Show on February 9, 1964, the Beatles had practiced their music in places like Liverpool and Hamburg, Germany for ten years. By February 9, 1964, the Beatles had exceeded the rule of 10,000 hours. In their first national appearance on American TV, they became overnight sensations.

As Commissioner of Agriculture, President of Southwest State, and Chancellor of the Minnesota State University System over 15 years, I had given countless speeches in almost every town. I had appeared many times in front of legislative committees. I had given interviews to hundreds of radio and TV stations. I had been interviewed for the nightly CBS national news several times—meaning that I had passed the 10,000 hours rule long ago.

On Friday, March 21, 1986, the Board of Regents interviewed Ruth Ann and me. That afternoon, I received a call from the Chair of the Board of Regents, Sandra McMullen, offering me the job. I accepted the job as the new President. Our family, including our two sons, Skipp and Andy, were now looking forward to moving to Manhattan, Kansas on July 1, 1986.

Introduction

A BRIEF HISTORY OF KANSAS STATE FROM 1863 TO 1986

Introduction

A BRIEF HISTORY OF KANSAS STATE FROM 1863 TO 1986

I heard many stories about the history of Kansas State during my years as president. In doing research after I retired, I realized the challenges I faced after July 1, 1986 were far more serious than I had imagined. In reading history books about Kansas State from 1863 to 1986, I came to understand why our school lagged so badly in the national rankings of land grant universities from World War II to the present.

My research on the earlier history of Kansas State revealed some stunning news. Four of the first five presidents had been fired between 1873 and 1909. They were summarily dismissed because all four had pressed the school's Board of Regents to embrace more programs in the liberal arts and classical studies.

I was shocked something like this could happen in the school's early years. For 23 years, my office was in a building named after its second president, John Anderson.

Although he was only the president from 1873 to 1879, John Anderson had set Kansas State firmly on a course for decades to be essentially a vocational institute. It was a mission that persisted for almost three-quarters of a century until Milton Eisenhower became president in 1943.

JOHN ANDERSON'S MISSION FOR KANSAS STATE

During his six years as president, John Anderson implemented his incredibly strict mission for this new Kansas State College: one, to emphasize academic programs in agriculture and the mechanic arts; and two, to de-emphasize programs in the liberal arts and classical studies. Anderson's narrow mission lasted for over seven decades.

Few people today recall that Kansas State had its own Board of Regents from 1863 to 1913. During much of this era, stern and unyielding farmer members dominated this new land grant college board. Over the next forty years, these regents elected to rigidly interpret the meaning of the 1862 Morrill Land Grant Act. For decades, a healthy majority of regents agreed with Anderson's central mantra—that the new college essentially existed to train farmers and mechanics.

KU CHARTED A RADICALLY DIFFERENT MISSION

Meanwhile, 90 miles down the road, the University of Kansas and its own Board of Regents were charting a course to emulate Ivy League schools like Harvard, Yale, and Princeton. From 1875 to 1901, Chancellors James Marvin, Joshua Lippincott, and Francis Snow underscored KU's central mission to be a rigorous, diverse, comprehensive, and scholarly academic institution.

These three Kansas Chancellors declared their university should have a great library, hire excellent research scholars and teachers, and celebrate the importance of the liberal arts.

Elite land grant colleges like Purdue, Ohio State, Iowa State, Cornell, Texas A&M, and Michigan State also promoted programs in agriculture and the mechanic arts. However, in contrast to Kansas State, these colleges aspired to become more comprehensive, modern, and diverse from the late 19th century on.

These up and coming land grant colleges fixed to be excellent in the sciences and the liberal arts. From the late 19th century, the nation's best land grants were becoming more research based, more comprehensive, building impressive libraries, hiring top-notch scholars, and offering a liberal arts curriculum. However, Kansas State was moving in quite another direction.

Kansas State's progress in becoming a highly ranked land grant college had been severely stifled by the college's second president, John Anderson. In fact, the college's mission did not fundamentally change until Milton Eisenhower became Kansas State's President in 1943—when he started mandating major new programs in the sciences and the liberal arts.

By World War II, the Kansas State Agricultural College had slipped far behind its counterpart 90 miles down the road. It also had lost serious ground to major land grant colleges like Iowa State, Purdue, Michigan State, Ohio State, Texas A&M, and Cornell.

In his history of Kansas State published in 1977, James Carey wrote about this new land grant college established in July of 1863. Under the Morrill Land Grant Act passed in 1862, Carey explains that the original mission of the new land grant colleges was "to benefit agriculture and the mechanic arts and to promote the liberal and practical education of the industrial classes in the several pursuits and professions in life."[3]

On July 23, 1863, the Reverend Joseph Denison was picked as the first President. The new college had one building, a small faculty, and several thousand books in its library. At the end of Denison's ten years, only 15 students had graduated. The highest number of students for any one semester was 125 students. In 1871, ten students were enrolled in agricultural classes. Ironically, 14 were enrolled in literature classes. The majority of faculty members were scholars in the arts and the classics.

During the ten years that Joseph Denison was President of Kansas State, the school accented the liberal arts and classical studies. But academic programs in agriculture and the mechanic arts were also an important and integral part of the curriculum.

Even though Joseph Denison was president for ten years, the future direction of the college was quite uncertain. Adding to that uncertainty, a new farm movement in Kansas appeared. It was called the Grange. Increasingly, its farm leaders and members focused their attention on the little land grant college in Manhattan.

AN IMPORTANT NEW FARM MOVEMENT: THE GRANGE

By the late 1860's and early 1870's, the Grange was becoming an influential farm organization. The Grangers developed a keen interest in Kansas State. In his 1909 book, J.D. Walters stressed the implications of this new farm movement: "The farmers began to interest themselves in political, sociological, and educational matters. Their 'school' in Manhattan was investigated and the conclusion was reached that it required a change of policy. . .The horny-handed Grangers and their political leaders finally agreed that 'something' should be done to fulfill its evident mission."[4]

By 1872, the Grange leaders were firmly committed to changing the land grant mission of Kansas State. The decisions of this new farm movement triggered a paradigm shift for this new college in Manhattan. The truth is this—no farm organization and no political party in the state's history has ever had a greater impact on the future course of Kansas State. The school would not recover from their collective actions for many, many decades.

THE HISTORIC DECISIONS OF JOHN ANDERSON

On September 1, 1873, President Joseph Denison was "handed" his walking papers. The Board of Regents, which included influential Grange members, decided that John Anderson, who was a preacher, journalist, and politician in Junction City, should be the school's new president.

Regent N.A. Adams, a major Grange champion, asked John Anderson to study how the college could become more closely integrated with agricultural and mechanical coursework. In his response to Regent Adams, Anderson declared "that he would bust (the new college) from stem to gudgeon." Regent Adams replied: "You are the man we are looking for."[5]

Over his six years as president, John Anderson played hardball. It was his way or else. Indeed, Anderson accumulated more power and influence than any president in the history of Kansas State. Knowing that he and the regents were in lock step, the new president immediately demanded the college stop teaching the classics like Greek and Latin Studies and many courses in the arts and sciences.

Two days after becoming president, John Anderson abruptly required the school's faculty to submit to the regents three new "courses of study": the first program was for students who desired to be farmers; the second was for students who wanted to be skilled workmen and artisans; and the third was for "young ladies" who would be trained in household economics.[6]

The Kansas State Agricultural College was one of the first two land grant colleges to be organized under the 1862 Morrill Land Grant Act. The legislation passed in the middle of the Civil War accented the importance of teaching "such branches of learning as are related to agriculture and the mechanic arts."

The act also stated that these programs should not exclude scientific and classical studies. Importantly, the legislation prescribed state legislatures to steadfastly promote "the liberal and practical education of the industrial classes in the several pursuits and professions in life."

THREE KANSAS STATE PRESIDENTS WERE FIRED AFTER 1879

The three presidents who followed John Anderson after 1879 discovered a hard truth. If you were not totally on board with his educational world-view, you would be dismissed. Anderson's legacy led to the firing of three presidents down the road: President George Fairchild in 1897; President Thomas Will in 1899; and President Ernest Nichols in 1909. President Anderson had cast a dark shadow on Kansas State that would last for decades.[7]

Although all three presidents collided with John Anderson's academic philosophy, it was Ernest R. Nichols who was victimized the most by his legacy. Nichols was selected as president in 1899.

A year later, the program in mechanics was replaced by engineering. Then, in 1901, Kansas State and KU began quarreling on funding for the emerging program of engineering. James Carey reported on this growing feud: "As early as 1906, the leaders on Mt. Oread considered Kansas State's development in engineering as a real challenge to the University's 'pre-eminence in engineering.'"[8]

The KU Chancellor, Frank Strong, asked the state legislature for $200,000 for a new engineering building. President Ernest Nichols followed suit by requesting $100,000 for a new engineering building in Manhattan. Strong became furious with Nichols. In a nasty turn of events, Nichols was stunned when he was also severely criticized by several members of his own Kansas State College Board of Regents for downgrading the school's agricultural programs.

While KU received an appropriation of $200,000 for its new engineering building, Kansas State had to settle for $80,000 for its building. Even with this disparity in funding, Chancellor Strong remained bitter with Kansas State and Nichols: "I hope that all friends of the University are going to keep in mind the contest which is sure to come before long with the Agricultural College. This is the only dark cloud that hangs over the future of the University, and it presents a very difficult challenge."[9]

Ramping up his negative rhetoric, Frank Strong insisted that Kansas State's engineering program "should restrict itself to training in the mechanic arts in the limited sense of occupations in which operators are given skill in following the designs prepared by others, while the University should be left the training of those who originate designs through the higher imagination and creative powers, this constituting the work of an engineer."[10]

With more than a touch of hubris, the KU Chancellor reminded legislators in the state "the cow college"should restrict itself to vocational programs. In Strong's mind, KU should be the "only" school that graduates engineers who design big things like factories, buildings, bridges, and power plants. Strong could just as well have directly quoted John Anderson that Kansas State should restrict its mission to agriculture and the mechanic arts.

For President Nichols, it only got worse. Governor Edward W. Hoch sided with KU's Chancellor that Kansas State should be a "great agricultural school" while KU should be a "great university." Edwin Taylor, a Kansas State Regent, delivered a stinging rebuke to Ernest Nichols by sending a petition to the State Senate "asking that body to consider placing restrictions on engineering work at Manhattan while limiting the courses there primarily to the realm of agriculture."

Adding insult to injury, F.D. Colburn, Secretary of the State Board of Agriculture and a former Kansas State Regent, summed up his feelings about President Nichols with these harsh comments: Kansas State "had been without a president for the past ten years" and he "was not fitted for the place."[11]

At a Board of Regents meeting on March 21, 1908, Regent Edwin Taylor moved that a committee of three regents start looking for a new president. I seriously doubt that any Kansas State president in history has ever been treated worse by a governing board.

Still, Nichols ended his presidency with no rancor. He was a quintessential gentleman and an outstanding academic leader. President Ernest Nichols left his school a much better place than he found it in 1899. He will always be regarded as an outstanding Kansas State President.

On July 1, 1909, Henry Jackson Waters became the next president of Kansas State. Like many of Nichols' critics, the KU Chancellor became a big backer of Henry Waters. After the Kansas State Regents picked Waters, Frank Strong was quoted as saying "that the two schools would now enter into an era of good feeling."

In two surrealistic decisions, Waters invited Chancellor Strong to give a major speech at his inauguration. In 1909, Waters then awarded the KU chancellor an honorary LL.D degree to help cement this new era.

Many Kansas State faculty members were outraged by President Waters' recognition of Frank Strong. Faculty members recalled that the KU Chancellor had proclaimed Kansas State to be a "peculiar institution" because it offered three different kinds of work: "elementary-school courses such as reading, writing, spelling, and arithmetic; high school work in such subjects such as algebra, bookkeeping. . ." and "even pretended to offer graduate study. . .that might rightfully come in a high school course."

Chancellor Strong even insisted that Kansas State College's prized BS degree in Agriculture "was merely a cheap degree." If Twitter had existed in 1909, there would have been a million angry tweets from Kansas State alumni.[12]

THE THREE PRESIDENTS FROM 1909 TO 1942 MAINLY ADHERED TO THE POLICIES OF PRESIDENT JOHN ANDERSON

Despite the elimination of separate Boards of Regents for the University of Kansas and Kansas State College in 1913, Presidents Henry J. Waters, William M. Jardine, and Francis D. Farrell continued the academic priorities of President Anderson from 1913 to 1943.

In 1913, the state legislature passed a law discontinuing the separate Boards of Regents for the two schools and the Emporia Normal School Board. This new arrangement set up a Board of Administration to exercise the powers of the former boards.

In the 1925 legislative session, Governor Ben S. Paulen signed legislation on March 7, 1925 setting up a new Board of Regents. Nine member regents would be appointed by the governor and would be given rotating four-year terms. The Board of Regents became the governing board for KU, Kansas State, and the teachers colleges at Emporia, Hays, and Pittsburg. This Board of Regents has lasted to the present.[13]

From 1913 to 1943, Presidents Henry Waters, William Jardine, and Francis Farrell led Kansas State almost as if they reported to the same old Kansas State Board of Regents—meaning that our school had three presidents in a row that closely followed John Anderson's view of the college as mainly a technical-vocational institute.

Years before Francis Farrell became president in 1925, a multitude of faculty members had demanded a Bachelor of Arts degree with no success. On May 4, 1925, the faculty in the humanities and social sciences met to back the creation of a new Bachelor of Arts degree.

Declaring that this would never happen on his watch, President Farrell's reply was swift: "This College would not offer a B.A. degree unless conditions change. The fundamental mission of this school is not to cater to the largest number of students, but to promote the hardest educational ideal in the world—the combination of vocation and culture."[14]

James Carey penned these words about the state's land grant college: "Until the Second World War, Kansas State was still a small somewhat parochial college which basically emphasized only agriculture, engineering, home economics, and veterinary medicine."[15]

For the first forty years of the 20th century, Kansas State College Presidents seldom mentioned words like comprehensive, modern, basic research, and the liberal arts. Kansas State College continued to fall further behind KU and the best land grant universities in America. For the future of Kansas State, there is no question that catching up would be incredibly difficult.

UNDER PRESIDENTS EISENHOWER, MCCAIN, AND ACKER KANSAS STATE GAINED IN ACADEMIC PRESTIGE

When Kansas State College selected Milton S. Eisenhower as its ninth president in May of 1943, the school experienced major changes. From his first day, Eisenhower knew that his school was far behind the best land grant colleges.

Milton's inaugural address was broadcast nationally on September 30, 1943. The new president was crystal clear—Kansas State had to become more modern, more diverse, and more comprehensive and it had to embrace the arts and sciences.

Eisenhower was articulate, intelligent, and knowledgeable. He was the first native Kansan and the first graduate of Kansas State to be its president. While his brother Dwight was leading the Allied Forces in Europe, Milton had spent several years as the assistant director of the Office of War Information in Washington D.C.

Milton was an inveterate reader. He had become an expert on world issues. It is doubtful that any president in the history of Kansas State ever understood the people of Kansas better than Milton Eisenhower.

The Eisenhower Administration kicked off early in 1944 a planning process that would alter the academic programming of Kansas State College for years to come. Milton decided to chair the general Committee on Post-War Planning because he was determined to accomplish one overriding goal—to liberalize the entire curriculum.

According to Stephen Ambrose and Richard H. Immerman in their book on Milton Eisenhower, he always "had the zeal of a reformer." Faculty members in the arts and sciences knew they had the unequivocal support of the college's president.[16]

Since 1863, Kansas State presidents and its regents had many debates about the meaning of the Morrill Land Grant Act. James Carey summed up Milton's world-view: "Eisenhower's philosophy of education for the twentieth century was a rejection of the narrow interpretation of John A. Anderson's ideals. Eisenhower's liberal views were in keeping with the broader interpretation of the Morrill land-grant wording which had provided for an education that was both liberal and practical."[17]

After Eisenhower left Kansas State to become the president of Penn State in 1950, every succeding president has embraced the centrality of the liberal arts for the college and the need to be comprehensive. Milton Eisenhower was one of Kansas State's greatest presidents.

The Kansas Board of Regents started a national search for a new president. The regents selected the forty-two-year-old president of the University of Montana, James A. McCain. He was the first president to argue Kansas State should become more of a research institution.

In his 1960's report to the faculty, McCain noted that the school's research funding had increased from $4 million in 1960 to over $10 million by 1970. The number of graduate students had increased from 749 graduate students in 1950 to 1517 in 1960. During the 1950's, ten new departments were authorized to grant the Ph.D degree. By 1961, Kansas State had 24 departments offering doctoral degrees.[18]

During the McCain years, new academic programs were set up in restaurant management, nuclear engineering, and industrial engineering. A new Department of Biochemistry was created. By 1963, the school had over 8,000 students and 1300 faculty and staff members.

In 1959, the state legislature changed the name of Kansas State College of Agriculture and Applied Science to the Kansas State University of Agriculture and Applied Science.[19] James McCain was determined to broaden the mission of Kansas State. Like Eisenhower, McCain insisted the college should become more diverse and modern by expanding programs in the liberal arts.

President McCain's counterpart for most of his time was one of KU's greatest leaders, Chancellor Franklin Murphy. In his history of KU, Clifford Griffin wrote that the University of Kansas had become by 1960 "a modern American state university that had outrun its founders' rosiest dreams. It had nine professional schools and an undergraduate college, a library of 1,100,000 volumes, impressive laboratories, over 100 buildings, 15,000 students, and almost 1,000 faculty, many of them professionally eminent. Taken together, it was one of the greater glories of the Sunflower State."[20]

There is no doubt on this score: President James McCain dramatically improved every facet of the university, including huge increases in enrollment, upgrading the scholarship and research of the faculty, improving the school's private giving, and constructing many new buildings for the university over 25 years. James McCain will be remembered as one of Kansas State University's best presidents.

Duane C. Acker became the next president of Kansas State on July 1, 1975. Like many of our presidents, Acker came from an agricultural background. Growing up on a farm near Atlantic, Iowa, he received his B.S. degree in animal science from Iowa State University in 1952 and his Ph.D in animal science from Oklahoma State University in 1957.

Later, Acker became the Associate Dean of Agriculture at Kansas State, the Dean of Agriculture and Director of Extension at South Dakota State University, and the Vice President of Agriculture and Natural Resources at the University of Nebraska. Duane had a 1929 Model A Ford. A Kansas State friend, John Krider, said this car fit him "well" and, like the 1929 automobile, the 11th president of Kansas State was "solid, reliable, and uncomplicated."[21]

Few presidents ever had a better grasp of the role of agriculture in American life and its relevance for the nation's land grant colleges. In his 1975 state of the university address, President Acker spoke about the importance of research at Kansas State. In addition to supporting an expanded research mission, he also wanted a vibrant program in the liberal arts. He was pleased that Kansas State's extramural funding had increased from $8 million in 1975 to $20 million in 1986.[22]

Many excellent things happened during Duane Acker's 11 years. In his good 2010 book entitled TWO AT A TIME, he mentions a number of them. The new buildings constructed included Durland Hall, funds for Rathbone Hall, the third building of the Veterinary Complex, the King International Center, the Peters Recreation Complex, the Weber Hall addition, Bluemont Hall, the first part of Throckmorton Hall, and the funds to build the Bramlage Basketball Arena. During his 11 years, 12 students won the Fulbright scholarship; 9 students won the Truman scholarship; and 3 won the Rhodes scholarship.[23]

Before leaving after 11 years, President Duane Acker had some thoughtful parting words: "As I review our own plans and the processes of our thoughts that led to these plans, they illustrate our philosophy that life is a relatively long journey over a maze of roadways. This maze provides options for many turns, many hills and valleys, and many vistas. There are many flowers and a few thornbushes along the road, and many people line the road. Each of these provides opportunity for acquaintance, interaction, pleasure, challenge, and satisfaction."[24]

Under the leadership of Presidents Eisenhower, McCain, and Acker, Kansas State was becoming a more comprehensive, diverse, research based, and modern university. From 1943 to 1986, there were large number of new buildings constructed—including the building of a new basketball arena in 1950 and a new football stadium in 1968. The campus was transformed. The school's basketball program became a national powerhouse between 1950 and 1986.

During these 43 years, student enrollment increased dramatically. The quality of both undergraduate and graduate students improved sharply. Kansas State's research programs were upgraded and improved. Research funding was increased. A number of new Ph.D programs were implemented. Private giving became a higher priority in the 1950's. During the era of Presidents Eisenhower, McCain, and Acker, Kansas State was becoming recognized as an important national land-grant university.

A SUMMARY OF THE YEARS FROM 1863 TO 1986

From 1863 to 1986, Kansas State had eleven presidents. Four of the first five presidents were fired. It would be difficult to find another land-grant school in the nation where something like this happened. One of those first five presidents, John Anderson, had the biggest impact of any president in the history of Kansas State.

Anderson spoke loudly and carried a big stick. His mission became the mission of Kansas State for seven decades—namely, that the land grant college in Manhattan should be a vocational-technical institute that trained farmers and mechanics.

Despite the many positive and important changes from 1943 to 1986, Kansas State still had arguably fallen at least a generation behind the University of Kansas in library holdings, research and extramural funding, private giving, and national academic rankings.

In my first several years as K-State's president, I often wondered why so many K-Staters seemed to have a kind of "Avis" mentality—a mind-set of our school either being in second place and always trying to catch up—or being one step away from a disaster of one kind or another. Many worried that their alma mater would remain in second place behind their rival 90 miles down the road.

From 1875 to 1901, KU Chancellors James Marvin, Joshua Lippincott, and Francis Snow had one major goal: to emulate schools in the Ivy League. In 1900, the Ivy League colleges led the way in founding the nationally elite Association of American Universities (AAU). Today, there are 61 research universities with memberships in the AAU—59 in the United States and two in Canada.

The goal of the three late 19th century KU chancellors paid off in just a few years when their school was selected in 1909 to become a member of the AAU. In 1932, KU became a charter member of the Association of Research Libraries (ARL). By the 1920's, KU had a national-class library and an excellent art museum. KU had also developed a nationally ranked medical school and law school. The center of their campus was called Mt. Oread. KU had arguably become the "Harvard of the Middle West" long before 1945.

Given the history of our school for the first 75 years, I now find it easier to understand why Kansas State has fared so poorly in various national academic rankings since 1945. It would be almost impossible for any major land grant university today to make up for 75 years of being a vocational-technical institute.

After I came to Kansas State in 1986, I realized our university had no chance of becoming a member of the Association of American Universities (AAU). I found out that K-State was the only university in the Big 8 not a member of the Association of Research Libraries (ARL). And I also discovered that K-State was the only school in the Big 8 without an art museum.

Many of our sports fans would probably emphasize far more the standing of our mediocre football program for decades. These many facets of Kansas State's history from 1863 to 1986 help explain why a sense of confidence was so hard to come by for so long.

But I know now that in 1986 our new administration was staring right into the heart and soul of the school's history. I knew that Kansas State had a long way to go to become one of the elite and nationally ranked land-grant universities in America. I also recognized that it would take several new Kansas State University presidents to achieve that laudable goal.

NOTE:
THE CHAPTERS THAT FOLLOW ON MY 23 YEARS AS PRESIDENT ARE AUTOBIOGRAPHICAL

Chapter 1

The Challenges Facing K-State In 1986

ON JUNE 27, 1985, Duane Acker announced he would be retiring on June 30, 1986. I applied for the position of president at Kansas State University early in 1986. If I had known what was going on at the school, I might not have applied. I had no idea that so many K-State supporters believed the school was going south so rapidly.

I did not know that the well-known columnist for the TOPEKA CAPITOL JOURNAL, Jim Suber, was predicting the virtual demise of K-State. In July of 1985, he was suggesting that Kansas State might become a subsidiary of the University of Kansas. This was not the first time this possibility had been mentioned.

The former KU Chancellor, Frank Strong, argued in 1908 that Kansas State should merge with his school and become one of its colleges. Governor Edward Hoch never refuted the idea. But this was 1985. This prediction came from a journalist who loved Kansas State. If I had heard any of these suggestions floating around the state in 1985, I would have been worried.

Some administrators in 1985 believed that the school's enrollment might fall to about 11,000 students. A number of alums felt the Big 8 might purge Kansas State. For some, Wichita State was on the verge of replacing K-State as the 2nd best university in Kansas. K-Staters' worst nightmare was to imagine their school with 11,000 students, no football team, and membership in a mid-major conference.

David Hacker, the editor of the MANHATTAN MERCURY, penned a column on July 23, 1985 entitled a "Sense of Urgency." He argued Kansas State had not achieved "an identity in the post-Acker era."[25]

I was aware of many of the challenges facing Kansas State University in the summer of 1986. I did worry about the fears and concerns of K-Staters. But I did not know the school required an identity fix as well. That would have taken my breath away.

In a WICHITA EAGLE column on August 6, 1985, the editor said agricultural programs dominated the university.[26] On August 4, 1985, the MERCURY'S David Hacker urged K-State to embrace a wider mission: "Now the task is to make KSU No. 1 in all other departments such as engineering, business, journalism, architecture, health, physical education, recreation, and so on."[27]

In his autobiography entitled OPPORTUNITY KNOCKED AND I LISTENED, John Dunbar, a former Dean of Agriculture, wrote about one of his Council of Deans' monthly meetings in the spring of 1985. He reported that the academic deans had running arguments about the high priority assigned the College of Agriculture.

The Dean of Engineering, Don Rathbone, was furious that the College of Agriculture was always the top priority. He said: "I don't see why Agriculture always gets all the money for everything. Every year, they get all the money! We need money for other things, too. Our libraries are underfunded. And other things, too!"[28]

THE VIEWS OF THE BOARD OF REGENTS CHAIRMAN IN 1985

Keep in mind the year is not 1909 or 1958. It is the spring of 1985. On April 18, 1985, the Chairman of the Board of Regents, a K-State graduate, and a former Speaker of the House, Wendell Lady, spoke to the Manhattan Rotary Club. He called his speech "Stick to your knitting." Regent Lady declared that K-State should continue to "stick to its knitting" by focusing on the "programs of agriculture and engineering."[29] Lady was reflecting the words of President John Anderson 112 years later.

In the late summer of 1986, I started receiving letters from the Chair of the Dean of Agriculture's Advisory Committee, Dana Cox. He wanted me to reinstate the position of Vice President for Agriculture. In 1965, President McCain created that position for the first time in Kansas State's history. Glenn Beck was a superb vice-president for agriculture until his retirement in 1975. Roger Mitchell replaced Beck. In the spring of 1980, President Acker replaced that position with a more typical Dean of Agriculture.

In my response, I explained the position of dean was working well. I thought my letter to Cox would take care of it. I was wrong. In January of 1987, Dana Cox and his advisory committee demanded a meeting. On a Saturday morning, Chuck Reagan and I met with them in the Student Union.

For 45 minutes, I listened to their arguments. I said no twice. Then, I told Cox the next time the job of president opens up he should apply. The meeting with Dana Cox represented the last gasp of the John Anderson legacy. This issue never came up again.

FROM PESSIMISM TO SOLVING PROBLEMS IN MY FIRST YEAR

In the summer of 1986, I started thinking that K-State would be difficult to turn around. Whenever I offered some possible solutions in Anderson Hall in the summer and fall of 1986 to a variety of problems, the views of many veteran staff were similar: "We do not have the money." "The enrollment was headed down regardless." "Football could never be revitalized." I told Ruth Ann I might have made a mistake in coming to Kansas State University.

The problems facing K-State in 1986 were quite long actually. In fact, they were chillingly enormous. When I was doing reseach on my book after 2009, I thought back to an ancient Greek metaphor from the 4th century B.C. called the Gordian Knot.

This metaphor from ancient Greece became synonymous with words like vexing and stubborn to impossible, immovable, and intractable. But no matter how you define a Gordian Knot, it has to be unraveled and solved.

When I stared at the stiffest challenges facing me in 1986, I knew they had to be unraveled and fixed. Some of the problems were simply vexing and stubborn. Other problems that had evolved over decades ranged from the intractable to the impossible.

When I look back at the stubborn issues facing K-State in 1986, some of them were unraveled in a year or two. The more intractable problems took 10 years, and even longer to unravel. These problems represented the equivalent of Gordian Knots.

I defined several of the challenges confronting K-State after 1986 as truly intractable because they had not been solved by a multitude of school leaders for decades. If they had been solved even partially in the decades before 1986, I would not have needed to use a word like intractable.

The problems facing us in the fall of 1986 ranged from vexing to intractable. They included the following: K-State's enrollment had plummeted since 1981; its library was the worst in the Big 8; it was the only school in the Big 8 without an art museum; it was a school that had focused mainly on the teaching of undergraduates from 1900 to 1990; its basic research funding was mediocre from 1945 to 1990; its Information Technology program was at ground zero; its private giving was behind Wichita State; its football complex and its football team were the worst in the United States of America.

THE TWO IMMEDIATE MAJOR CHALLENGES

The two biggest and immediate challenges I had to solve in 1986 were mainly vexing—namely to hire a new leadership team and to solve the declining enrollment problem. But first I had another overall challenge. I had to first restore hope for the entire university. In the decade before I came to K-State, an air of pessimism permeated the university.

Napoleon Bonaparte once said: "A leader is a dealer in hope." Mother Teresa embodied the concept of hope even better: "Optimism is the faith that leads to achievement. Nothing can be done without hope or confidence."

If I could not get our faculty, staff, and students to be hopeful about the future, the job might have been impossible. In order to generate an air of optimism, I had to project confidence and hope myself. Otherwise, K-State might have continued in a downward spiral.

THE NEED TO HIRE A NEW ADMINISTRATIVE TEAM

From 1986 to 1988, I hired a new team in Anderson Hall. I had to figure out who should stay on and who should move on. All presidential transitions are difficult—especially when you have to make changes. The key positions in Anderson Hall included the Provost, the Vice President for Administration and Finance, the Vice President for Student Affairs, the Director for Legislative Relations, a Chief of Staff, and a Director of Recruiting.

The people I met after July 1, 1986 in Anderson Hall were dedicated and hard working. But I sensed many of them lacked confidence and enthusiasm. Indeed, many were quite pessimistic. Whenever I suggested a plan of action on any front, most had a simple response: No! Do not even think about it. For most of them, the challenges were quite unsolvable. In my mind's eye, I often thought about this quote from Winston Churchill: "A pessimist sees the difficulty in every opportunity; an optimist sees the opportunity in every difficulty."

Although most of the "holdovers" I met in Anderson Hall were not brimming with confidence, optimism, and a sense of hope, I was fortunate to meet up and coming leaders like Jim Coffman, Chuck Reagan, and Pat Bosco. All of them became pivotal leaders for our new leadership team. But there was another "holdover" administrator who came to my attention in the summer of 1986: Bob Kruh. He had been at Kansas State since the late 1960's. From 1986 to the early 1990's, Kruh played an invaluable role as the Dean of the Graduate School and Associate Provost.

Bob Kruh helped our new team figure out where we had to go in two crucial areas: to improve the school's basic research funding and to develop a new Information Technology program. Then, in 1991, we convinced Bob to come out of retirement to Chair our 1992 North Central Accreditation report. After the report was finished, a member of the North Central Accreditation Team declared that K-State's Report was the best report given by a university in his twenty years of accreditation visits. Everyone who worked with Bob over the years always remarked on his dedication and his love for K-State.

In my first six months, I also faced an element of hostility from a number of holdover administrators—mainly because of my strategy to increase enrollment. After I was picked as the new president in March of 1986, I asked George Miller, the Vice President for Administration and Finance, to reallocate $250,000 out of next year's state budget to develop a new enrollment program.

Some criticism was inevitable. I requested this reallocation in the spring of 1986 so we could hire new admission representatives. The critics reminded me of the budget reductions of $500,000 for the past two years. I quickly explained to the critics these cuts had resulted from declining enrollment.

Only a few people in Anderson Hall in the summer of 1986 believed our enrollment could be turned around. Many of the holdovers argued that K-State was destined for an enrollment of 11,000 to 12,000 students. The main opponent of my enrollment strategy was the Director of Legislative Relations under President Duane Acker, Michael Johnson. He was against using any state funds for student recruitment.

Later, I discovered that Mike Johnson was severely lampooning our enrollment strategy to powerful members of the Kansas State Senate and the House of Representatives—and most important to Governor Mike Hayden and his top staff. Johnson thought my plan would be a waste of time, money, and produce no results.

MY FIRST TWO APPOINTMENTS

There were some people who were positive about the future. Some understood a creative game plan was needed to move the school forward. One was Charles Reagan. As one of several faculty members on the search committee, he had given Ruth Ann and I a ride to Manhattan from Kansas City after my second interview in February of 1986.

With a Ph.D in philosophy from KU, Chuck Reagan was an impressive scholar, the former head of the Philosophy Department, and a former president of the Kansas State Faculty Senate. Jerry Frieman, who had chaired the search committee, suggested I should hire Chuck to be my new chief of staff. He became my first hire. Chuck

Reagan and I both showed up for work on July 1, 1986.

Neither one of us believed he would work for me for 23 years as a major advisor. Chuck became a visionary and a trouble-shooter on many different fronts. In the next few years, I had the Landon Lecture Series, the McCain Auditorium, the Beach Art Museum, the University Attorneys, the Affirmative Action Office, and the KSU-Salina Aviation Program directly reporting to him. In appointing a new team, I was off to a good start.

In my first two weeks, I met with Pat Bosco. Immediately, I liked his enthusiasm, passion, and common sense. I asked Pat why he had been stuck as a third level bureaucrat in student affairs for years. He was not sure. I was. Bosco had too much energy, confidence, and ambition to be on the first team. His work ethic and dedication were off the charts.

After a short meeting, I asked Pat Bosco to be our first Director of Enrollment Management. Quickly accepting, he took to this challenge like a duck to water. Pat was soon working seven days a week. Every note was written in purple. He even bought a purple car. Pat Bosco became an MVP for K-State in the next two years.

THE KEY POSITION OF PROVOST: MY BEST APPOINTMENT EVER

Everyone agreed the most important position to fill would be the new provost. Owen Koeppe had been the provost since 1980. Early in August of 1986, I set up an appointment with Owen to discuss his future. I did not say much. Always a gentleman, he said he was fine with a reassignment to the Department of Biochemistry. To the day he passed away years later, I respected Owen Koeppe.

In October of 1986, I set up a search committee. It was the most important search committee in my 23 years. Three candidates were interviewed in February of 1987. None of them caught our fancy. In March of 1987, the committee invited Milton Glick, the Dean of the College of Arts and Sciences at Missouri. I offered him the job. But I am still thankful today that he rejected it.

Sometimes you are lucky in life. Sometimes you make a few good decisions. In this case, I was lucky. At times, there are people right around you who are simply outstanding. Yet they never get on the radar screen. Many people had told me Jim Coffman was a great Dean of the College of Veterinary Medicine.

In the spring of 1987, I met with Jim and asked him to be our interim provost. He agreed. From day one, I saw that he had a ton of virtues. He was keenly intelligent. He was an optimist. He was a born leader. He knew how to win friends. He was the best listener I ever worked with. In fact, he never heard a "dumb" idea. It was all topped off with his great Kansas sense of humor.

I knew I would never find a better provost. After consulting with key faculty senate leaders and deans, they were unanimous: "Go ahead and appoint Jim Coffman. We have had a year-long search and he will make a first-rate Provost."

We hired a multitude of excellent administrators, staff, and coaches from 1986 to 2009. But listen up: Jim Coffman was my most important hire in any area of the entire university in my 23 years. I knew that if I had a mediocre Provost, I would not succeed. Without a great Provost, I knew that our academic process would implode.

Without him, I would not have lasted for over two decades as president. I will always feel blessed Jim Coffman was my provost for seventeen years. He is the best provost in the history of Kansas State and he is the Most Valuable Player in my tenure.

A TERRIFIC NEW V.P. FOR INSITUTIONAL ADVANCEMENT

Early on, I knew the Vice-President for Educational and Student Services since August of 1985, Bill Sutton, would not be a good fit. Our school had to improve in student services and enrollment. In June of 1987, Bill Sutton moved to the Division of Biology.

Shortly before July 1, 1986, I announced we would be creating a new Vice-President for Institutional Advancement position. With a green light from the Acker Administration, I set up a search committee in May of 1986.

After interviewing four candidates, I hired Robert S. Krause in mid-July. When I became President of Southwest State in 1977, Bob was the Vice-President for Student Services. He was excellent on all counts. From 1977 on, Bob Krause and I became close friends. We worked together for 32 years. When I became Chancellor of the State University System five years later in 1982, I selected Bob as the system's Vice-President for Student Services. Once again, he did a superb job.

Bob Krause was exactly the kind of person Kansas State needed. In every way, he did an excellent job. Coming to work at 5:00 a.m. every day and leaving late, his work ethic was legendary. He was totally dedicated. He was a quick study. He was a terrific problem solver for the entire university. He became an exceptional leader in working with K-State students.

Fitting right in with our new team, Bob had a major impact on Kansas State over the next two decades. He was a leader in our enrollment turnaround. He was a prime mover in the rebuilding of our football complex. He played a pivotal role for the new K-State Olathe campus and the DHS selection of K-State for NBAF. For 23 years, Bob Krause was an invaluable player in the transformation of K-State.

TWO MORE TOP-NOTCH LEADERS ARE HIRED

We needed to make a change in the position of Vice-President for Administration and Finance as well. George Miller had held that job since the spring of 1984. I saw that he was personable, utterly decent, and a team player. But he was not a good fit. I talked to him about a reassignment in 1988. He soon left for another university.

Now I had to find a crackerjack Vice-President for Administration and Finance. A national search was launched. In the search process, Tom Rawson's name increasingly came up. He was a graduate of Kansas State. He had a Ph.D from New Mexico. He had worked as the Director of Fiscal Affairs for the Board of Regents from 1974 to 1987. He was KU's Director of Fiscal Affairs until 1989.

Tom Rawson was exactly the right hire to be our Vice President for Administration and Finance. He was extremely intelligent. Like Bob Krause, he redefined the words "work ethic." He came to work every morning at 5:00 a.m. as well. His mantra was simple: he wanted everyone in his area of operations to solve problems.

Tom Rawson became the best day-to-day problem solver I ever worked with. When a faculty member called him early in the morning to solve an electrical problem or to repair a broken door, Tom quickly dispatched somebody to fix the problem. His sense of urgency was second to none.

Tom could take a complicated budget and explain it to anybody. When he appeared before the Board of Regents or a key legislative committee, he was clear, concise, on target, and understandable. He could answer any questions on the budget or finances. Tom Rawson became a brilliant Vice President for Administration and Finance.

There was still one missing piece. K-State needed a new Director of Legislative Relations. I inherited a dentist from Abilene, Kansas. From day one, Mike Johnson conveyed the impression that no one could replace President Acker. I had a number of lunches with him. Normally, I could turn most people around. But I could never win him over.

Then, I found out about his opposition to our enrollment program. In the fall of 1986, I discovered Johnson was talking to some key members of the Senate Ways and Means Committee and the House Appropriations Subcommittee on Public Higher Education as well as top staff members in Governor Mike Hayden's office. He was essentially telling them that our admission recruiters would take any students regardless of their scores or grades.

During the 1987 legislative session, Warren Armstrong, the President of Wichita State University, called me to report that Mike Johnson was criticizing our new enrollment program with key legislators and the Governor's office. In the next few years, I found out how much damage he had done in Topeka. A change was necessary. Johnson made it easier when he decided to run for the Kansas State Senate in 1988.

We needed to find a new Director of Governmental Relations. We learned that Susan Peterson, the Governor's Executive Assistant for Governmental Relations, might be interested in becoming K-State's new Director of Governmental Relations. Sue was a KSU graduate. She loved politics. When she accepted our offer, we were ecstatic.

For Sue Peterson, it did not make any difference whether the legislators were Republicans or Democrats. She knew exactly what to say to legislators and how to say it. She could talk about sports, the weather, and politics in a nonpartisan way. She became a "secret weapon" for K-State in and out of the legislature.

Sue Peterson became an authority on our budget. We put Sue Peterson in charge of both our state and federal relations. She did a first-rate job in both areas. Whether it was our Congressional delegation or anyone in the state legislature from both parties, all of them respected, liked, and listened to her.

In either Topeka or Washington D.C., Sue Peterson became a superb Director of Governmental Relations. On campus, she was respected and well liked. From 1989 to 2009, she became the finest legislative director for any university in Kansas or anywhere else.

By 1989, our new Anderson Hall team was mainly in place. I rather doubt that any Kansas State president had ever assembled a better administrative team. This was a leadership team committed to excellence and hard work. It was a team of problem solvers who could do the impossible. The words—"no, it can't be done"—had been employed too many times by Kansas State administrators over many years. Our team never used those terms.

On December 22, 2015, Dolph Simons, the Editor of the LAWRENCE JOURNAL WORLD, wrote about the K-State leadership team we put together in 1986 and 1987. Dolph and his entire family are graduates of the University of Kansas. They are all passionate and committed Jayhawkers. Calling our team a "Unique Team," Dolph contends that: "The special inner circle recruited by Kansas State University President Jon Wefald helped build KSU into the thriving university it is today."

Dolph Simons concluded his December 22, 2015 column this

way: The Wefald Leadership Team "was a powerful group in every respect, one that should serve as a model for other universities. Some schools have it; others don't. It requires hard work, vision, and true leadership, but the dividends of such commitment are rewarding for all parties. Consider what took place at Kansas State."

We had a very good leadership team for several reasons: it was small; we operated as a team; all of us empowered hundreds of people on all levels to make decisions; and we basically trusted those leaders to make good decisions. Because most schools today do not operate this way, few of them "have it and most don't."

For me, it meant if you could dream it, you could do it. The historic poem of Oliver Wendell Holmes summed up our leadership spirit: "I find the great thing in this world is not so much where we stand, as in what direction we are moving: to reach the port of heaven, we must sail sometimes with the wind and sometimes against it—But we must sail, not drift, nor lie at anchor."

THE FIRST CHALLENGE WAS TO SOLVE DECLINING ENROLLMENT

On July 1, 1986, our highest priority was to increase Kansas State's enrollment. The former administration had five years to solve the plummeting enrollment. They even had a Manhattan Chamber of Commerce delegation pressing the Acker administration to stop the enrollment decline. It never happened. If this challenge was so easy to unravel, it would have been solved between 1981 and 1986.

After I reassigned Pat Bosco to untangle our enrollment challenge in July of 1986, I knew success was inevitable. Pat and I were believers. First, we would never permit the enrollment to drop to 11,000 students. Second, we were resolved to increase the school's enrollment to over 20,000 in five years.

Pat and I approached this challenge with a sense of urgency, clarity, and a full-court press. We swiftly hired nine bright seniors from our 1986 graduating class by the last week of July. Because all of them had the K-State work ethic, Pat coached them up quickly. We divided the state into geographic regions and placed our recruiters in exactly the right regions.

Pat Bosco's plan was simple: the nine new recruiters would visit each high school in the state twice a year—once in the fall and once in the spring. They would meet eyeball to eyeball with all interested students in every school district in Kansas. They would get to know every single K-State prospect. They called them often. They employed purple pens to send handwritten letters.

The state of Kansas had never ever seen a student recruiting team like the one we assembled in 1986-87. We were recruiting pioneers. The school superintendants and principals of the state were shocked and thrilled at how fast we built our recruiting program.

Our recruiters approached each new prospect one student at a time. Each prospect was treated with total respect. Unlike some other school recruiters who told a student prospect "if you want to come here fine, if not, that is fine too," our team deployed a full-court press on every single prospect.

Pat's recruiters covered the state like a blanket. We soon heard from high school principals from all over the state. There comments were similar: "Where has K-State been all these years?" "And why did it take K-State so many years to come up with this program?"

THE ENROLLMENT INCREASE HAPPENED FAST AND A GOOD FOOTBALL TEAM HAD NOTHING TO DO WITH IT!

Kansas State's enrollment was about 19,000 in 1981. By 1986, the school's enrollment had slipped to about 16,500. It had dropped by 484 students in 1982, 1,027 students in 1983, 378 students in 1984, 512 students in 1985, and 118 students in 1986. We stopped that decline immediately.

In the fall of 1987, K-State enrolled 597 new students. In 1988, we added 1,242 additional students. In 1989, we enrolled 709 new students. In 1990, we gained an additional 1,027 students. Our enrollment exceeded 20,000 students by 1990 for the first time—meaning that we accomplished our enrollment goal in four years.

There are KSU sports fans and sports writers today who still believe it was a winning football team that increased our enrollment. That view is absurd. The K-State football team won two games in 1986. It lost every game in 1987 and 1988. In 1989, the football team won one game. The truth is we did not have a superb football program until 1993. Meanwhile, K-State added about 5,000 new students from 1986 to 1991.[30]

Two years before our football program became a ranked team in 1993, K-State had become the state university of choice for high school seniors in almost every county in the state.

From 1986 to 1989, the number of traditional-aged first-time freshmen from the state of Kansas enrolled at K-State increased by 53.4%. Our market share increased in those three years from 6.5% to almost 10%. By 1989, one out of every five college bound Kansas high school graduates enrolled at K-State.

Our predecessors had been pessimistic about recruiting high school students in the urban and suburban areas of the state. From 1986 to 1989, K-State's largest gains were in the three most urban counties: our enrollment was up 60.4% in Johnson County; up 122.3% in Shawnee County; and up 64.7% in Sedgwick County.[31]

By 1999, K-State had 21,543 students. By 2009, Kansas State University had an all-time high enrollment of 23,581 students. Pat Bosco and his recruiters had put together the best admissions program of any school in the history of Kansas. It still is.[32]

HOW ENROLLMENT WAS FUNDED

In the state university system, there was a direct correlation between student enrollment and university budgets. Kansas State had lost over $500,000 in 1986 and 1987 due to declining enrollments suffered in preceding years. But now K-State was reporting record enrollments from 1986 to 1991.

An analyst for the Legislative Research Department's fiscal staff created the enrollment corridor adjustment system in 1981. This system involved a new methodology that would adjust university budgets for actual student credit hour growth that occurred from one fiscal year to another. It was titled the enrollment corridor adjustment system.[33]

The enrollment corridor ranged between 1.5% down and 1.5% up. If any of the six state universities reported modest increases or modest decreases within that range, there were no budget adjustments. If any of them fell below 1.5%, that school received a budget reduction. If a university went above 1.5%, that school received a positive budget adjustment.

Because our enrollment went up almost 600 students in the fall of 1987, the university received $697,000 two years later the proper adjustment funds from the state. With one healthy year in enrollment, K-State recovered the $250,000 that we had reallocated in the spring of 1986 to stem our enrollment decline.[34]

THE STUNNING INCREASE IN ENROLLMENT IN 1988

In the fall of 1988, K-State shocked the Board of Regents and the Governor's Office by enrolling about 1,300 new students over the fall of 1987. K-State had enrolled its largest freshman class in history. With the enrollment adjustment system, K-State was now in line to receive about $5 million in the spring of 1990.

In my university presentation on September 12, 1989, I was optimistic about the future because the state of Kansas owed our school about $5 million. In my report, I stated: "Relief is on the way. The funding formula is such that there is a two-year lag between enrollment growth and appropriations to address the growth. By next year, we will have the largest budgetary increase enrollment growth in the history of any state university."[35]

At Kansas State, we were also very excited about the Board of Regents plan for a three-year plan called the Margin of Excellence. It called for higher faculty salaries and program improvements. It would include $6 million in faculty salary increases and $5.5 million in program improvements for the six state universities over three years.

With respect to faculty salaries for the first two years of the Margin of Excellence, the university received $1.8 million in 1989 and

$2.1 million for 1990. These totals were above the normal 5 per cent cost of living increases—meaning that average faculty salaries increased more than 8 percent for each of the first two years.

K-State also received over $3 million in program improvements in the first two years of the Margin of Excellence. For fiscal year 1988, Kansas State received $299,000 in one-time funds from fees. In 1989, our university received over $1 million in one-time fee release funds. It had been literally years since Kansas State had two outstanding years in a row of good funding.[36]

THE BOTTOM FELL OUT IN 1990

During the 1990 legislative session, the bottom fell out. No one at K-State could have predicted that a financial nightmare was on its way. The Margin of Excellence for faculty salaries and program improvements came to a screeching halt.

In the final hours of the 1990 session, our school lost $1.9 million in an across the board budget reduction. This reduction came after Governor Mike Hayden ordered a mid-year budget recision in January of 1990 of $1.2 million. We did not quarrel with these reductions. Every state university was treated the same.[37]

THEN, MIKE HAYDEN CHANGED THE ENROLLMENT SYSTEM

But we never imagined this stunning development—Governor Mike Hayden abruptly threw out the window the widely accepted enrollment corridor adjustment system. Kansas State now faced a financial nightmare over the next three years. Every state legislature had backed this bipartisan system since 1981.

With our increased enrollment of 1,300 students in the fall of 1988, Kansas State was legally and ethically due to receive an enrollment adjustment in the 1990 session of $4.69 million. Instead, the Governor, a K-State graduate, arbitrarily changed the entire enrollment corridor system.[38]

In a heartbreaking decision for us, Mike Hayden made a ruling to provide K-State only 55% of the funds we were owed. Instead of receiving $4.69 million, we got only $2.55 million. Governor Hayden failed to realize those students had been enrolled at KSU for two years. Even worse, our leadership team had already decided where the full $4.69 million would be allocated.[39]

For years to come, this decision was an unmitigated disaster for Kansas State University. We had planned on $1.1 million of the $4.69 million going to instructional programs for the students already in school. The remainder would go for needed funds for the library, academic programs, academic computing, and infrastructure.

I never dreamed that Governor Hayden would leave his alma mater so high and dry. Our leadership team launched a major letter writing campaign. Hundreds of K-Staters wrote letters to Governor Mike Hayden. Hundreds of calls were made. Doyle Rahjes, the Kansas Farm Bureau President, called him and pleaded for fairness. None of this worked. The letters and calls fell on deaf ears.

THE FINANCIAL NIGHTMARE DEEPENS

With the future of the enrollment adjustment corridor in doubt, the financial nightmare intensified for K-State. The Board of Regents sensed Governor Hayden and key state legislative leaders were backing away from the enrollment corridor system adopted in 1981. The Regents buckled and responded with a revised system.

The Regents decision also did enormous harm to K-State. Prior to the Governor's decision, there had been no complaints about the corridor system from 1981 to 1990—until KSU started racking up enrollment increases. If KU had sharply increased their enrollment, they likely would have gotten the funds owed them.

In the fall of 1989, Kansas State enrolled an additional 709 new students. Under the 1981 formula, KSU was owed $3.6 million in enrollment adjustment funds. But, under the new Board of Regents plan and with the Governor's backing, the amount owed to K-State was arbitrarily reduced from $3.6 million to $1.9 million.

The Governor, the state legislature, and the Board of Regents left us in a small canoe with one broken paddle. Shockingly, it got even worse. K-State did not even get the $1.9 million. I still cannot believe Mike Hayden and the legislature allocated absolutely zero for our new 709 students. KSU had received some hard right hands to the head from the Governor and the Regents.[40]

KANSAS STATE WAS TREATED HORRIBLY IN 1989-90

What does all this mean? From 1987 to 1990, K-State had enrolled about 4,500 additional students. But we received new state funding for only 1,000 of them. This was an unmitigated disaster for us. No Board of Regents university had been treated this badly since 1925.

K-State now had zero state funding for 3,500 students. This was hardly fair. The end result—despite the increase of about 6,000 students between 1986 and 2009, K-State actually had fewer instructional faculty members in 2009 than it had in 1986. Our school had been kicked in the head.

KSU HAD FEWER FACULTY IN 2009 THAN IT HAD IN 1986

In the fall of 1986, Kansas State had a total of 999.2 instructional faculty members. In the fall of 2008, the school had a total of 948.64 faculty members. I doubt that anyone can name a major university in America that enrolled 6,000 more students and ended up 22 years later with 51 fewer instructional faculty members—and, with these major constraints, we still made major advances in research.[41]

For K-State, the financial nightmare persisted. In the fall of 1990, we enrolled 1,027 new students. Under the old corridor, we would have received about $3 million. Tom Rawson explained what this meant: "After 'due consideration' the legislature appropriated KSU a total of $1.7 million in enrollment adjustment funding for FY 1993—which really represented a two-year budgetary adjustment since no additional funding was appropriated the previous year."[42]

KSU WAS DENIED OVER $7 MILLION IN ENROLLMENT FUNDS

Under the 1981 enrollment adjustment funding system, Kansas State should have received about $11.3 million for the three fiscal years of 1991, 1992, and 1993. Instead, we received only $4.3 million. This meant that our FY 1993 base budget was short $7 million under the original enrollment adjustment system. The $7 million shortfall would equate to about $14 million in 2009 dollars—or about $18 million today. How does K-State make up for this kind of damage? The answer is: it never will.

With Governor Mike Hayden's decisions on our enrollment increases, K-State would never recover from his decisions. I rather doubt that any Governor has ever treated any state university more unfairly in the history of the state of Kansas.[43]

A SENSE OF OPTIMISM WAS STILL NEEDED

Despite this stream of bad news, I had to convey a sense of optimism to our entire academic community. As hard as it was, I had no choice. A leader has to embody hope. I told our team in 1990 and 1991 a positive and optimistic approach was crucial.

Kansas State was in dire need of better strategic planning. Some serious reorganization and even mergers would have to be considered. In a statement on September 11, 1990, I stated: "There is a great temptation for university administrators to allow all academic programs to slowly sink into mediocrity. I am requesting faculty, staff, and students to begin the process of developing a plan for reorganization which will insure the academic vitality of Kansas State well into the 21st century."[44]

THE MISTAKE I MADE ON REORGANIZATION

In my 23 years as Kansas State's President, I made a number of mistakes. Two decisions stand out. My first major mistake was to try and merge two colleges with two other colleges in October of 1990. My second major mistake occurred in 2008 when I stupidly let our outstanding athletic director, Tim Weiser, move on to take the position of Deputy Commissioner in the Big 12. Both decisions came as a result of arrogance. Leaders can sometimes believe that they are smarter than they really are.

After the legislative session of 1990, everyone at K-State was upset with the decisions of the Governor and the State Legislature. I should have remembered what the best coaches tell their players after a bad loss: "Do not let this loss lead you to still another loss in the next game." I did anyway. I let our losses suffered in the recent legislative sessions lead me right into another loss with the badly conceived reorganization plan of October 1990.

Our leadership team in the fall of 1990 had several meetings with the university strategic planning committee and the Faculty Senate Leadership Group about reorganization. Jim Coffman and I started moving towards a plan for reorganization. The proposed plan was to merge the College of Human Ecology with the College of Business and several other colleges and merge the College of Architecture, Planning, and Design with the College of Engineering.[45]

If this reorganization plan took place, Jim Coffman and I concluded that the savings would be over $3 million. The funds would be reallocated to the College of Arts and Sciences and the library. One-half of the $3 million would go to the College of Arts and Sciences because the bulk of our unfunded 4,500 new students had beeen taking classes in that college for their first two years. The college needed dozens of new faculty positions.

In the fall of 1990, Coffman and I met with the Faculty Senate Leadership Group and—I can say this now—all of them backed the plan of trying to save $3 million by reorganization.[46]

IT WAS A STUPID AND ARROGANT MISTAKE

I had taken a number of calculated risks since 1986. Most worked. Any good leader has to take calculated risks. Success can often lead to arrogance. This happened to me. As I think about our plan of reorganization today, I still cannot believe how addlebrained I was to promote this radical plan. The DAILY KANSAN correctly quoted me on November 2, 1990: "It was a very, very, very dumb idea." Some people might have seen the movie "Dumb and Dumber." Well, I played the lead role.[47]

On Wednesday, October 31, 1990, Provost Jim Coffman and I released a written draft of the plan. The faculty, staff, and students in the Colleges of Human Ecology and the College of Architecture, Planning, and Design were already angry.

Even before the written draft was released, students from both colleges were showing up inside Anderson Hall to denounce it. I remember how hundreds of students gathered in the middle of the Anderson Hall lawn to protest our plan the next day.

Jim Coffman and I were summoned to meet with faculty, staff, and students from the two colleges on Friday, November 2, 1990. It was scheduled for 1:30 p.m. on the steps of Seaton Hall. Over 1,000 students showed up. The questions were hostile. There were no satisfactory answers. In a situation like this, it is impossible to articulate any coherent answers. I certainly could not.[48]

THE MEETING IN MCCAIN ON NOVEMBER 5, 1990

Right after this Friday session, I called a meeting for the following Monday morning, November 5, 1990 at 9:00 a.m. It would be held at McCain Auditorium for all interested faculty, staff, and students.

On Monday morning, November 5, 1990, I made the decision to stand in the well of McCain Auditorium by myself. Because Jim Coffman was better informed on the key issues, I would have preferred he join me. But I was the one who made the decision to move forward with the plan. This happened on my watch. I could not shirk my responsibility. I had to make the decisions on how we would proceed on Monday morning.

By about 9:00 a.m. there were about 1,500 faculty, staff, and students in attendance. There were more pointed questions. I did my best to answer those questions. But I had no satisfactory answers—none at all.

I WITHDREW THE REORGANIZATION PLAN AND APOLOGIZED

When the meeting started, I announced that I was withdrawing the reorganization plan. I apologized to the two colleges and the entire university for even considering the plan. I did recall a multitude of political, business, and educational leaders in American history who could never apologize for anything.

If they did, most of them could only say something feeble like this: "If I offended anyone, I apologize." This is not an apology. It can only be labeled as an offensive "limited hangout apology." I could never say anything like "If I offended anyone, I apologize." I had offended the entire university. My apology was absolute: "I fully apologize and nothing like this will ever happen again as long as I am president of Kansas State University."[49]

As a student of history, I did think about President Richard Nixon and his failure to apologize for the Watergate Crisis in June of 1972. All of us can recall prominent political leaders, personalities, and athletes who could never apologize for anything. The list includes talented people like Bill Clinton, Martha Stewart, Pete Rose, Jamie Diamond, Lance Armstrong, Hillary Clinton, Barack Obama, George W. Bush, and Donald Trump.

I knew that the American people have always been willing to forgive someone who is sincerely contrite and apologizes for their actions. After several days, I had totally withdrawn the entire plan—and I had categorically apologized to the people of Kansas State and the faculty, staff, and students of the two colleges.

In retrospect, this crisis was a telling moment for my future at Kansas State. If I had been unwilling to admit I had made a mistake and if I had not been able to completely apologize, my days at Kansas State would have been numbered. Instead, I was at K-State for almost another 20 years.

Most people realized that I was sincerely sorry. They accepted my apologies and moved on. The crisis ended rather quickly. Within a short period of time, my leadership team and I regained the trust of faculty and students. That continued to grow and deepen over the years. Ralph Waldo Emerson was exactly right: "Meet your failure nobly and it will not differ much from success."

K-State had made some remarkable progress in my first four years. Randy Martin, who was the President of the Manhattan Chamber of Commerce from 1989 to 1996, sent me a note in the spring of 2011 on his observations: "After seven years at the Chamber and another 12 years in private business in Manhattan, I am struck with the completeness of the vision inspired by Jon Wefald. It is one thing to sit around and dream up ideas. It is something else to see what needs to happen, to plot the steps over time to accomplish it, and then to execute the vision. Wefald and his team made things happen. The entire community began to reflect the vibrancy we are experiencing in the new millennium."[50]

Dan Bolen was a Jayhawk who watched what we did over 23 years. Dan graduated from KU and the University of Virginia Law School. For several years, he was a general counsel for the U.S. Senate. He became the CEO of the Bank of Prairie Village in Johnson County. In the fall of 2011, Dan talked about our first four or five years. His take: "I was born with a genetic predisposition making me wary of the color purple. I was informed early that Manhattan, Kansas was an insurgent citadel. You can appreciate my surprise when I found myself marrying a Manhattan girl. Prior to President Wefald, I privately viewed the Kansas State community as adrift."

After Dan moved back to Kansas in 1989, he saw the changes taking place at K-State: "An anticipatory buzz had commenced at the university. Viewing myself as a competitor, I detected a fierce renewed sense of determination with the 'Wefald Executive Team.' Wearing purple became fashionable. Whenever I returned to Manhattan after 1989, it was as if every KSU battle station was being manned and every weapon fired. The Bill Snyder gridiron miracle was one of many miracles during Jon Wefald's Presidency. It was perhaps the most visible, but not the most dramatic. I will always view K-State as a competitor. However, as a Kansan, I will likewise forever view Jon Wefald's successful presidency as the one which all other modern university leaders should be measured."[51]

In our first several years, we identified the short-term problems and challenges—including instilling a mood of optimism and hope; hiring an outstanding new administrative team; and turning the enrollment around.

Our new leadership team not only embraced an attitude of optimism and hope, but they became excellent problem-solvers who had a sense of urgency and teamwork. We had assembled the best administrative team in the history of the school. In four years, Pat Bosco and our student recruiters had increased Kansas State's enrollment to over 20,000 students. By the late 1980's, our leadership team was ready to take on the more intractable challenges.

Chapter 2

Empowerment And Delegation Of Authority: Two Principles That Guided My 23 Years As President

As I reflect back on my years growing up in the towns of Excelsior, Minnesota, Garretson, South Dakota, and Minot, North Dakota, I never had any reason to think I was better than anyone else. I certainly knew that I was not smarter than anyone else. Even with the different jobs I had in the years ahead, I still feel exactly the same way today.

Our family, which included my mom and dad, two brothers, and one sister, was always quite poor. In Excelsior, Minnesota, while my dad was a state grain inspector in Minneapolis, we lived in three different rented homes—two of which had outhouses. We also lived for several months in a tiny motel.

My dad got a job as a grain inspector in Sioux Falls, South Dakota. Our family moved to Garretson, a small farm town with no stoplights and 16 miles from Sioux Falls. The six of us lived in a miserable second story apartment above a furniture store on Main Street. I have many memories from this small town.

But one sticks with me. While I was in the sixth grade, a friend and I were out shooting single shot twenty-two rifles in the area of the Jesse James Bridge Park just outside of Garretson. Trying to come close, my comrade accidently shot me in the left shoulder blade. It was a close call. But I still have that bullet in my left shoulder today.

After four years in Garretson, South Dakota, our family moved to Minot, North Dakota. My dad was offered the opportunity to set up a private grain inspection point in Minot. The Great Northern and Soo Line railroads brought in carload after carload of spring wheat, barley, and oats that came in from eastern Montana and northwestern North Dakota.

The grain samplers took five-pound sacks of grain from each car into my dad's office where he inspected each sample. The inspection results were sent directly from Minot by a Great Northern train to Minneapolis where the inspection results were posted at the Minneapolis Grain Exchange. My dad worked six days a week.

During our first year or so in Minot, our family lived in Pat's Motel just outside of town. We shared two "tiny" rooms. My parents' room served as their bedroom and the kitchen area. The four kids lived in the other room. There was no living room. My mom prepared meals on a hot plate. After living in this tiny motel, our family was likely viewed by many as living "on the other side of the tracks" during the time I lived in Minot.

A HIGH SCHOOL TEACHER TOLD ME: "FORGET COLLEGE"

Unlike my two brothers and sister who did very well in school, I was never a good student. I was a C student. In high school, I took one math class and one science class. I received an A in typing.

In my junior year, several teachers asked me about my future plans. Ron Davy, the school's vocational teacher, asked me if I wanted to join the school's Distributive Education program and be a clerk intern at a local department store—meaning that I was not projected as a college student. Davy probably checked my 10th grade transcript and saw I had received a score of 108 on a high school IQ test.

It got worse. As a senior, Ann Ackerman, my high school English teacher, asked me what I was going to do after graduation. After telling her I wanted to attend college, she said curtly: "Jon, you are not smart enough to go to any college anywhere. You should join the army or get a job at Woolworth's."

I did not take her advice. By my junior and senior years, my dad was making enough money to send all of us to college. One May Sunday morning, I was looking at college bulletins in the basement of the First Lutheran Church. I spotted a handsome bulletin from Pacific Lutheran College in Tacoma, Washington.

PLC was probably taking any Norwegian-American high school seniors who applied. Even though I was a C student, I was accepted. I took the Great Northern from Minot to Tacoma, Washington. In late August of 1955, I remember standing in front of the Old Main Building and meeting students from Seattle, Tacoma, Portland, San Francisco, and Los Angeles. Then, it dawned on me. I would now have to match wits with good students up and down the West Coast.

At the end of my first semester, I had a 2.5 grade point. For my second semester, I compiled a 3.0 grade point. Then, one day I looked in the mirror and decided I could compete with anyone. In the next 3 years, I received mainly A's. I graduated Cum Laude with a 3.3 grade point in 1959. Meanwhile, since 1959, I have thought about Ann Ackerman's advice to me at least a million times.

After PLC, I thought I could do most anything. I finally realized how vital it was to adhere to the values of hard work, willpower, and passion. I received a MA degree in history from Washington State University in 1961. By 1965, I had a Ph.D from the University of Michigan in history. I taught at Gustavus Adolphus College in St. Peter, Minnesota for the next five years. I had left Pat's Motel and Minot High School in my rear view mirror.

THE LEADERSHIP SKILLS I LEARNED AS MINNESOTA'S COMMISSIONER OF AGRICULTURE

In my first year as the new Commissioner of Agriculture in 1971, I had to figure out how to be a leader. At Gustavus Adolphus College, I had never been a department head. I had never managed a secretary. My experience as a leader of any kind was non-existent.

At age 32, I found myself as the commissioner of a large state agency. The Department of Agriculture had over 400 employees. The departments included grain inspection, meat inspection, dairy inspection, food inspection, and marketing.

I inherited solid department heads. They were veterans. It did not take me long to understand how I would lead this large department. I had no choice. I had to trust the department heads. I came to call this style of management "pragmatic empowerment."

This was a philosophy that I followed in every job I held from 1971 to 2009. I found it easy to hire excellent people and delegate authority because I knew I was never the "smartest guy in the room." I came to know how vital it was to be surrounded by people who were smarter than me. For me, this was easy because I knew most people were smarter.

"PRAGMATIC EMPOWERMENT" WORKED

In 1971, as the new commissioner, I decided to concentrate initially on speaking out for the state's farmers. After a year on the job, I noticed something—the department heads were pleased with my management style. They knew I trusted them. It worked.

Meanwhile, the governor's staff and key state legislators noticed that the department was running efficiently and in a nonpartisan fashion. In my fourth year, the Commissioner of Administration, Richard Brubacher, called me to his office. He said that the Governor had told him that I was one of their best commissioners.

After six and one-half years in the Department of Agriculture from 1971 to 1977, I learned more about leadership and management strategies as President of Southwest State University from 1977 to 1982 and as Chancellor of the Minnesota State University System from 1982 to 1986. In both positions, I continued to practice the management concept of "pragmatic empowerment."

MY LEADERSHIP PRINCIPLES AS KSU'S NEW PRESIDENT IN 1986

As the new president in 1986, I knew from studying American history that every situation is unique. For me, history was never irreversible. I learned that one person can make a difference; that leadership is not necessarily a rare skill; and that most people have the potential to be a good leader.

Knowing that I had only scored an I.Q. of 108 in the tenth grade, I concluded there might be different ways to become a good leader. I found out how important it was to have a strong work ethic, willpower, passion, and a never-give-up attitude. It was important to have a good sense of humor. If you cannot laugh at yourself, you will not be a leader too long.

THE IMPORTANCE OF EMOTIONAL INTELLIGENCE

In his book entitled EMOTIONAL INTELLIGENCE: WHY IT CAN MATTER MORE THAN IQ, Daniel Goleman wrote: "A view of human nature that ignores the power of emotions is sadly shortsighted. . .As we all know from experience, when it comes to shaping our decisions and our actions, feeling counts every bit as much—and often more—than thought. We have gone too far in emphasizing the value and import of the purely rational—of what IQ measures—in human life."[52]

Count me in as a major Goleman supporter. I came to see treating everyone with respect, empathy, and kindness pretty much trumps everything else. Most of our successful American presidents embodied these values.

In a book by Elizabeth Haas Edersheim entitled THE DEFINITIVE DRUCKER, she explains Peter Drucker's views of what makes for a good leader: "The most important thing anybody in a leadership position can do is to ask what needs to be done. And make sure that what needs to be done is understood." Drucker often said in his speeches: "Good leaders never start out with the question of 'What do I want?' Rather, good leaders ask, 'What needs to be done?'"[53]

I followed Drucker's advice. I asked every K-State constituency what needed to be done? Too many leaders in business, politics, and higher education assumed their positions with a preconceived plan. I wanted to find out from everyone what needed to be done.

For that to work, I empowered all of K-State's leaders, including vice-presidents, associate vice presidents, deans, department heads, faculty leaders, and student leaders. I always believed that empowerment would lead to success.

EMPOWERMENT AND FLAT MANAGEMENT WORKS

Empowerment would become a new definition of leadership for the entire school. I wanted our leaders to get things done—not next year or next week, but right now. That could only be done if we delegated authority to the lowest level. I wanted everyone up and down the line to have a sense of urgency and quick action. Problems should be solved that day, not tomorrow or the next day. None of this would happen if our leaders were not empowered.

MOST TOP UNIVERSITIES FOLLOWED THE CORPORATE MODEL

From 1945 on, most leading universities in America hired presidents and chancellors who mainly paid lip service to the concepts of empowerment and shared governance. Most of them embraced the "Corporate Model" of leadership. I did not. This centralized model was followed increasingly in many of the major state universities from the 1960's to the present. It mirrored the big business model dominating American corporations after 1945.

Many university boards of regents preferred a centralized model of governance so they could monitor the actions of their CEO's. Many of these university regents either had a "to do" list or a politically correct agenda that enhanced centralization. Many university presidents claim they practice the delegation of authority and responsibility. The truth is most never practice those concepts. Those views are only played out in their dreams.

In his book A UNIVERSITY FOR THE 21ST CENTURY, James Duderstadt, the University of Michigan President from 1988 to 1996, explained how tough it was to be a major university president. He argued the average tenure of major public university presidents was about five to six years. Many of these presidents stalled out because they practiced overscheduling, micro-management, and highly centralized management.[54]

Chuck Reagan wrote about Ross Perot's Landon Lecture at Kansas State on January 24, 1995. Perot was a huge stockholder in General Motors in the 1990's. He became a member of the GM Board of Directors. Several years later, Ross argued that too many of the GM executives and vice-presidents were essentially bureaucrats going from one meeting to another. Perot made this telling and humorous comment: "You guys are scheduled every 15 minutes. If I wanted to do that, I would have been a dentist."[55]

IN RETROSPECT, CHARLES KOCH'S GOOD CONCEPTS IN RUNNNG KOCH INDUSTRIES FROM 1968 TO THE PRESENT

In 2014, I read the new book by Daniel Schulman entitled SONS OF WICHITA. He wrote a history of the Koch family. He focused on the top leader of Koch Industries with its corporate headquarters in Wichita, Kansas: Charles Koch. Although Schulman analyzed the entire Koch family and its history, I was most intrigued with his chapter on Charles' management strategy after he became the CEO of Koch Industries in 1968. Charles quickly embraced a strategy of delegation of authority, empowerment, and a flat management structure.

I had not thought very much about Charles Koch in the five years since I retired. I read many newspaper articles about the Koch brothers—particularly in their roles as leaders and board members of Americans for Prosperity. Schulman outlines how the Koch brothers played pivotal roles in distributing campaign funds to a multitude of conservative groups all over America. But I have had little interest in Charles Koch's politics before 2009 or after.

I drove to Wichita two or three times in the 1990's to meet with Charles and his top advisors. I thought that K-State and Koch Industries could work out a mutually beneficial partnership. Koch had employed a large number of our graduates who had degrees in engineering, agriculture, and business from 1986 to 2009. The company still hires a huge number of K-State graduates.

From about 1993 to 2009, the KSU Foundation, the College of Business Dean, Yar Ebadi, and my office tried to develop a partnership with Koch Industries. Dean Ebadi and the College of Business submitted several proposals for Koch Chairs over the years. Because Charles Koch was a major voice for America's free enterprise system, the first chair proposal submitted by Dean Ebadi was for a Koch Chair in Free Enterprise. It was turned down.

Then, several Koch leaders said they would like to see a Koch Chair in Accounting. About a month later, Dean Ebadi submitted a second proposal for a Koch Chair in Accounting. Even though the company hired a ton of our graduates in finance and accounting, the Koch leaders were not interested in this proposal either. The College of Business did not submit any more proposals for a Koch Chair in anything up to 2009.

In reading Schulman's book in 2014, however, I realized that I had led K-State from 1986 to 2009 very similar to the way Charles ran Koch Industries from the 1970's to the present. Schulman specifically explains how Charles Koch rejected the "Corporate Model" of business leadership. He insisted on adhering to the concept of decentralized decision-making as the corporation's CEO.

Unlike General Motors and most of the FORTUNE MAGAZINE TOP 500 Corporations that employed a top-down model—including most of the huge banks in America like JP Morgan Chase, Citigroup, Bank of America, and Wells Fargo—Charles Koch absolutely rejected the highly centralized model of most major American corporations.

He brilliantly deployed a flat management strategy for all of the Koch business enterprises throughout America. Charles understood how very few American corporations utilized the concept of empowerment.

Charles Koch pushed his theory of "flat management" to the lowest levels of the entire company. He wanted the maximum number of employees to have the authority to solve problems at the very lowest level. He genuinely believed that Koch's key local employees knew far more about the "problems" in their respective areas—especially compared to some manager in a central office or in some far off Koch company location.

Koch insisted that his company should depend on their local managers, supervisors, mechanics, factory workers, and even mail clerks. He has never deviated from that belief. Charles preached to all of his employees that his company valued their input and that they were free to make decisions. He firmly believed that his key local rank and file employees around the nation had superior knowledge about what should be done in their areas. He wanted them to make decisions, act quickly, and solve problems. When they did, they were promoted and paid a higher salary.[56]

How well did these business principles work for Charles Koch and Koch Industries? Between 1960 and 2006, the revenues of this private corporation grew from $70 million to $90 billion. Daniel Schulman summed up the success of Koch Industries under Charles Koch this way: "During that time-frame, an original investment of $1,000 in Koch Industries would have swelled to $2 million, a rate of growth that outperformed the S&P 500 formula by a factor of 16, This was not dumb luck. Charles had a formula."[57]

Because Charles Koch utilized the business model of empowerment, he had a great deal of time to spend on American politics. Many pundits might wonder how Charles spent so much time promoting conservative causes and leading his Americans for Prosperity national organization. He had the time because his company hired superb leaders who could make decisions at every level of the company.

I could say ditto for the way I ran K-State. All of the vice-presidents, deans, department heads, faculty and student leaders who worked for me were empowered to make decisions. Because I delegated authority to hundreds of people at every level in my 23 years, I had plenty of "extra" time to assist the school's debate team, the speech squad, the theatre program, and the marching band. I also had the time to help recruit student athletes for football, men's basketball, women's basketball, and volleyball.

MY "LEAN AND MEAN" APPROACH TO MANAGEMENT

This is the approach I took at K-State. In a paper submitted to the Regents on my goals for 2001-02, I wrote: "Of all the nation's major research universities, K-State might very well have the smallest, the leanest, and the meanest administrative structure anywhere. Even though the number of students had grown from about 16,000 students in 1986 to over 22,000 students by 2001, K-State still had the same number of central administrators we had in 1987. Thus, K-State has one of the lowest administrative cost ratios for any of the major universities in America. The truth is we spent only about 4.5 cents out of every dollar on central administration."[58]

Our institutional researchers discovered in 2001 that many big-time universities often spent about 20 cents out of every dollar on central administration. For example, the president of Virginia Tech announced their school had the lowest amount of spending on central administration of any university in the Big East Conference because they only spent 22 cents out of every dollar.

Because only a handful of new bureaucrats were added over my tenure, we kept our administrative cost ratios historically low. In sixteen out of the seventeen years that Jim Coffman was the Provost, the average percentage of faculty salaries was always higher than the average percentage of administrative salaries. Jim and I can only remember one year where central staff had a greater percentage salary increase than the faculty.

While K-State only had a provost and two vice-presidents in 2001, the University of Minnesota had at least eight vice-presidents (one of them was a position listed as the Vice-President for Scholarly and Cultural Affairs); Florida had eight; Michigan had nine; California at Davis had six; and the University of Texas had eight. K-State only needed a few central administrators—mainly because we had people at the lowest local level with the authority to solve specific problems.[59]

In June of 2008, we found out how important our mantra of "flat" management and delegation of authority worked. Our campus was severely hit by a F-2 tornado on June 11, 2008. I found out again when you have a history of everyone up and down the line making decisions and solving problems, it works. In short, when you have people on "the ground" making timely and urgent decisions, I found out that 99% of the time things usually work out fine.

This tornado's destruction covered a third of our campus. Roofs were torn up and thousands of windows were blown out. Many mature trees were blown over. In three minutes, this storm had heavily damaged four buildings and seriously damaged 40 others. The date was June 11, 2008—meaning we only had about two and one-half months to repair the campus.

Ed Rice, our Associate Vice-President for Facilities and our key decision maker on the ground, explained how our electricians, plumbers, painters, roofers, and carpenters teamed up to work six days a week from June 11, 2008 to September 1, 2008. Our administration delegated extraordinary authority to Ed Rice and his staff to get the job done. I would use the word "magical" to describe the outcome of their good work.

Ed rightfully complimented all of his main staff members and facilities workers for "magically" restoring our campus by the time classes started in mid August—including Tom Rawson, Bruce Shubert, Ed Heptig, and Dale Boggs.

Ed Rice told me about two of his employees that made a crucial difference: Mark Loberg and Kevin Minnihan, two project managers for facilities. Ed Rice said about them: "Mark and Kevin pulled off the greatest project management achievement in Kansas history."[60]

Who were they? I did not even know them. But these two K-State employees prove that every organization best succeeds and solves problems when people at the local level are given the authority to act and make decisions.

The truth is that if we had called the federal agency FEMA and asked them to be the leader in the rebuilding and renovation of our K-State campus, the job might have taken a year or more—instead of getting it done in 65 days or so.

Because so many university and business CEO's favor a top-down and centralized approach, I need to explain in detail how well our policy of empowerment worked during my 23 years. It is imperative I provide factual evidence on the reactions of a whole host of K-State policy makers to our strategy of "flat management."

Under two Provosts, Jim Coffman and Duane Nellis, our academic administration consistently practiced a "flat management style." We delegated considerable authority and responsibility to our academic deans and department heads on every front.

HOW OUR NEW ADMINISTRATORS SUPPORTED EMPOWERMENT

Over 23 years, we found that university administrators, deans, department heads, and faculty members backed our "flat" and decentralized decision-making. A newly hired administrator, Elizabeth Unger, who was appointed as the new Information Technology leader in 1994, was one of those who liked our style of empowerment.

After Beth retired in 2009, she thought back to our 1994 pledge that she would run IT: "Well, I had often heard this from my superiors in my 35-year career to that date. Sure, I said. But Jon really meant it. He was a breath of fresh air. He never once told me how to do my job."[61]

In May of 1987, Jim Coffman hired Mel Chastain as the new Director of the Kansas Regents Educational Communications Center. The ECC was housed on the KSU campus and served all Regents schools. I rarely worked directly with Mel. In his retirement letter to me on September 27, 2008, Mel mentioned he had worked in the University of California System under Chancellor Clark Kerr and the Texas A&M University System under Chancellor Frank Hubert.

Still, Mel found my leadership style refreshing: "President Wefald, I must say to you in all candor that in my 45 years in the business of leading a higher education unit, I have never learned more about leadership and management than I have during my 19-plus years at Kansas State. I've heard other leaders describe their leadership style in the same way that you describe yours: hire good people; give them a clear understanding of their mission; and get out of the way. None that I can recall have actually had the courage to live by that philosophy. I can say that you have allowed me to lead, to take chances, and learn from my mistakes."[62]

DEANS, TOO, LIKED THE IDEA OF EMPOWERMENT

Provost Coffman appointed Yar Ebadi the Dean of the College of

Business in March of 1996. He served in that position until July 1, 2010. Dean Ebadi did a superb job over 14 years. He and his top staff increased the number of faculty fellowships from six to 33. In 1996, the College of Business had no endowed chairs. In the years ahead, Yar and his team raised funds for ten fully funded endowed chairs. In 2010, the college's MBA was ranked among the Global 100 Best in the Aspen's Institute's Beyond Grey Pinstripes biennial survey.

Dean Ebadi stressed how important the concept of trust was to his deanship: "For 23 years, I was privileged to watch President Wefald lead through his empowerment of others. He was astute in assembling the right people to do the best job in building supportive levels of corporate success. Wefald had the confidence of his convictions in empowering others to do their jobs without interference. His example of empowering leadership is the style I have adopted as I have advanced in the ranks of higher education. It allows individuals to rise and fall on their own merits."[63]

Mike Holen was the Dean of the College of Education during virtually my entire tenure. If I had ever handed out a MVP trophy to someone in the Council of Deans, it would have gone to Dean Holen. He was a fine scholar and teacher. He was savvy; he had common sense in spades; and he related positively with all of the deans and faculty members. Mike's accomplishments as the Dean of the College of Education from 1990 to 2011 were many and impressive. In his 40 years at Kansas State, Holen was a professor, department head, and associate dean before becoming the dean in 1990.

Dean Holen outlined why he stayed at K-State for so many years: "President Wefald was a special person for an administrator to serve. I doubt I would have remained at K-State for so long had I not been allowed by Jon and his team to use my own creativity, intellect, and leadership skills to contribute to the success of the institution. Frankly, if Jon Wefald or his team had insisted on approving most of my decisions, I can easily imagine I would be retiring as a President or a Provost at some other university. No other president in Kansas State's history has come close to the improvements he has championed for teaching, research, and service."[64]

From 1995 to 2009, Dennis Law was the Dean of the College of Architecture, Planning, and Design. He will be remembered as one of the best deans for that college. He led it with distinction, grace, and a sense of humor. For years, the college's departments had been rated in the top ten nationally in every category. They still are.

Dennis Law explained his support for our leadership model: "I think it was not only the DELEGATION of authority, but also the DISTRIBUTION of authority that made the system so successful. I did not have to answer to any other dean or vice-president, but was allowed to work collaboratively on solving problems within my unit and for the common good of the university."[65]

Terry King was a first-rate Dean for the College of Engineering from 1997 to 2006. No engineering college in the region produced more excellent and well-prepared undergraduates who were highly prized by engineering firms all over the nation. Terry is now the provost at Ball State University in Muncie, Indiana.

Terry King talked about his years at KSU: "I learned many key leadership lessons at K-State but none more important than this: If a complex organization is tightly controlled from the top, then, the organization is only as intelligent as the leader. If, on the other hand, the leader empowers those in the organization to be creative and show initiative, then, the organization can be much smarter than any single person in the organization. The leader must have the self confidence to give up complete control and have the talents to guide creative people in the organization."[66]

FACULTY SENATE PRESIDENTS BACKED EMPOWERMENT

Faculty Senate presidents at Kansas State always played a crucial leadership role in my 23 years. Our administration developed a special partnership with our faculty senate colleagues. They reacted favorably to our model of "distributed leadership."

The Faculty Senate Leadership group was made up of seven faculty members elected by their peers. Our administration met once a month during the academic year with their leadership group. The faculty could put any item on the monthly agenda. We did the same. Our goal was to work with the faculty leaders to solve problems. Many of those problems were solved on the spot.

Fred Fairchild, a Professor of Grain Science and Industry, was the most recent Faculty Senate President I worked with. He served in that position during the school year, 2008-2009.

Fred talked about the meetings we had and what we got done: "Jon was always willing to listen to my inputs and have open dialogue that benefited the relationship between the faculty senate and the administration. As President of the Faculty Senate, I had many opportunities to work with him. We openly shared and discussed many issues. He always had an open door."[67]

Like most faculty leaders, Professor Fairchild believed that the highest priority of the faculty senate over the years was "to keep salaries moving up and benefits competitive and sufficient." He was a member of the faculty senate from 2001 to 2010. In 2004-2005 and 2007-2008, Fairchild served as the chair of the senate's academic affairs committee.

Professor Fairchild focused on three faculty successes. All three of these requests came directly from the faculty senate leadership group. Our role was to find a way to make them happen.

In 2003, the faculty leadership wanted to establish faculty spouse and dependent tuition awards. A special committee of faculty members was set up to devise a plan to allow spouses and dependents to take three credit hours of class work at no cost. It needed the approval of the Board of Regents. After it was approved, we set aside funds in the foundation to cover the program costs. By 2009, tuition awards to faculty spouses and dependents were increased to 7 credit hours per semester for each participant.

The establishment of a "targeted salary enhancement plan" was another Faculty Senate plan to reward highly productive faculty regardless of rank. Bob Zabel was the faculty leader who had vigorously backed this plan for several years as a full professor in the College of Education. But a way had to be found to pay for this meritorious plan. We did and we called it the Zabel Plan.

Professor Fairchild reported on its workings: "The plan would supplement normal merit increases in increments of $2,500 a year. Those monies were added to a faculty member's base salary." Fred reported that about "250 award increments were given to the college deans to distribute to the best faculty each year as long as a funding source was available. This allowed many faculty members to attain more competitive salaries as compared to peer institutions and their faculty."

The Faculty Senate Leadership group backed a plan that Wichita State had adopted to upgrade faculty salaries. It was a "Professorial Performance Award." Fairchild argued that it was a plan for "the most productive tenured full professors. Before, tenured full professors had no way, other than normal merit raises, to increase their incomes. They had reached the top income increment in their appointment when they were promoted to Professor. With this new plan, a full professor could apply for this award every six years."[68]

James C. Legg, a Professor of Physics and the President of the Faculty Senate for the school year 1995-1996, wrote a letter to THE MANHATTAN MERCURY on March 4, 1996. After going to Board of Regents meetings for a year, he said: "Kansas State has very able administrators—the best team in Kansas."[69]

Buddy Gray, a Professor of History, was the president of the faculty senate from 1999-2000. In Bob Shoop's book, Gray stated: "From a faculty perspective, one of Jon Wefald's outstanding qualities is his respect for shared governance. He recognizes the Faculty Senate as the voice of the faculty. He often states publicly that the faculty are the most valuable asset of the university."[70]

Mickey Ransom, a professor of agronomy, was the Faculty Senate president during the year 2000-2001. In a letter to me in 2001, Ransom wrote: "I greatly appreciate the opportunity to work with such an outstanding leader, scholar, and friend. We are so fortunate to have you as President of Kansas State University. Your vision, drive, and dedication to shared governance are truly exemplary."[71]

STUDENT LEADERS ALSO LIKED DELEGATION OF AUTHORITY

Chris Hansen, the Student Body President for 1996-1997 and a senior in nuclear engineering, told the COLLEGIAN how he enjoyed working with an administrative team that gave the students a voice in the operation of the school: "President Wefald has empowered student government to make decisions and play an important role on campus. That definitely is not the case at most other schools."[72]

In the summer of 1986, I told the student senate leaders they would have the final authority to decide how student fees were allocated. On September 10, 1996, the COLLEGIAN editor had a nice column about that idea and our administration: "The president has done a great deal to give students a say in the governing of K-State. Wefald has given more power to students by increasing the duties of the student body president and Student Senate. It was his idea to hand the fee-payment issue to Senate."[73]

WHY I LASTED FOR 23 YEARS

The central reason I remained K-State's President for so long is because I followed for 23 years the management principles of empowerment, a "flat" management structure, trust, and the delegation of authority.

Andrew Carnegie, the president of the Carnegie Steel Company in Pittsburgh, Pennsylvania in the late 19th century, consistently insisted on hiring talented, smart, and strong individuals. Carnegie's enthusiasm for hiring the best and brightest was so intense that he told his associates what he wanted on his tombstone: "Here lies a man who attracted better people into his service than he was himself."

I can easily identify with his thoughts because I certainly was never the smartest guy in the room—meaning it was never a problem for me to hire people who were much smarter and more talented than me. I would recommend for any future leader in any field of activity to take seriously what Andrew Carnegie said about hiring the best and the brightest people they can find.

Terry King's comments from his time as our Dean of Engineering from 1997 to 2006, need to be reaffirmed: "I learned many key leadership lessons at K-State but none more important than this—If a complex organization is tightly controlled from the top, then, the organization is only as intelligent as the leader. If, on the other hand, the leader empowers those in the organization to be creative and show initiative, then, the organization can be much smarter than any single person in the organization."

I think that Dean Terry King explains our "magic" of delegation and empowerment as well as anyone who worked with me over the years. King came to understand that K-State was unique in public higher education because he knew that our school had hundreds of leaders making decisions every day. He recognized, moreover, that most of them never came to my attention at all because I trusted them to do a superb job. When any of our leaders failed to act or if they made a number of poor decisions, we either reassigned them or asked them to move on. That did not happen very often.

But, equally important, King's comments also reveal so well why I had the time to focus in on some areas that ordinarily would not get the attention of any president—mainly because so many of them were micro-managing the entire campus.

In short, Terry's analysis succinctly explains how I found the time to help programs and departments that were normally out of sight and mind. That would include the Speech Squad, the Debate Team, the Theatre program, and the Marching Band. It also helps elucidate how I increasingly found the time after 1990 to help recruit student athletes for four different teams.

Chapter 3

Two Major Strategic Initiatives—Upgrading Our Research And Graduate Programs And Initiating A New Information Technology Program

Provost Jim Coffman led our academic reforms in the decade of the 1990's. During that decade, K-State's strategic priorities focused more on university-wide initiatives rather than specific college and department programs. Our leadership team was intent on improving academic programs for the whole university. That would take most of the first ten years. Those university-wide academic priorities were set by a combination of strategic planning and administrative action.

Our leadership team listened carefully to the deans, department heads, faculty leaders, and student leaders. We decided our most important strategic inititiatives to enhance our national ranking among land-grant universites were two-fold: one, to improve our Research and Graduate education; and two, to initiate a major effort in Information Technology.

OUR RESEARCH AND GRADUATE PROGRAMS HAD TO IMPROVE

The single biggest university-wide academic program challenge in the late 1980's and 1990's was the urgent need to thoroughly upgrade our university research and graduate education programs. Kansas State had no choice. Our goal was to seriously enhance our national academic reputation—meaning that we had to completely ramp up our basic research program and improve our graduate school programs.

In 1986, Kansas State was ranked about 105th among America's public universities in competitive research grants and research expenditures. Among the nation's major public universities, Kansas State was way behind in basic research and peer-driven grants.

It is important to remember that our school had been mainly a vocational-technical institute for its first 75 years. Few land grant universities in the nation could have overcome eight decades of being a vocational institute.

Meanwhile, Kansas and its Chancellors had been stressing from 1875 on that their university should have a national class library, hire the best research scholars and teachers, and celebrate the importance of the liberal arts.

The elite Ivy League schools formed the prestigious Association of American Universities (AAU) in 1900. Importantly, KU was admitted into the AAU in 1909. In 1932, KU helped start the Association of Research Libraries (ARL). Kansas State is still not a member of either the AAU or the ARL.

Even more important for Kansas State's standing, our major land grant competitors like Iowa State, Purdue, and Texas A&M from early in the 20th century were championing the importance of having excellent research libraries, hiring top-notch researchers and scholars, and striving to be more comprehensive, modern, and diverse. These facts help explain why Iowa State became an AAU school in 1958, Purdue in 1958, and Texas A&M in 2001.

KANSAS STATE WAS MAINLY AN UNDERGRADUATE SCHOOL FROM 1900 TO 1990: MORE GORDIAN KNOTS

In contrast to these land grant schools, Kansas State fell further and further behind in the 20th century for at least three reasons. First, Kansas State was largely a vocational institute from 1873 to 1943. Second, our school mainly emphasized programs in agriculture and engineering from 1900 to 1986. Third, our school was largely an undergraduate teaching institution from 1900 to 1990. Taken together, these three historic patterns represented a Gordian Knot of challenges that had to be unraveled.

During my 23 years, we met all three of these historic trends head on. Indeed, we made great progress in unraveling all three challenges. But I seriously doubt that any of these historic trends can be totally unraveled completely in my lifetime or any lifetime.

After World War II, the Colleges of Engineering, Agriculture, and Veterinary Medicine at Iowa State, Purdue, Colorado State, and Texas A&M increasingly expanded their major research programs and competitive research grants.

Kansas State did not aggressively promote competitive research grant programs until the late 1980's and early 1990's. This was especially true for the three colleges that were most vital for our school to be a major research university—namely, the Colleges of Engineering, Agriculture, and Veterinary Medicine. Indeed, the truth is that the majority of graduate students at Kansas State in the late 1980's were in the College of Education.

There is no doubt that our academic programs in engineering, agriculture, and veterinary medicine had outstanding teachers and teaching excellence from 1900 to 1990. There is no doubt that these three colleges did an excellent job of producing highly skilled, literate, and educated undergraduate and professional students who were highly sought after by America's best businesses.

It is important to remember, however, that the College of Agriculture was garnering a multitude of congressional earmarks and formula-driven funds for various agricultural research programs from the United States Department of Agriculture from 1945 to the present.

THE COLLEGE OF AGRICULTURE AND ITS APPLIED RESEARCH

K-State's College of Agriculture had a much different history in basic applied research compared to the Colleges of Engineering and Veterinary Medicine. These two important colleges received some formula funding over these years—but not much.

From 1945 and even in the years before to the present, the College of Agriculture did compelling, original, and outstanding applied basic research. Importantly, the bulk of the funding for these research projects in agriculture came from directed federal and state appropriations. They are called formula-driven earmarks.

As president of a land grant university, I was reminded many times about two crucial pieces of historic Congressional legislation: the Hatch Act of 1887 and the Smith-Lever Act of 1914. The Hatch Act was enacted to establish agricultural experiment stations for every land grant school. Kansas State had experiment stations for agricultural research in Hays and Manhattan.

The Smith-Lever Act of 1914 started the entire process of federal funding for cooperative extension. Like Kansas State, each land grant school received federal funding to hire extension county agents for the counties in their states. This 1914 legislation was set up on a national basis to have county agents in virtually every county to advise farmers and ranchers on the best practices.[74]

Our College of Agriculture researchers have been developing superb new wheat varieties for decades. The Hays Experiment Station has produced an amazing number of wheat hybrids for the farmers and ranchers of western Kansas—including wheat varieties like Kiowa, Bison, Arkan, Dodge, Lakin, and Tiger.

Focusing on wheat adapted to central and eastern Kansas, the Manhattan Experiment Station has produced popular and premier wheat varieties like Newton, Karl, Jagger, 2137, Overly, and Everest. I became acquainted with these nationally recognized wheat hybrids produced in the 1980's and 1990's.[75]

These new wheat hybrids propelled Kansas to the top of all wheat producing states in America. Since World War II, Kansas has been recognized as the wheat capital of America and even the world. Between 1997 and 2009, the wheat farmers of Kansas averaged about 400 million bushels of winter wheat per year.

Bikram Gill, a first-rate University Distinguished Professor of Plant Pathology, used some humor to explain the importance of these new wheat hybrids: "It's funny that some Kansas residents expect two things from K-State—to educate their children and to produce wheat varieties."[76]

Much of the vital Kansas State agricultural research funds after 1945 came from directed state appropriations and formula-driven earmarks from the USDA under the umbrella of the Hatch Act of 1887. To say the least, these grants have had a lasting and profound impact on the state's agriculture and its farmers.

In 1998, Ron Trewyn, the Vice Provost for Research and Dean of the Graduate School, released a publication documenting the results of our researchers and scientists in wheat, sorghum, beef, and meat processing. It shows that the economic value from our applied agricultural research totaled over $1 billion for just 1998.

The figure of $1 billion would only grow in the years ahead. For 1998, some important examples of the value-added agricultural research from the work of K-State's top agricultural researchers included: research on range management, $96 million; meat processing research for the beef processing plants in Dodge City, Garden City, and Liberal, $296 million; research on feedlot performance and livestock implants, $250 million; and improved wheat varieties, well over $100 million, etc.[77]

Although this $1 billion was a huge bonus for the economy of Kansas every year, ratings publications like U.S. NEWS AND REPORT ignored this kind of applied research because it came from directed state appropriations and federal USDA earmarks instead of competitive grants from the NSF and the NIH.

From research to teaching to extension, some of the most wonderful people I met over 23 years were in the College of Agriculture.

WHY OTHER LAND GRANTS WERE GRADED HIGHER THAN KSU

K-State and our new leadership team after 1986 had to focus on sharply improving the quality and volume of peer-driven competitive research. This focus was imperative if our goal was to make Kansas State one of the nation's best land grant schools.

Increasingly, the major rating services and publications like U.S. NEWS AND WORLD REPORT from the 1970's to the present graded the premier land grant universities at the highest level because of their excellent Ph.D programs, their first-rate research libraries, and the volume of their competitive research grants.

By 1986, K-State was way behind elite land grants like Texas A&M, Purdue, and Iowa State in extramural funding. But our school had also fallen behind three other land grant universities that we should have been competitive with by 1986—Colorado State, Oregon

State, and Washington State. In 1987, Jim Coffman and our entire team knew our competitive research grants had to be jacked up.

The best land-grant universities had been gearing up for basic research and peer-driven grants from 1945 to 1986. Schools like Texas A&M, Purdue, Iowa State, Oregon State, and Colorado State had been securing their fair share of competitive grants for decades—especially in their three Colleges of Engineering, Agriculture, and Veterinary Medicine.

The meaning of all this is straightforward. If we were going to take a major step up in extramural funding and competitive research grants, K-State absolutely needed the Colleges of Engineering, Agriculture, and Veterinary Medicine to play leadership roles. We were confident this would happen.

THE HISTORIC RESEARCH SUCCESSES OF TWO DEPARTMENTS IN THE COLLEGE OF ARTS AND SCIENCES: PHYSICS AND BIOLOGY

Meanwhile, there were two outstanding academic programs right in the middle of our school that had become basic research powerhouses as early as the 1960's and 1970's—the Department of Physics and the Division of Biology. In the two decades before I came to K-State in 1986, those two departments had already become genuine pacesetters for peer-driven competitive research years before any of the university's major colleges.

In 1964, the McCain administration created a University Distinguished Professor program for research scholars. The first UDP was selected in 1964. For reasons unknown, Kansas State only selected 4 more UDP's between 1964 and 1986.

In 1987, Jim Coffman and the new Vice Provost for Research, Tim Donoghue, decided that we had to get into the national game of competitive grants. Knowing how vital it was to encourage the school's brightest researchers, Jim and Tim elevated the importance of the UDP program from 1987 to 2009.

Everyone agreed that the new UDP's would be chosen for excellence in research, scholarship, teaching, and creative endeavors. In 1995, Jim Coffman and Tim Donoghue decided to fund at least two UDP's a year. Each new recipient would receive an additional $10,000 base salary adjustment. Importantly, for the future of our research efforts, K-State added 57 new University Distinguished Professors from 1987 to 2009.[78]

In 1995, Provost Coffman and the deans created another award to enhance our support for academic excellence. We created a University Distinguished Teaching Scholars Award. Later, this award was rightfully named after our outstanding provost, Jim Coffman.

Initially, the award stipend was $2,500. By 2003, each winner received a base stipend of $5,000. The teaching scholar award was for excellence in undergraduate teaching and learning. Between 1995 and 2008, 13 faculty members were selected for this award.[79]

In reviewing these two awards, I was hardly surprised to see how many excellent researchers and scientists were in the Department of Physics and the Division of Biology. Out of the 57 University Distinguished Professors chosen between 1987 and 2008, nine were Physics professors and seven were Biology professors. Between 1995 and 2008, there were 13 professors selected for the Coffman Chair for Teaching Scholars—with three in physics and two in biology.[80]

Two professors in physics deserve special mention: Dean Zollman and Chris Sorensen. They achieved a classic academic trifecta. They were both selected for the University Distinguished Professor, a Coffman Chair for University Distinguished Teaching Scholars, and selected in separate years for the CASE/CARNEGIE NATIONAL PROFESSOR OF THE YEAR AWARD—meaning both professors were the equivalent of First Team All-American scholars.[81]

THE EXCELLENT RESEARCH RECORD IN PHYSICS

The Department of Physics became the first major research-intensive department in the university beginning in the 1960's. Over the next two decades, the physics department built national class and vital research programs in atomic, molecular, and optical physics, high-energy physics, and cosmology.

From the 1960's on, the Department of Physics hired a multitude of first-class researchers and scholars—including Dudley Williams, R. Dean Dragsdorf, Brock Dale, Chandra Bhalla, Lew Cocke, Bob Leachman, Jim Legg, Patrick Richard, Jim McDonald, Chris Sorensen, Dean Zollman, and many others. With so many brilliant teachers and researchers, the Department of Physics peer-driven grants grew from $2 million in 1990 to $7 million by 2009.

Several physics professors reminded me the research funding for their department came from only 27 permanent permanent faculty members—while North Carolina State, one of our peer schools, had almost double the number of permanent faculty members.[82]

THE NEW AND SUPERB DIVISION OF BIOLOGY IN 1967

John Chalmers, the Dean of the College of Arts and Sciences, created the Division of Biology in 1967. The departments of botany, zoology, and bacteriology were combined into a new Division. In the next 40 years, the Division developed strengths in ecological genomics, biology, cellular and developmental biology, gravitational biology, ecological research, basic cancer research, and biomedical research.

From 1967 on, the division hired many national class researchers including—L. Evans Roth; Lloyd Hubert; Dick Marzolf; Richard Consigli (Dick received the CASE National Professor of the Year Silver Medal Award in both 1985 and 1986); Terry Johnson; John Zimmerman; Robert Robel; Brian Spooner; Gary Conrad; Rob Dennell; Larry Takemoto; John Blair; Walter Dodds; Anne Stalheim-Smith; David Rintoul; Larry Williams; Beth Montelone, David Hartnett; Anthony Joern; and Alan Knapp.

Given biology's superior researchers and teachers, the program attracted over 700 undergraduate majors and 60 graduate students by 2009. The 63 faculty members in the Division of Biology by 2009 were publishing up to 125 papers in peer-reviewed journals annually, about 20 book chapters, and many review articles annually. Thus, the Division of Biology was excelling in both research and teaching by the late 1960's and early 1970's.[83]

THE STAGGERING RESEARCH FUNDING IN BIOLOGY SINCE 1967

From 1967 to 2009, the Division of Biology became a leader among all of the university departments and colleges in terms of generating millions in peer-driven competitive research grants year after year.

From 1995 to 2009, under the leadership of Brian Spooner who became the director in 1994, the Division of Biology generated a huge figure of over $126 million in basic research funding. Brian and his staff compiled the following figures for those 15 years—the research grants totaled $33.7 million from 1995 to 1999; $42.6 million from 2000 to 2004; and $49.5 million from 2005 to 2009.[84]

The extramural funding came from a Division of Biology program averaging 39 tenure-track faculty members a year. This number does not include non-tenure track faculty who were mainly teaching faculty and unclassified non-research professionals.

Brian Spooner explained the division's research success this way: "If the 2004-09 annual average of $9.9 million is divided by 39 tenured-track faculty members a per year, the division is generating over $254,000 per tenured/tenure track faculty member a year."[85]

When you consider the research funding per tenure-track faculty members combined with the excellent teaching of over 700 undergraduate majors, the conclusion is straightforward. The Division of Biology became the pacesetter in the past generation among all departments and colleges at K-State from 1970 to 2009.

In my 23 years as K-State president, my candidate for a MVP department head is Professor Brian Spooner. He has been a scholar, teacher, and leader—and a boss that expects excellence in both research and teaching from everyone.

FOR KANSAS STATE AFTER 1960, THE QUESTION IS—WHAT IF?

When you reflect back to 1960, you can only think of what if? What if the Colleges of Engineering, Veterinary Medicine, and Agriculture had hired more basic research faculty members similar to what Physics and Biology had done since the 1960's and 1970's?

If that had happened, K-State's competitive grants by 2009 might be equal today to that of the premier land grant peer universities.

In 2009, North Carolina State's competitive grants were $380 million; Iowa State had $224 million; Colorado State had $304 million; Washington State had $285 million; and Oregon State had $209 million. In 2009, K-State's competitive grants were $134 million.[86]

THE IMPORTANCE OF IMPROVING OUR RESEARCH AND GRADUATE EDUCATION PROGRAMS AFTER 1986

With all of this in mind, Provost Coffman appointed Howard Erickson, a Professor of Anatomy and Physiology in the College of Veterinary Medicine, to chair a new task force in 1987. Its mission was to make recommendations for new approaches in research and graduate education. The recommendation was to combine the two areas of research and graduate education into one key position: a Vice-Provost for Research and Dean of the Graduate School.

After a long search process, Coffman appointed Tim Donoghue to that position in late 1988. He was a Professor of Physics and Co-Director of the Van de Graaff Accelerator Lab at Ohio State University. He was highly regarded for his vision in creating numerous interdisciplinary campus-wide research initiatives. Tim Donoghue became a key leader in kick-starting the school's quest to become a leader in competitive research grants.[87]

THE INITIAL DIFFICULTIES IN UPGRADING OUR RESEARCH

Early on, Coffman and Donoghue saw how difficult the process was for our researchers—most especially getting our research grant proposals out the door. For many of our research faculty, they often viewed the school's research door as closed or sometimes even locked—mainly because our system was so inefficient and subject to delays and even errors.

The initial expansion of research funding and graduate education was largely funded by the reallocation of funds. Coffman transferred $1.5 million from the provost's office and various cost centers to the new operation in research and graduate education. As extramural funding started to grow, the new research funding generated new overhead monies (SRO)—which were reinvested in the new research office and the research infrastructure in the primary academic departments.

In 1992, Tim Donoghue set up an important new research position. For the first time, an assistant research director position for pre-award services was hired: Paul Lowe. He was a superb hire. In the Biology program, Paul had gained experience in directing proposal development, award management, and fiscal affairs.[88]

From 1993 to 2009, Paul Lowe and his colleagues launched many new strategies for upgrading our research efforts. They included the following: the development of streamlined electronic and procedural resources; the adoption of more seamless policies and procedures for our faculty to submit competitive grants; the deployment of targeted research training for the deans and their faculty members; the enhancement of the service mission of the office; and the encouragement of cross-department cooperation across the whole university.[89]

THE HIRING IN 1994 OF A KEY RESEARCH LEADER: RON TREWYN

From 1989 to 1993, Tim Donoghue had several interim associate vice-provosts for research. In 1994, he appointed Ron Trewyn as the new Associate Vice-Provost for Research. Ron was a magna cum laude graduate of Wisconsin State University with a B.S. in biology and a Ph.D in biochemistry and genetics from Oregon State.

Ron Trewyn had been a Professor of Medical Biochemistry, Director of the Biochemistry graduate program, and Director of the Ohio State Cancer Center's Tissue Procurement Service. Tim was bullish about Ron's credentials: "Dr. Trewyn has considerable experience in securing extramural funding for his cancer-related research programs, which is a highly competitive area. That experience will be very valuable in providing guidance to new faculty submitting proposals for the first time."[90]

MORE IMPORTANT CHANGES IN RESEARCH

Trewyn's first job was to ensure that the entire research operation was sufficiently staffed and focused on the service mission of the office. The research office, for example, needed to expand the university's compliance capabilities. Trewyn added an excellent new compliance officer, Jerry Jaax. In 1998, Jim Guikema was appointed as the associate dean of the graduate school. Then, in 2001, Jim became the associate dean for research. As a top scholar, Guikema had conducted research in gravitational biology in the Division of Biology since 1981.

When Tim Donoghue retired in 1998, Ron Trewyn was promoted by Jim Coffman to be the interim Vice-Provost for Research and Dean of the Graduate School. Ron became a dynamic leader for our research efforts and competitive research grants program. In 2007, the new Provost, Duane Nellis, and I appointed Ron Trewyn as the school's first Vice-President for Research. Trewyn, then, appointed Jim Guikema as the new Associate Vice-President for Research.

Ron Trewyn, Jim Guikema, and Paul Lowe developed an excellent partnership. The three research leaders worked together to enhance our research programs by hiring some additional excellent full-service support personnel for K-State's grant seeking efforts. By 2008, the pre-award services office had been upgraded to include a talented group of 13 FTE professional staff, two graduate students, and five undergraduate students.

This group of professionals came to include vital research personnel, including grant and contract specialists, professional contract negotiators, data managers, budget analysts, and other support staff. They were all dedicated to the mission of providing timely and focused assistance in the development of research proposals for the faculty scholars of Kansas State University.[91]

Between 2000 and 2009, a first-rate central research support system had been established. It would benefit the university for years to come. Led by Trewyn, Guikema, and Lowe, these research leaders knocked down virtually all of the barriers that had discouraged faculty researchers in the past from seeking external sponsorship of Kansas State's research capabilities.

About the central research team, Paul Lowe said: "We performed very deliberate recruitments, procured software and hardware to support the shift to electronic proposal development, and accelerated the submission of federal funding opportunities. We also worked closely with departments to encourage proactive support at the department/experiment station/college level, along with increasing the promotion of faculty successes. These efforts resulted in a very high quality package that allowed the K-State faculty's scholarship to shine during peer-reviewed competition."[92]

K-STATE PASSES KU, LAWRENCE IN RESEARCH FUNDING BY 2009

In 1986, Kansas State had total annual extramural funding of about $18 to $20 million. K-State was light-years behind KU in research grants funded. After K-State first passed $50 million in 1994, Paul Lowe declared: "Our school has not looked back." In 1994, Kansas State submitted about 800 proposals a year. By 2010, KSU was advancing about 1,400 proposals per year requesting in excess of $480 million.

After 1987, Provost Jim Coffman and our research leaders were confident that the three vital Colleges of Engineering, Veterinary Medicine, and Agriculture would dramatically increase their basic research and peer-driven grants. That happened.

While all three colleges continued their superb teaching, they also made outstanding progress in the important arena of competitive basic research. From 1990 to 2009, the College of Engineering increased its competitive research funding from $5.5 million to $22.7 million. The College of Veterinary Medicine improved its competitive research awards from $1 million to $13.6 million. And the College of Agriculture increased its competitive research awards from $7.2 million to $29 million.[93]

By 2008, K-State in Manhattan had caught up to KU in Lawrence in total research funding. By 2009, K-State in Manhattan actually passed KU in Lawrence in total "sponsored activity." In 2008, KU in Lawrence had research awards of $124 million compared to KSU's total of $118 million. By 2009, KSU had a total of $133.6 million in research awards compared to KU's research awards of $126.3 million.

To this day, I am still astounded that our university could compile these extraordinary advances in basic research grants by 2009—in spite of the challenges of 6,000 new students and 51 fewer instructional faculty members than we had in 1986.[94]

Kansas State had become a major land grant university. It had taken 23 years. But our leadership team had hired the right people from 1988 to 2009 to produce an historic turnaround in research funding and awards. We were catching up to many of the major land-grant universities in America.

With $20 million in extramural funding in 1986, Kansas State was ranked about 105th among public universities in research expenditures.

But with the $134 million in research funding in 2009, the Arizona State University Center for Measuring University Performance now ranked Kansas State 75th of the Top 100 public universities in research expenditures. This means that K-State had moved up at least 25 to 30 spots in the ASU Center for Measuring University Performance over our 23 years.[95]

Paul Lowe reflected on K-State's progress in research successes from 1986 to 2009. He stated: "Who knows where Kansas State would be sitting today if not for the visionary leadership of the

Wefald Administration. K-State was able to achieve greatness in this research area while also exerting great effort to control costs and remain accountable to the taxpayers of Kansas. The 'lean and mean' administrative structure deployed at K-State during the Wefald Administration allowed this enormous growth in research infrastructure at a cost much less than that of its peers."[96]

THE HUGE CHALLENGES FACING K-STATE IN 1986

After 1987, K-State needed a dramatically juiced up program in information technology. It was still another severe intractable problem. For years, these two areas of administrative and academic computing had been located in separate silos. Actually, the people in each silo were at war with one another.

I could not help at all because I had no IT skills. In this new emerging world of IT, I was basically ignorant. Indeed, I was a 19th century Luddite. In 1987, Provost Jim Coffman had far more IT skills than I did. From 1987 to 1993, he saw the two warring camps at work. Despite his skills at working with individuals or groups, Jim knew he was literally confronting an entrenched and almost Old World bureaucracy.

WHAT CHANGES WERE IMMEDIATELY NECESSARY?

In late 1992, Provost Coffman was able to craft a new position to provide leadership for the new IT effort. The position was called the Vice-Provost for Academic Services and Technology and the Dean of Continuing Education (VPAST/DCE). Jim had to find exactly the right person to fill this job. The school had struck out several times. Coffman reminded me that in 1992 it was advantageous for these two units to be under one roof due to the emerging importance of distance education—which over time became a program of huge importance at K-State.

In 1992, the candidate interviewed was either a specialist in continuing education with a modest IT background or vice versa. But many people on the search committee kept saying that the right person for the job was already here—Elizabeth Unger. She had a BS in Engineering and an MS in mathematics from Michigan State University and a Ph.D in Computer Science from KU.

Jim Coffman had to convince Beth Unger she could do a good job. Indeed, she became exactly the right person and the right fit for the job. Beth faced a school that was at ground zero in IT in 1993.

In her first couple of years, she had to deal with quite a few combative and cantankerous IT staff members on both sides. She had to fire many of them. We learned quickly that Beth Unger was up to the challenge.

Ordinarily, Jim Coffman does not rave about people. He came to see Beth as a visionary, a decision maker, and exceptionally talented. The respect between Coffman and Unger was mutual. Beth wrote that: "Jim Coffman was the finest administrator I have ever worked with. He was brilliant, an innovator, wise, a peacemaker, and honest as the day is long."

Beth Unger was excellent in selecting her new team. She did not care if the hire was a recent hotshot college graduate or an IT veteran of many years. Like Thomas Edison, Beth wanted people who were creative and innovative. She did exactly that when she hired young college graduates like Rob Caffey, Scott Finkeldei, and Danny Fonce and veterans like Harvard Townsend, Fred Damkroger, Rebecca Gould, Sue Maes, Kelly Moon, David Stewart, Betty Stevens, and Mel Chastain.

OUR RESEARCHERS NEEDED HIGH PERFORMANCE COMPUTING

By 1993 and 1994, our best researchers, scientists, engineers, and scholars were demanding high performance computing. Beth Unger heard them loud and clear: K-State had to immediately jump on the bandwagon of high performance computing.

Sizing up the huge problems facing computing services, Beth was incredibly blunt: "K-State was not even experimentally looking at the new World Wide Web concepts; electronic communication (primarily email) was spotty around campus and not heavily used; there was no experimentation with course management systems; and there was no central support for people trying to use the computing resources that were available. My own philosophy was to hire the best people and get out of the way."[97]

The new strategy for IT and Beth Unger was to leave the vertical silo syndrome behind and transition to a more modern horizontal program. In a horizontal model, the computing staff would have to team up with employees from every cost center in computing services. Everyone had to embrace a simple historic fact. Change had to be the one constant for computing and continuing education.

A new chart for the horizontally organized units was adopted. It included the following: (1) User Services—later called ITAC; (2) Division of Continuing Education and Technology in teaching and learning; (3) Applications—now called the Information Systems Office; (4) Data and Information Organization; (5) Computing—now called Computing Technical Services; and (6) The Educational Communications Center. Each functional unit depended directly on the ones next to them in the hierarchy.[98]

I was an old-fashioned teacher. I needed only chalkboards and chalk. I taught a history course in 1990 on American history from 1945 to the present. I had 30 students. I outlined my lecture on three chalkboards. I lectured off the chalkboards. I never used a PowerPoint presentation. It was too dull. By 2007, I was the only president in the state university system giving an annual presentation without an overhead.

In my 23 years, I never used a laptop. I never had a cell phone. By the late 1990's, I was receiving emails. But my excellent administrative assistant, Dana Hastings, received the emails for me in the president's office and I dictated a response.

My ignorance of IT landed me in big-time trouble at least once. In 1999, I was surprised how one badly handled email could cause such a huge problem. On September 29, 1999, some fan sent me an email written by a sportswriter from THE SPORTING NEWS. The writer, Will Leatch, had written a story about our upcoming football game between K-State and Texas.

Leatch said some nasty things about our football team. He wrote that most fans in America would be cheering for Texas. I should have left it alone. But I sent an email response. I told Will Leatch something like this: "Outside of Texas, very few people cheer for the Longhorns because the University of Texas represents in most people's minds both incredible wealth and arrogance."

Will Leatch was the only person who had a copy of my absurd email. From time to time, I did a stupid thing. I told Dana Hastings to put my email on the KSU athletic website. I was hoping that K-State's football fans would like my criticism of the SPORTING NEWS article.

I might as well have sent my email to the General Secretary of the United Nations, the Pope, or to the UT President, Larry Faulkner. My office soon got irate phone calls from many UT fans. I learned, again, that if you make a mistake, you should immediately apologize.

I did that. I called Faulkner and I talked to the editor of the Texas student newspaper. I told them that my comments were pure nonsense. I totally apologized. I learned when you put an email on an athletic department website, you had better be praising the Founding Fathers or Abraham Lincoln.

I went to the UT game in Austin. No one recognized me. At half-time, I went to the men's room near the visiting athletic director's suite. There were two Texas alums in the restroom. One of them said to the other: "Well, we might not beat K-State today, but it sure is nice to be both arrogant and rich."

MANY CLASSROOMS HAD TO BE RENOVATED FOR I.T.

For K-State's emerging distance education programs, Beth Unger's goal was "to capture the activities in a classroom and deliver this to distance students either synchronously or asynchronously." In the spring of 1995, Unger and several of her staff members visited schools like Harvard, Rensselaer Polytechnic University, and Notre Dame.

Harvard provided Kansas State the architectural specs for the "tiered classroom design." RPI provided the specs for a "studio classroom concept" that aided K-State in creating introductory biology, English, engineering, and statistics studio classrooms. Notre Dame helped with the concepts of "video capture and delivery."[99]

To create easy to use classroom technology in renovated classrooms, Beth and her staff initially identified the larger classrooms seating 100 students or more. The goal was to improve the spaces that emphasized the lecture style.

In 1995, the first classroom scheduled as an IT enhanced lecture hall was Williams Auditorium. It was the largest lecture hall on campus with about 425 seats. In 2010, the Williams Auditorium was completely redesigned at a cost of about $1 million to a discussion style model.

By the end of her tenure, Beth Unger could proclaim: "K-State now had 70 new technologically upgraded classrooms on campus by 2009. These classrooms helped faculty members move to more interactive teaching and allowed the introduction of new media tools that enhanced learning."[100]

THE GROWTH OF DISTANCE EDUCATION PROGRAMS

The distance education programs mushroomed at the same time. After 1994, these programs quickly grew to include 22 master's degrees, nine bachelor's degrees, and one doctoral degree. In addition, 19 certificate programs became available online. By 2008-2009, Kansas State was offering over 50 academic degrees and certificates to students throughout the nation and the world.[101]

During Beth Unger's tenure from 1994 to 2009, the IT budget increased from $2.3 million dollars in 1994 to over $30 million in 2009. By 1995, 26,000 messages were sent per day; by 2000, it was 215,000 messages a day; and by 2007, it was 749,000 messages a day. By 1995, seventy-five per cent of the faculty offices had been wired for the campus network and internet access.[102]

By 1996, virtually all of the students had email accounts and 62% of the faculty and staff had email accounts and access to the internet through the World Wide Web (WWW). By 1997, all colleges had a

WWW page; 61 out of 62 academic departments had a WWW page; and 62 per cent of administrative units had a WWW page.

In 1997, K-State was ranked 85th of America's Most Wired Universities. In 2001, YAHOO! INTERNET LIFE ranked K-State as 31st of the100 Most Wired Universities. In 2004, the PRINCETON REVIEW ranked Kansas State 15th in the nation of the most wired campuses. From 1994 when our school was at ground zero in IT to 2004, K-State had become an elite wired campus.[103]

By 2007, the number of students using KSOL exceeded the number of enrolled students. By 2007, 100% of all teaching spaces, faculty offices, and residence halls were served with wireless computing.

In the 2008 edition of PC MAGAZINE, AMERICA'S TOP WIRED COLLEGES, which evaluated schools on data collected by the PRINCETON REVIEW, the magazine ranked K-State as the No. 2 wired college in the United States. The University of Illinois was ranked first in this 2008 edition of PC MAGAZINE.[104]

Rightfully, Beth Unger called this high ranking by PC MAGAZINE in 2008 "the culminating award for the staff, faculty, and administration for the years that I was VPAST/DCE from 1994 to 2009. It recognized both the IT infrastructure and the IT tools people could use but also the outstanding uses the K-State community was making of IT. It recognized both academic and administrative computing which were now fully integrated as the user experienced the IT world at K-State."[105]

From 1993 to 2009, Kansas State had made historic progress in Information Technology. In December of 2014, Jim Coffman and I were having coffee. I asked Jim, how in the world did Beth Unger get so much done in her tenure. He said: "I have no idea." I did not know either.

But the two of us agreed on several words for Beth's great work for K-State—"It was magical." Neither one of us knew exactly how she had done it—meaning Beth Unger was totally empowered to lead and manage our IT program for 16 years.

In the 1990's, we had two major goals—to upgrade our research and graduate programs and to implement a new program in information technology. These goals were met head on. During the decade of the 1990's, the university had made enormous progress on many fronts. Kansas State University was now much better prepared for the challenges of the 21st century.

Chapter 4

In The 1990's, More Notable Changes Occur: In Diversity, The Foundation, And The Alumni Association

From July of 1986 on, our entire leadership team understood how far behind Kansas State was in the area of diversity. But there were a number of dynamic leaders intent on improving the diversity of our faculty, staff, and student body. They included faculty and staff like Jim Boyer, Juanita McGowan, Kathy Greene, and Veryl Switzer.

But there was one singular leader, Jim Boyer. An excellent teacher in the College of Education, he was K-State's most passionate leader for diversity. From 1971 to 1997, Boyer carried the torch of equality for people of color at Kansas State. In his retirement statement on November 25, 1997, I declared: "If Martin Luther King Jr. was the drum major for peace and the nation's trumpet for social justice, Jim Boyer was an inspired disciple."[106]

In 1988, Jim Coffman and Bob Krause recommended a new Task Force for Retention to upgrade our efforts in diversity. It was this task force that forced us to look at graduation rates among minority students and to improve the recruiting of all minority students, especially African-American and Hispanic students.

Chaired by Ken Gowdy, an Associate Dean in Engineering, and Susan Scott, an Associate Dean in Student Life, the findings of this 1990 task force on minority student retention and recruitment led our team to set up an Office of Diversity and Dual Career Development. This study had uncovered many uncomfortable truths about K-State and our lack of success in diversity.[107]

I often wondered why I became such a strong advocate for diversity. After all, I had grown up in Minot, North Dakota, a city of about 20,000 in 1960. It only had a handful of African-Americans.

By my eighth and ninth grades, I had become a fanatical supporter of the Brooklyn Dodgers. In the ninth grade, I could name every starter for the Brooklyn Dodgers. I still can. I liked the Dodgers—mainly because they were the first team to play blacks.

I was excited to see a team that had outstanding African-American players like Jackie Robinson, Roy Campanella, Don Newcombe,

Junior Gilliam, and Sandy Amaros. In the summer of my tenth grade, I talked my dad into letting me take the train from Minot, North Dakota to Milwaukee, Wisconsin to see the Milwaukee Braves and the Brooklyn Dodgers. I do not know of any other Minot kid that took a train to Milwaukee to see a major league game.

In the summer of 1956, I organized a fast pitch softball team. We had a number of my former American Legion teammates on the team. Lacking an excellent pitcher, somebody told me about a young African-American business leader who could pitch. He was the only black player in that summer softball league. I have developed great friendships with people of color ever since.

The findings of the Gowdy-Scott Task Force represented a tipping point for all of us in Anderson Hall. Diversity had to become a high priority. Having created the new position of Associate Provost for Diversity and Dual Career Development, K-State was fortunate to hire Mordean Taylor-Archer from VCU. Appointed on June 7, 1990, Mordean became a great leader for K-State for diversity.[108]

In the fall of 1988, K-State had enrolled 164 new African-American students, 99 new Hispanic students, 14 new Native American students, and 50 new Asian students. Pat Bosco and his admission representatives were aggressively recruiting students from everywhere in Kansas.

The school did modestly well in recruiting new minority students from 1986 to 1990. But we made little progress in recruiting new African-American and Hispanic faculty and staff during our first four years.

In the spring of 1992, the K-State Black Student Union issued a stiff challenge to me to sharply improve the number of minority faculty and staff members by the fall of 1993. The BSU demanded that we hire at least ten faculty of color by that fall.

Fortunately, we were able to hire 14 faculty of color, including seven African-American, Native American, and Hispanic faculty, and seven Asian Americans by the fall of 1992. In the fall of 1994, we hired ten new African-American faculty and ten new African-American staff members.[109]

After 1990, Mordean and her staff implemented two major strategies: one, to increase the recruitment and retention of faculty and staff of color; and two, to develop and implement strategies to facilitate the recruitment, retention, and graduation rates of students of color.

Over 23 years, I consistently preached that diversity for the entire school was not only an end in itself—it was the means to the end as well. By improving diversity, the entire school would benefit.

In her years as our leader for enhancing diversity, Mordean Taylor-Archer worked well with everyone on campus and off campus. Her office was viewed as vital for the entire school. The number of new African-American and Hispanic faculty, staff, and students was going up. In her 12 years as K-State's Assistant Provost for Diversity, Mordean Taylor-Archer did an exceptional job.

In 2002, Provost Coffman selected Myra Gordon to be the new Associate Provost for Diversity. Myra had a BS degree from Cornell University and M.S. and Ph.D degrees from the State University of New York at Buffalo. When she arrived from Virginia Tech in 2002, I saw that Myra Gordon had a keen intellect, an excellent sense of history, and a powerful commitment to diversity.

With an undeniable passion to advance all aspects of diversity, Myra wanted to get things done right now. Myra Gordon did an extraordinary job and dramatically improved Kansas State in all areas of diversity.[110]

Throughout its history, the state of Kansas has had a relatively small population of African-Americans. This meant K-State had to work much harder than most universities in other states to improve its diversity.

Still, K-State did quite well in recruiting African-American students. In 1988, K-State had about 400 African-American students. The number of African-American students at Kansas State increased to over 900 in 2009.

With African American faculty, there was an increase from two faculty members in 1987 to 27 in 2009. With Hispanic faculty, the numbers improved from five faculty members in 1987 to 34 in 2009.

With female faculty, there was a major change from 169 faculty members in 1987 to 353 in 2009.

In 1986, Kansas State had a modest number of staff members who were African-American and Hispanic. By 2009, our school had over 110 African-American staff members and over 95 Hispanic staff members. When you combine the number of faculty and staff members for the fall of 2009, the university had about 137 African-Americans and about 130 Hispanics.[111]

I remember attending university diversity meetings held in the K-State Student Union Ballroom every April from 1987 to 1992. Hardly anyone was there. K-State was not even close to having a critical mass of people of color. It was like going to the poorly repaired tomb of U. S. Grant in New York City in the 1960's. No one was there either.

When Myra Gordon became the Associate Provost for Diversity in 2002, she ramped up the spring diversity meetings. Myra eagerly invited deans, department heads, administrators, faculty, staff, and students to attend the spring meeting.

By 2008, the school had a critical mass of 270 people of color on the faculty and in staff positions combined with almost 900 African-American students and over 800 Hispanic students. Gordon invited good musical groups to entertain the crowd. She had superb speakers to address the issues of diversity for Kansas State.

The annual spring diversity meetings became more contagious, electric, and fun. The people who came to those meetings in 2007, 2008, and 2009 clearly realized that diversity at our school had improved nicely. Kansas State was making good progress in the area of diversity.

By 2009, there was more hope and promise for Kansas State University and its goals for increasing the number of people of color for the student body, the faculty, and the staff.[112]

THE STATE OF THE KSU FOUNDATION IN 1986

After World War II, America's public universities were creating endowment associations and foundations to raise private funds. With declining state funding, fund raising groups became more important by the 1980's. Kansas State's Endowment Association started in March of 1944. Yet the school lacked a full-time director until Kenneth Haywood was hired in 1956.

When I came to K-State in 1986, over 50% of our annual budget came from state appropriated funds. By the fall of 2009, the state provided less than 20% of our annual budget. By December of 1986, KU was in the midst of a major fund-raising campaign. K-State had yet to launch its first major fund-raising campaign.[113]

IN 1986, ART LOUB WAS THE FOUNDATION PRESIDENT

In 1986, Arthur F. Loub was the President of the Kansas State Foundation. As a capable and solid fund-raiser, Art and his staff had raised funds for a $750,000 renovation of Shellenberger Hall for Grain Science and Industry, conducted a $500,000 campaign for Phase II of the College of Engineering, and initiated a $760,000 campaign for a new synthetic turf and indoor workout complex for the football program.[114]

The Telefund campaign was kicked off in 1980. This first student-led Telefund involved students and alums from the Colleges of Engineering, Agriculture, and Arts and Sciences. These volunteers manned a bank of 15 telephones in the KSU Union where they called alumni across the nation. The initial effort raised $140,000.

This telefund program grew into a national model. By 1993, the number of volunteers grew to 1,400 student callers. Over 200,000 alumni pledged more than $6 million. Between 1983 and 1986, the Foundation raised over $6 million of private funds to help build a new $17 million Bramlage Coliseum. By 1993, the KSU Foundation was raising $21 million annually.[115]

From 1986 to 2009, I worked with many excellent Foundation Trustees and with its Executive Committee of 15 members. This key committee met twice in the fall and twice in the spring. In 23 years, I only missed a few meetings. Because there were so many talented and extraordinary K-Staters on the Executive Committee, the meetings were enlightening, lively, and productive.

All of the members brought considerable expertise to the meetings; they contributed good ideas for improved fund-raising; and they were generous to the university to boot. In my first year, there were two leaders of the Executive Committee that I was fortunate to work with: Jack Goldstein of Manhattan and Fred Bramlage of Junction City. Both were giants.

Art Loub and the Executive Committee were dedicated to make my tenure a success. Jack Goldstein, the CEO of Steel and Pipe and the Chair of the Executive Committee, made sure I would have a running start. At my first meeting on September 23, 1986, Jack got a unanimous vote to provide $700,000 of privately raised funds for the president's office. Jack was a dear friend for years.

Most of this new funding was allocated to student recruitment, academic scholarships, and faculty development. The Executive Committee reaffirmed that funding every year. This funding played a vital role in all of our successes from 1986 to 2009.

In 1987, the KU Endowment Association announced the successful completion of a five-year fund-raising campaign of over $150 million. KU organized their endowment association in 1891. By the 1920's, KU was raising millions of dollars every year.[116]

In early 1987, the Wichita State Foundation announced their campaign to raise over $100 million. But the KSU Foundation had no plans for a major fund-raising campaign. Prior to 1987, the largest Foundation campaign was to raise $6 million for a new basketball arena. In 1987, K-State was raising about $7 million a year.

THE FIRST FOUNDATION CAMPAIGN WAS A BIG SUCCESS

K-State had no choice in 1987. Its fund-raising had to be seriously ramped up. With KU and WSU in the midst of raising $150 million and $100 million respectively, K-State's private giving campaign had to be ratcheted up by a factor of 20. Our school absolutely needed a fund-raising campaign to raise $125 million—if for no other reason than to cement our image as one of the state's two flagship schools.

In 1988, the Foundation introduced the silent phase of the new Essential Edge Campaign to raise at least $125 million. On April 21, 1990, the Foundation hosted a public black tie gathering of more than 800 alumni and friends in the Bramlage Coliseum. Gordon Jump, a well-known television actor and KSU graduate, was the Master of Ceremonies.

The chair of the national campaign was Robert Hagans. He was a supremely generous K-Stater. Bob announced early in the evening that our campaign had already raised a total of over $52 million. The celebration was on. On June 30, 1993, the Essential Edge Campaign was closed out. Over $163 million had been raised for the benefit of Kansas State University. We were happy campers.[117]

THE NEW FOUNDATION PRESIDENT IN 1996: GARY HELLEBUST

When Art Loub retired in 1993, Mark Moore, who had served on the staff for 14 years, became the new president. After three years on the job, he resigned. In 1996, Gary Hellebust, the chief operating officer, was selected as the new Foundation President.

Everything changed. Gary Hellebust wanted to hire talented people and empower them. The KSU Foundation had a thin staff in 1996. More fund-raising specialists were needed. Gary knew every academic college would soon need at least one full-time fund-raiser. We helped him accomplish exactly that by 2001. The fund-raising team had to get bigger. It did.[118]

Gary Hellebust and I became partners. In Bob Shoop's book, A UNIVERSITY RENAISSANCE, Hellebust said: "The changes begun by the Foundation in 1996 were to be more aggressive, more visionary, and more risk-taking. . . Wefald's mindset was infectious. . . We have identified a vision, developed a plan, and assumed risk. I appreciate Jon and Ruth Ann Wefald's ability to make winners of everyone and to listen to all sides. The single most important concept

I have learned from Wefald's leadership style is the importance of empowering people."[119]

Gary put together an excellent, hard-working team of fund-raisers and staff members from 1996 to his retirement in 2009—including Mike Smith, Alan Klug, David Weaver, Julie Lea, and a number of other good staff members. The deans also became superb fund-raisers. The Alumni Association President, Amy Button Renz, and her board provided terrific support for Gary and his staff as well.

Everyone at the Foundation understood that it could only be as successful as the university. If our administration had not turned the university around from 1986 to 1999 academically and athletically, it would have been impossible for the Foundation to propose a $500 million dollar campaign by the year 2000.

The Foundation needed a visionary like Gary Hellebust and a number of talented staff members. That took place. The Executive Committee needed members who would consider major stretch goals. That happened. There would have to be a solid partnership with the KSU Alumni Association, its President Amy Button Renz, and its thousands of members. That occurred.

Our administration backed Gary Hellebust's strategy to establish a single source contract concept that would provide new fund-raisers in each college on a shared cost basis. With the deans and our Anderson Hall team supporting the cost sharing of new fund-raisers, Hellebust increased the Foundation staff from about 30 in 1996 to a staff of 100 by 2002. Major successes were on the horizon.[120]

IN 2008, THE KSU FOUNDATION RAISED $100 MILLION AND CAUGHT UP WITH KU

In 1986, the KSU Foundation was raising about $5 million a year. By 1996, it was $22 million a year. By 2000, it was $53 million a year. By 2006, it was $93 million a year.

By 2008, the KSU Foundation was raising about $100 million a year. For the first time in the history of the two schools, K-State was raising about the same amount in private giving as the University of Kansas.

In 1986, I rather doubt that there was one K-Stater anywhere who believed that our university could ever raise $100 million in annual fund-raising. By the end of Gary Hellebust's tenure in 2009, the Foundation had assets of $400 million. In Gary's 13 years, K-State became a major force in the important arena of fund-raising.[121] K-State had caught up with KU in annual fund-raising even though KU had two major advantages in private fund-raising. First, KU had started their endowment association in 1891—which meant that they had about a 50-year head start. Second, KU had two important institutions that K-State did not have: a superb law school and an excellent medical school.

In 1996, the Foundation kicked off a $50 million scholarship fund. To keep recruiting the best students, we needed to have a major academic scholarship campaign. On June 30, 2000, the Foundation hosted a $50 million academic scholarship celebration dinner in Overland Park, Kansas. Over 400 people attended. Our scholarship campaign raised over $63 million.[122]

On July 1, 2000, the Foundation entered into the silent phase of the Changing Lives Campaign. For K-Staters everywhere, it had an unprecedented goal: $500 million.

On December 31, 2007, the Foundation hosted a wonderful celebration in Bramlage Arena with a concert by Sarah Evans.

The announcement was made—the Changing Lives Campaign had raised well over half a billion dollars. K-State was red-hot.

The Foundation had made astounding progress in just a few years. In his 13 years as the Foundation President, Gary Hellebust and his outstanding staff had raised over $885 million. During those years, there was a reaffirmation of the K-State spirit—namely, if we worked as a team, our school could accomplish miracles.[123]

THE HISTORIC IMPORTANCE OF THE KSU ALUMNI ASSOCIATION

The Kansas State Alumni Association was founded in 1874 during the tenure of President John Anderson. In 1916, the association established dues at $1 annually or $20 for a life membership. In 1944, the Endowment Association was established as the official fundraising arm of Kansas State. In 1951, the first K-STATER magazine was published. In 1977, the first student ambassadors were chosen to represent the university at various functions. In 1983, the alumni fellows program was inaugurated.[124]

In 1991, the Alumni Association moved to the old Foundation center. It now had adequate space. Larry Weigel was the President of the Alumni Association. He had a great knack for meeting people and winning friends. Under Weigel's excellent leadership, the association gained more members.

From 1978 to 1988, Larry upgraded the Kansas State Alumni Association. From 1988 to 1994, Fred Thibodeau served as the President. He added more members and kept the ball rolling. In 1994, Thibodeau announced his resignation.[125]

AMY BUTTON RENZ BECAME THE NEW PRESIDENT IN 1994

Later that year, the Alumni Association Board picked a superb replacement to be the next President—Amy Button Renz. She was a graduate of K-State, a member of a long-time Wildcat family from Newton, Kansas, and the former vice-president.

The alumni board could not have found a better successor than Amy. She was keenly intelligent, always cheerful, and consistently positive.

From 1994 to 2009, Amy became a dear friend, a terrific problem-solver, and a leader with a tremendous vision. The association always had sterling board chairs. From 1986 to 2009, the chairs and the board members were hard working, dedicated, and excellent.

In the next several years, Amy Button Renz hired a solid staff, including Brad Seidner, Kelly Law, Terin Walters, Steve Logbeck, and Jodi Weiberg and she retained Tim Lindemuth, the editor of the K-STATER Magazine. She developed a harmonious relationship with all of the board chairs and members.

Amy invited me to give updates on K-State at the three meetings of the alumni board in Manhattan each year. Over 23 years, I gave countless talks about K-State to alumni association clubs all over the state—probably more than any president in history. The meetings were always fun and uplifting.[126]

When Amy Renz became the President in 1994, K-State had 32,774 alumni members. By the summer of 2010, there were over 40,000 alumni members. From 1996 to 2009, K-State was the No. 1 school in the Big 12 in the number of alumni members. It still is.

The enormous growth of the Alumni Association paralleled that of the university itself and our improved football team. Amy realized that the football games home and away represented a great venue to display our both the university and our football team.

After 1995, Amy and her staff were hosting excellent alumni events before the away games in Norman, Boulder, Lawrence, Lincoln, Ames, Columbia, and later in College Station, Waco, Austin, and Lubbock. I attended a ton of those events. From 1997 to 2003 when the football team was winning 11 games a year in six of those seven years, the enthusiasm was off the charts.[127]

Amy and many passionate alumni in Johnson County launched the Wabash Cannonball Scholarship program. At the first gala in Overland Park, Kansas in 2006, everyone was ecstatic when the event generated $170,000 for academic scholarships. By 2010, the scholarship program had raised over $1 million for student scholarships in the Kansas City area.[128]

THE BUILDING OF THE SPLENDID NEW ALUMNI BUILDING IN 2002

Amy Renz's quintessential achievement is the construction of the

Alumni Association Building in 2002. Initially, there was some dispute over where the new building should be located. Amy and her board favored the site directly south of the old football stadium. Although some people opposed that site, I supported Amy and her board. That was the best place. The new K-State Alumni building was unquestionably impressive, stunning, and beautiful.

It is difficult to single out one board member who played a defining role in the new building. But there was one—Curt Frasier from Beloit, Kansas. Curt was the chair of the Alumni Board from 1996 to 1997. He was there when the concept was hatched, discussed, and approved.

Because of his leadership and dedication, Curt Frazier was selected by his colleagues to be the chair of the new building project. From 1997 to 2002, Frasier and his advisory group brilliantly guided the construction of this splendid new building.

In a dream come true for thousands of alumni everywhere, K-State now had an iconic, elegant, and spacious new alumni building. It was dedicated on October 19, 2002. When people learned that the total cost of the building was $12.9 million—including the land, the building, and the furnishings—everyone was impressed. Under the leadership of Amy Button Renz and her stalwart Alumni Association Board, the future held great promise.[129]

During the decade of the 1990's, K-Staters everywhere were mirroring a greater sense of optimism and confidence. Kansas State was improving on every level. The new leaders in the Office of Diversity, the Foundation, and the Alumni Association during those ten years all had a great deal to do with the enhanced national prestige of Kansas State University.

Chapter 5

Half Is Not Good Enough: Building A New National Class Library And Creating A New Art Museum

There were two more extraordinary challenges for revitalizing and transforming Kansas State after 1986. First, our leadership team had to find a way to construct a new first-rate library. Second, we totally understood the compelling need to build a new art museum.

If we had any chance of defining K-State as a major university that valued the liberal arts, a great new library and art museum were absolutely mandatory.

A brief history of Kansas State's library is necessary—because an excellent new research library for our school had not been seriously championed by any administration from 1863 to 1986.

For 75 years, Kansas State and its own Board of Regents defined the school as a technical institute. In 1932, 35 excellent universities founded the Association of Research Libraries (ARL). Kansas State was not one of those 35 schools.

From 1932 to 1986, Kansas State's national reputation suffered because its library was the only one in the Big 8 Conference lacking membership in the ARL. Equally embarrassing, Kansas State was the only university in the Big 8 in 1986 without an art museum.

FROM 1863 TO 1986, A GREAT LIBRARY WAS NEVER A PRIORITY

In 1986, the Kansas State University Library was in horrible shape. Our library was light-years removed from being a major research library. I worried more about the state of our library from 1986 to 1995 than I did about any other problem facing the school.

For me, the challenge of a new library was still another virtually intractable challenge. I do not use this metaphor lightly. I actually saw the status of the library as an almost intractable challenge in my first five years on the job. I came to believe that if we could not build a great new library, our future as a major university would be dire.

The best land grant universities in America had already spent several generations building up their libraries. After WWII, virtually every top-rated public and private university in America had an impressive library. Those top universities had already become members of the Association of Research Libraries (ARL).

By 1986, Iowa State, Oklahoma State, Nebraska, Missouri, Colorado, Oklahoma, and Kansas were all members of the ARL—the lone exception in the Big 8 Conference was Kansas State. Moreover, although governed by a State Board of Agriculture, Colorado State found the resources to be a member of the ARL. Our school was not in good company.[130]

THE SHORTCOMINGS OF THE 1927 LIBRARY

In April of 2010, Brice Hobrock, the Dean of Libraries for Kansas State from 1982 to 2004, wrote a short unpublished history of the university library. The Farrell Library was completed in 1927. It took about two years to construct.

It was designed in the splendid 'Collegiate Gothic' style. Paul Weigel, the lead architect, wanted to construct a double Gothic Tower in the grand reading room style of this era of library architecture.

Because of financial worries, Brice Hobrock reported: "The architects were forced into a modified design. This meant the construction of only one tower—the north tower. Even though the grand reading room of the north tower remains today as a beloved historical icon, the new Farrell Library was constructed to only about half the size of Weigel's design."

This unfortunate pattern for the school's library continued over the next generation—including the 1954 and 1969 additions to the Farrell Library. The 1927 new library started a trend in the 20th century for the K-State library that is best described as: 'Half is good enough.'"

THE FLAWS OF THE 1927 LIBRARY AND THE 1954 ADDITION

Brice Hobrock spelled out the idiosyncrasies of the 1927 Farrell Library: "Strangely, the eight tiers of stacks built into the 1927 library structure were characterized by low ceilings, four, five, and six feet high on three levels. Cast iron stacks relocated from Anderson Hall to Fairchild to the 1927 structure were still in place in tier stacks until the Hale reconstruction in 1994."

During his tenure from 1943 to 1950, Milton Eisenhower knew the need for expanded stack capacity in the library. Hobrock described what happened: "The 'south stacks' addition sought by Eisenhower was not constructed until 1954, albeit only with the west half completed with floors and shelving. Some public passageways between the 1927 and 1954 stacks were only four feet high. On the completion of the south stack shell in 1954, the entire complex was named in 1955 for Francis David Farrell."[131]

THE LIBRARY RENOVATION IN 1969: "HALF IS GOOD ENOUGH"

By the late 1950's and 1960's, Kansas State students were complaining about the limitations of the school's library. Many could not study in the library. Many found it impossible to gain access to the stacks for their research and term papers. The architects recommended 120,000 square feet for the 1969 library addition. The 1927 Farrell Library and its 1954 addition were constructed at only half of what the architects wanted. The librarians and the faculty had hoped that it would not happen again in 1969.

Hobrock reported the shortcomings of the 1969 library addition: "Of the 120,000 square feet recommended by the architects for the 1968-69 design, only half of the recommended net square feet was built on the southeast corner connected to the 1927 and 1954 'Farrell' phases."

Hobrock continued: "President McCain did not want to irritate the Legislature by insisting upon full funding for the entire project. The resulting budget for half the project included inexpensive construction materials, abrupt level changes, poor integration of space and materials, and a new 'carport' entrance one level below the main campus thoroughfare."[132]

From 1873 to the 1970's, the same pattern of "half is good enough"was equally applicable to the number of books and other library materials purchased for the library.

In 1863, the school's first library inherited 2,700 volumes from the old Bluemont College building. In 1877, Professor M.L. Ward transferred 1,225 books to Farm Machinery Hall. Fittingly, the first recorded book was entitled HOW TO GET A FARM AND WHERE TO FIND ONE by Edmund Morris in 1864.

From 1873 to 1913, the Kansas State Board of Regents defined the college as a technical institute. It did not include a good library. Dean Brice Hobrock studied the MINUTES OF THE KANSAS STATE BOARD OF REGENTS in the period from the Civil War to 1913. He found requests for library funding repeatedly denied.

In the minutes of one of those meetings in 1875, Hobrock talked about the school's librarian requesting $500 for new books. One of the ornery regents spewed out: "I don't believe that the faculty has yet read all the books that the library has."[133]

EVERY KU CHANCELLOR FROM 1875 ON EMPHASIZED THE NEED FOR A GREAT LIBRARY

In 1932, the Kansas State Library did not meet the requirements of the Association of Research Libraries. Eighty miles down the road, every Chancellor from 1875 to 1901 and beyond strongly argued that KU had to have a world-class library.

Joshua Lippincott, who was the KU Chancellor from 1883 to 1890, repeatedly declared that the University of Kansas should "foster original research" and it should "have a superb library, one excellent enough to attract scholars from afar."[134] From 1873 to 1986, no Kansas State President ever uttered a similar statement.

THE HUGE DISPARITY IN LIBRARY VOLUMES: KU and KSU

The disparity in the number of print volumes in the KU library and the Kansas State library has been wide and deep for decades. It was not close in 1900. It was not close in 1932. In 1961, the KU Library had over 1.1 million print volumes while the KSU Library had about 276,000 print volumes. The gap widened in the years ahead.

In 1986, the KU Library had about 2.5 million print volumes compared to Kansas State's 1.0 million print volumes. In 1995, the KU library had over 3.3 million print volumes while the Kansas State library had 1.3 million print volumes. In 2009, the KU Library possessed 4.2 million print volumes compared to Kansas State's 1.8 million print volumes.[135]

Brice Hobrock became the Dean of Libraries in 1982. His first challenge was to analyze a consulting study done in 1981 by Peat, Marwick, and Mitchell, Inc. The Joint Committee in Building Construction had authorized the study.

Key state legislators in 1969 had promised that "Phase II" of the design study for the expansion of Farrell Library would be fully funded in 1983. But the dreams of K-State's librarians were punctured again. The study declared that the Farrell Library had adequate space up to 2000. This space included 1,680 seats for users. Hobrock declared that this study was pure nonsense.[136]

The University of Kansas and Wichita State University had been the primary petitioners for the consulting study. KU wanted a new science library. WSU desired a major library addition.

Once again, KU won and K-State lost. Hobrock wrote: "The Legislature promptly provided full funding in 1983 to the University of Kansas for the Anschutz Library and to Wichita State for a major addition to the Ablah Library. The Kansas State Library received no new funding for library construction or planning."[137]

Kansas State was mired in third place. Moreover, Brice Hobrock now faced a new internal challenge. In 1985, the Acker leadership team had laid out a plan for new buildings for the entire campus over the next 20 years. Hobrock was shocked to find out that a design for a new library was almost a footnote in the plans.

About the 1985 20-year building plan, Hobrock said: "The priority for a new library was moved steadily downward on the list of proposed new buildings to 2010, 2027, and even 2050." Brice must have gotten a bad migraine headache when he read that a badly needed new library for Kansas State might be down the road somewhere between 42 and 65 years.[138]

In 1987, I was not optimistic that we would ever get the critical funds for a great new library. History was against us. Too many Kansas State leaders had ignored the importance of a great library. From the new Farrell Library in 1927 to the 1954 and 1969 additions, the motto always was: "Half is good enough."

In 1986, the truth is we would spend over ten years unraveling the multitude of historical and stubborn problems to build a great new library. Today, I can say I suffered far more headaches about the building of a new research library than I ever did about turning the football program around.

SHORT-TERM NEEDS HAD TO BE ADDRESSED

After 1987, I soon found out again how lucky we were to be led by Provost Jim Coffman and Dean Brice Hobrock to find the right strategy and the funding to go with it. With those two leading the way, we had a chance to fulfill our dream of building a great new research library.

Coffman and Hobrock were the key leaders who found the necessary funds in every single cost center to meet the ongoing needs of the library.

With the university facing a $3.5 million budget recision, for example, we protected it from cuts. In the fall of 1987, we allocated the library an additional base funding of $530,000 and a one-time allocation of $40,000.

In 1989 and 1990, we allocated the library about $200,000 in base funding from the first year of the Margin of Excellence and $140,000 in base funding from the second. In 1995, we added funds to upgrade the mainframe for university computing in the library.[139]

From 1987 to 1996, we reallocated close to $2 million in base funds and about $1.3 million in one-time funds to the Farrell Library. During three budget recisions over those eight years, the library was held harmless. For the future building, we set aside over $7 million in funds to guarantee that the new library would have the necessary and vital Information Technology systems.

Despite our actions, it would never be enough. Dean Hobrock wrote about our efforts to aid the library: "The Kansas State administration tried diligently during the period 1986-1996 to keep pace with inflation by allocating blocks of new funds annually to the Libraries. The utter failure to fund the school's library for over a hundred years could never be made up."[140]

THE VITAL IMPORTANCE OF STUDENT INVOLVEMENT

The university coalition of deans, faculty leaders, and student leaders after 1988 did an excellent job of getting the word out on our poor library to key political leaders. But it is impossible to overstate the importance of our student leaders.

It was student leaders who started the ball rolling towards a new library. In 1989, Todd Johnson was elected as the new K-State Student Body President. Fred Wingert became his top student advisor.

These two students started meeting with Brice Hobrock, Jim Coffman, and I. I met with them a number of times. Todd Johnson and Fred Wingert wanted Kansas State to have a new library—right now. They demanded it.

When we told them about the failed attempts over two generations to get a great new library, they quickly brushed that history aside. Initially, I viewed them as fanatics. But I came to realize how right they were.

I met with many student leaders over 23 years. But Todd Johnson and Fred Wingert were the two toughest, most formidable, and most unforgettable student leaders that I ever met. They talked like two big-time Chicago lawyers in their mid-thirties.

Actually, these two guys acted more like two key aides to Chicago's Mayor, Richard Daley, in the 1970's. With them, you could not engage in smoke and mirrors. They could see right through any mumbo-jumbo from me or anyone else.

Soon other student leaders joined in. The next two student body presidents became vibrant supporters of the new library too. Todd Heitschmidt was elected in 1990 and Jackie McClaskey was elected in 1991 and re-elected in 1992. Both of them articulated the case for a new library to key state legislators and the governor's office.

Because Jackie served for two terms, she had an even greater impact. Her election coincided with the election of a new governor in 1992, Joan Finney. And it was Governor Finney who became the ultimate game-changer leader for our march to a new library.

To this day, Todd Johnson, Fred Wingert, Todd Heitschmidt, and Jackie McClaskey are four of my greatest student heroes. Without them, the dedication of our beautiful and first-rate library in October of 1997 might never have happened. I doubt that any university has had more stellar student leadership.

In January of 1990, a student group called Students Helping Enhance Library Funding (SHELF) planned a sit-in in the president's office to get the attention of state policy makers. The protesters cleared their sit-in with Dean Brice Hobrock and me.

I told the student leaders their meeting should be in the library. I would follow up their sit-in by requesting the Board of Regents to hire a consultant to determine the costs for a major library expansion. The sit-in received good media coverage. It worked.[141]

ARCHITECTS HIRED FOR A NEW LIBRARY

In the next several weeks, the Regents selected consultants Peckham, Guyton, Albers, and Viets, an architectural firm in Kansas City, to determine the needs and costs for our new library. This firm had designed the Anschutz Library at KU and the Ellis Library expansion at the University of Missouri, Columbia. By designating these architectural consultants, the Board of Regents gave us the best news for our library in history.[142]

K-State now had the undivided attention of the Regents and the state's policy makers—maybe for the first time. The consultants' report determined that our library needed an additional 153,000 net square feet at a cost of $28 million.

This time, there would be absolutely no compromise on a new library. The library expansion this time would be at least 153,000 net square feet. The concept of "half is good enough" for our library was now dead and buried—period.[143]

THE TRIPARTITE STRATEGY FOR A NEW LIBRARY

Since 1989, we had advocated a "tripartite" funding strategy for funding the new library. This strategy in 1991 included the following sums: $5 million from student fees; $5 million from the University Foundation; and the remaining $18 million from state funds. The Student Government quickly authorized a referendum in November of 1991 to commit $5 million in student fees for the renovation of the Farrell Library. The $5 million referendum won by a 97% margin.[144]

The Foundation leadership now agreed to raise $5 million. Joe and Joyce Hale of Kansas City became the lead donors when they decided to contribute $2 million for the new library.

The student leadership traveled to Topeka early in the 1992 session of the Kansas Legislature to present a "large symbolic check of $10 million" to the state legislators.

In life, luck is always important. Luck happens in life when you prepare and work hard. Preparation meets opportunity. Harvey McKay, a national columnist, put it this way: "You want to get lucky. The harder you work, the luckier you will get."

Early in the 1992 legislative session, Governor Joan Finney announced that the federal government was distributing "windfall reimbursement funds" to a number of states. Kansas would receive roughly $80 million in one-time federal funds that would be allocated at the discretion of the Governor. The legislature would have final approval.

Thankfully, Joan Finney won the Governorship in 1990. Based on his decisions affecting K-State as Governor from 1986 to 1990, it is quite doubtful that Governor Mike Hayden would have backed any of those one-time federal funds for a K-State project.[145]

Governor Finney proposed that most of the one-time federal monies should be allocated to two construction projects at KU and K-State in 1992. Hit by lightning and burned down in April of 1991, the Hoch Auditorium at KU was targeted as one of the two projects. The two projects were approved by a large margin in the Kansas House in April of 1992.

In the Kansas Senate, however, the funds for the K-State library were almost struck from the bill. The Senate vote ended in a tie. Again, we were lucky. The President of the State Senate, Paul 'Bud' Burke, a KU graduate, cast the decisive vote for our new library.[146]

THE HISTORIC ROLE OF GOVERNOR JOAN FINNEY

There were many legislators to thank on both sides of the aisle. But Governor Finney was the key leader. She was the "decider" on the allocation of these one-time federal "windfall funds." She decided the K-State library project should receive $18 million. There should be no question on this point—all K-Staters should be forever grateful to Governor Joan Finney.

Without her decisive leadership, K-State might still be waiting for the critical funds to build our new library. She will always be one of K-State's angels. The $28 million was now in place for the new library. Energy conservation grants and some supplementary funding raised the total funding to over $30 million.

After good work by an astute library committee in the fall of 1992, the university selected an excellent partnership of two architectural firms: Brent Bowman (BBA) Associates in Manhattan, Kansas and Hammond, Beeby, and Babka (HBB) in Chicago, Illinois. This architectural partnership proved to be a Godsend for our library.

THE OCTOBER 22, 1993 GROUNDBREAKING

The groundbreaking ceremonies took place on October 22, 1993.

Joe and Joyce Hale, our two lead donors, were there along with a nice gathering—including Governor Joan Finney, deans, faculty and student leaders, and many others. Frankly, there should have been 1,000 people at the dedication. That only seems to happen at major universities when a sports facility is being dedicated.

Dean Hobrock and his colleagues understood that any library built in the 1990's had to be wired for the current state of electronic technology. At the time of construction, the architects made sure that category 5 cable for high-speed Internet would be installed everywhere.

The architects and the librarians agreed that at least two hundred hard-wired 100 Mb computer terminals would be installed in the new "Information Commons" area. It is vital to cover the details of our new library—because those basic details had been overlooked since 1927.[147]

THE STUBBORN CHALLENGES FACING THE ARCHITECTS

The two architectural firms faced an incredibly stubborn design challenge in constructing the new library. To begin with, the architects had to integrate the three older and contrasting phases of 1927, 1954, and 1969. This could have been an unsolvable task.

Anyone who toured the Farrell Library before 1997 would easily see the architectural hurdles. With the new library having an additional 153,000 gross square feet, the architects had to overcome a truly formidable challenge—namely, "external and internal architectural and functional coherence."[148]

The architects overcame the exterior architecture of the three earlier and different phases by brilliantly integrating the original Collegiate Gothic style of the 1927 Farrell Library all the way down from the north side to a revival of the Richardsonian Romanesque style on the south side. The architects deployed the large arches, towers, and loggias to unify the new library.

The Romanesque architecture is mirrored in Dickens Hall, Holton Hall, and Fairchild Hall today. The upshot: the Collegiate Gothic style on the north side was gracefully transitioned on the west side to the Richardsonian Romanesque style on the south side.

The architectural challenges in the building's interior were even more daunting and stubborn. To integrate the three earlier interior phases of the Farrell Library, the architects needed BA degrees in Magic.

The architects knew the 1927 library had eight tiers of stacks with low ceilings that were four, five, and six feet high on three different levels. In building the 1954 addition, a number of the public passageways between the 1927 and 1954 stacks were only four feet high.

In the 1950's and 1960's, students constantly complained about the library's idiosyncrasies. Many students said they found it almost impossible to gain access to the stacks for their research.

About their magical work, Hobrock wrote: "Internally, floor and ceiling designs defined pathways around book storage and shelf blocks directing the user in a 360-degree circle around the entire structure. A science library was created on the first floor. A 24-hour study facility was created and the overall design was adaptable to 24 x 7 operations. Two thousand student seats of a variety of styles met the continuing needs of students and faculty."[149]

The architects did a splendid job in designing the main entrance on the southwest corner of the Hale Library with a long loggia walkway right next to the main walking patterns. This walkway convinced students that the new library would be a welcoming gathering place.

The architects constructed a secondary entry called the "Sunflower Entrance" on the southeast side as well that would bring in foot traffic from the nearby dormitories.[150]

THE HALE LIBRARY WAS DEDICATED ON OCTOBER 5, 1997

The Hale Library was completed in April of 1997. The dedication of the library was set for October 5, 1997. After years of dreaming about a new library for Kansas State University, October 5 could not come soon enough.

The dedication came on a beautiful Saturday morning as the trees were changing into a variety of colors. In seeing the architectural masterpiece of the new Hale Library in October of 1997, most of us believed we were looking at one of the most elegant and beautiful public buildings ever constructed in the history of Kansas.

The library was named the Hale Library in honor of our two lead donors, Joe and Joyce Hale. Todd Johnson, who was the Student Body President in 1989-1990 and Jackie McClaskey, who was the Student Body President for two terms from 1991-1993, attended the dedication. Todd and Jackie were seated in the front row.

DEAN HOBROCK AND HIS STAFF EMBRACE NEW TECHNOLOGIES

The new world of information technology presented great opportunities for the library's future. Dean Hobrock interpreted these trends nicely: "Libraries began to change rapidly when electronic journals and books became available. Print book acquisitions stabilized. Print journal subscriptions were being replaced by electronic access. Hundreds of computer terminals in the K-State library and offices could begin to access these information sources simultaneously and remotely. By 2009, K-State offered 644,000 electronic books and 55,000 electronic scholarly journals to go with 19,000 print journal titles."[151]

THE LIBRARY IS RE-ENGINEERED

During the building of the Hale Library, Brice used the phrase "the management technique of re-engineering." His world-view on the new library came into focus at a Council of Deans meeting in the spring of 1997. Prior to the meeting, Hobrock jotted the following ideas on an envelope:

"Libraries are designed as vast warehouses, collecting man's scholarly output, JUST IN CASE somebody needs it sometime."

"A book may sit on the shelf for generations before it is needed or never. Data are available to show that the 'average book' is accessed only once every five years."

"Libraries should be re-engineered so that materials may be acquired JUST IN TIME to meet the users' needs."[152]

Today, the Hale Library is considered a major library player comparable to the ARL libraries in the Big 12 and the Great Western Library Alliance. Our libraries became a leader in the Great Western Library Alliance because we implemented the entire information access process. The ARL benchmark was used as a standard for our library system.[153]

This time, Kansas State did not settle for "half is good enough." Instead, K-Staters on and off campus knew the school finally had achieved a national class library.

The splendid and graceful Hale Library provided a lift in confidence and pride for K-Staters everywhere. As Frank Lloyd Wright said: "The thing always happens that you really believe in; and the belief in a thing makes it happen." In so many ways, that is the history of the Hale Library.

THE ARDUOUS PATH TO A NEW KANSAS STATE ART MUSEUM

The journey to a new Kansas State University art museum followed a pathway quite similar to the new Hale Library. Both took a decade to accomplish. Both were viewed as almost intractable. From World War I to 1986, no administration had argued for a new art museum. But K-State could not become a leading land-grant university that celebrated the arts and humanities without its own special art museum.

THE HISTORIC ROLE OF JOHN HELM

Professor John Helm was the first curator of the Kansas State art collection. From the 1920's until his death in 1973, he selflessly worked on enhancing the university's art collection. In 1934, Helm and his colleagues started a group known as the Friends of Art. By the 1950's and 1960's, Kansas State was able to purchase important works by some of the nation's leading regionalists such as John Steuart Curry, Thomas Hart Benton, and Grant Wood.[154]

When Ruth Ann and I arrived in Manhattan in July of 1986, the Friends of Art group was inactive. Jessica Reichman had been hired as curator of the university's art collection in 1983. She wanted to locate all of the artworks, assess their condition, develop a computerized cataloguing system, and set up a central storage space for the art collection. But Jessica discovered that the art collection was in bad shape.

The collection was scattered to the winds. The best paintings were located in various buildings from the student union to the dining halls. Jessica wrote: "During the eighteen-month campus-wide search, I found many valuable artworks languishing in deplorable conditions. The most severely damaged paintings were salvaged when they were sent to a professional conservator."[155]

Ruth Ann was always an extraordinary supporter of the arts. Early on, she knew that KSU was the only school in the Big 8 without an art museum—and that the KU Spencer Museum of Art was established in 1928 with well over 30,000 works. She did not need to know more than that.

Shortly after we arrived in Manhattan, Charles Stroh, Jessica Reichman, and Ruth Ann set up a meeting to figure out a game plan for a new art museum. After talking with the Foundation President, Art Loub, Ruth Ann and her two colleagues decided they had to do two things—make K-Staters aware of the university's art collection and make a convincing case for a new art museum.

In 1986, many K-Staters were indifferent to a new art museum. Ruth Ann never let indifference stop her. After 1987, the Alumni Association helped organize local community efforts in Kansas to promote the new museum. Ruth Ann and Jessica started scheduling art museum events in various towns.

They showcased the art collection and the talent of excellent students in art and music. In 1987 and 1988, their goal was to highlight the school's art collection. In 1989 and 1990, their goal shifted to raising funds.

During these four years, the K-State group visited many communities, including Salina, Topeka, Wichita, Dodge City, Garden City, Hays, Lawrence, and communities in Johnson County. They were met with enthusiasm.[156]

In 1989, Ruth Ann and I flew to Coffeyville, Kansas to meet with R.M. Seaton. He was a K-State graduate and the owner of the COFFEYVILLE JOURNAL, the MANHATTAN MERCURY, and several radio stations. We hoped that R.M. would share our vision for a new art museum.

R.M. responded with an historic metaphor: "The idea of an art museum at my school is sort of like finding the 'the holy grail'—everyone seems to think it is a great idea, but no one has ever been able to find it." Hearing those words, I knew that Ruth Ann would become the exact leader to find "the holy grail."[157]

K-STATE'S QUINTESSENTIAL VOLUNTEER: RUTH ANN WEFALD

Ruth Ann became the quintessential volunteer for Kansas State University for 23 years. She never asked for or received a paid position in all those years. She volunteered at least thirty hours a week every year. She played a pivotal leadership role for the new art museum.

She also raised funds to expand the International Student Center; to build three new dance studios for the Theatre and Dance Program in the 1990's; and to construct a new Boathouse for the women's crew team in the 21st century. She did that and more. Ruth Ann's love for K-State was boundless.

Ruth Ann knew one day she would soon find the key to "the holy grail." That day occurred late in 1988 when K-State's art museum group met in Hays, Kansas. On that singular day, serendipity struck. A very special person had attended their meeting—Marianna Kistler Beach. She was enthused. She soon shared that ardor with her husband and best friend, Ross.

OUR HISTORIC MEETING WITH THE BEACHES

Ruth Ann and I were eager to host a dinner for the Beaches. In January of 1989, Ruth Ann and I hosted a dinner for Ross and Marianna Beach to determine the level of their interest in becoming the lead donors. Bob Hagans, the Chairman of the Foundation Executive Committee, and Gary Hellebust, the Director of Corporate Relations, joined the Beaches and us.

Ross Beach was President of Kansas Natural Gas, Inc. of Hays, Kansas, and the Chairman of the Douglas County Bank of Lawrence, Kansas. After dinner, Ruth Ann and I asked Ross if he might consider a lead gift for a new art museum.

We shared a rough architectural rendering of what the new museum might look like. Ross and Marianna were rather taken with it. After looking closely at the sketch, Ross suggested that he would consider the idea of a lead gift.

After a few nervewracking minutes, Ross said he would provide a $1 million dollar lead gift in the near future. He had been pondering a naming opportunity for Marianna in honor of their fiftieth wedding anniversary.

But it almost never happened. After Ross suggested a figure, Bob Hagans said the Foundation would need a lead gift of at least $3 million for a naming opportunity. Before I could say anything, Ross said: "If you need a lead gift of that amount, you will have to look elsewhere."

I almost fell off my chair. I managed to blurt out that a $1 million dollar lead gift would work just fine. After all, if Ross Beach wanted a naming opportunity for Marianna in honor of their 50th wedding anniversary, I sensed that he would provide more funding in the future. Everyone took a deep breath. No one said anything. Then, Ross, said, "If you can accept a lead gift of this amount, count us in."

In a moment Ruth Ann and I would always remember, all six of us signed the architectural rendering. I could not wait to sign it. Ruth Ann signed first. A public announcement of the gift would come later. At the end of the dinner, Ruth Ann and I could truly believe in the possibility of a new Kansas State art museum for the first time in history. We knew the Beaches would make it happen.[158]

Ross and Marianna Beach were getting closer to making a significant lead gift. The time arrived for a big announcement. On Friday, September 13, 1991, at a reception hosted by the Friends of Art, R.M. Seaton announced that Ross Beach had committed $2 million dollars for a new art museum. Ruth Ann was beaming. She could see the dream of the art museum becoming a reality.

More than 300 people attended the reception. This extraordinary gift from Ross Beach increased the art museum cash gifts and pledges to $3.4 million. The total of deferred gifts had reached $1.1 million. With their heroic gift, Ross and Marianna Beach became two of the greatest angels in the history of Kansas State.[159]

Meanwhile, R.M. Seaton agreed to become the chair of the Art Museum Campaign Development Committee. I will always remember R.M. Seaton fondly. Always gracious, he was one of the most impressive business leaders I have ever met. R.M. Seaton donated $500,000 for the construction of a new art museum. With the financial support of Ross Beach and R.M. Seaton, a Marianna Kistler Beach Museum of Art was just on the horizon.[160]

The former excellent Director of the Beach Museum of Art from 1999 to 2011, Lorne Render, sent me his comments on the role of Ruth Ann Wefald in achieving the new Beach Museum of Art: "Kansas State had a glaring void in the cultural life it offered by not having an art museum. It was the vision, passion, and determination of Ruth Ann Wefald that got the job done. She led the work of raising awareness and support, traveling the state, and encouraging people in creating an art museum. And she succeeded! The Marianna Kistler Beach Museum of Art opened in 1996 and is a showcase for Kansas and regional art and a major contributor to the artistic and cultural life on campus. Ruth Ann's outstanding leadership helped to make this dream possible and is deeply appreciated by so many today."[161]

THE SEARCH FOR A NEW ART MUSEUM DIRECTOR

With the critical funds to initiate a national search for the first art museum director, a search committee was set up in 1992. The Director of the East Carolina University Art Museum, Nelson C. Britt, was selected. Britt had a BA degree in art history from the State University of New York College at Buffalo, New York and a MFA degree from the Rhode Island School of Design. From September 1, 1992 to June 30, 1997, Nelson Britt did an outstanding job.[162]

With the hiring of Nelson in September of 1992, the search for a museum architect was launched. Although a number of excellent design proposals were submitted, the Moore/Andersson architectural firm from Austin, Texas won the job.

Arthur Andersson became the project's lead architect. A building site near the edge of campus that featured excellent exposure for both the community and campus was selected. On May 6, 1994, a groundbreaking ceremony was held. Ironically, this site was near the place where Ross had proposed to Marianna.[163]

Arthur Andersson talked about the future location for the new museum: "When I first visited KSU's campus in 1991, it was wintertime and beautifully austere. It was a grey day. There were no leaves on the trees. All of the limestone buildings were a crème color, most of them with silver-gray asphalt roofs. The campus looked like a slightly tinted black-and white photograph."[164]

K-State had hired a superb architect with a poetic sense. Under his direction, the architects designed a post-modern building of 26,000 square feet. They utilized the native limestone. The new museum contained five galleries, an auditorium, a classroom, offices, art storage places, and workspaces. The Moore/Andersson architects and the Eby Construction Company of Wichita did a brilliant job in building the Marianna Kistler Beach Museum of Art.[165]

THE MEMORABLE DEDICATION ON OCTOBER 13, 1996

On the Saturday morning of October 13, 1996, the weather was clear, sunny, and beautiful. The dedication was impressive. The Beach Museum of Art quickly became one of the most beautiful buildings on the campus. A nice crowd assembled by the museum's classic archway. For the arts and humanities faculty and students, the day was truly historic.

In addition to Ross and Marianna Beach, donors like R.M. Seaton, Jack and Donna Vanier, Lou Ann McKinnon Dunn, Jack and Joann Goldstein, R. Crosby Kemper and Bebe Kemper, Caroline Peine, Perry Peine, and Barbara Wilson were at the dedication. For many K-Staters, this was a dream come true. The university had a stunning new art museum for the first time in history.[166]

Beth Unger was in attendance with her husband, Sam. She was an engineer and a computer scientist and he was an economist. She told me after the dedication how the new Beach Museum of Art was so special for them. Beth summed up their heartfelt feelings on that Saturday morning: "Sam and I were so full of emotion as we stood there. With misty eyes, Sam said, 'People can no longer say we are a cow college. Today, K-State is finally a university.'"[167]

THE HISTORIC NATURE OF THE BEACHS' GIFT

There were many people to thank on this beautiful Saturday morning. Ross and Marianna Beach of Hays, Kansas will be remembered forever for their magnificent gifts. Without them, the new art museum might not have happened for decades.

Ruth Ann championed this crusade for a decade. She convinced many donors to step forward to help fund the new Beach Museum of Art—including R.M. Seaton and his family, R. Crosby Kemper, Jack and Donna Vanier, Orval Hempler, Tom and Lou Ann McKinnon Dunn, Robert and Barbara Wilson, and Jack and Joann Goldstein.

Jack Goldstein and R. Crosby Kemper, the Chairman of the UMB Bank in Kansas City, thrilled the Beach Museum of Art supporters by giving the funds for a magnificent Dale Chihuly glass sculpture. Installed in the stairway tower, this beautiful glass sculpture would be visible to everyone looking at the Beach Museum of Art. Today, it is like a beacon light for the fine arts.[168]

When the Marianna Kistler Beach Museum of Art opened in October of 1996, three boards were in place—including a museum advisory board, a national board of visitors, and the Friends of the Beach Museum of Art Board. They were raising about $50,000 a year by 2009. These funds are used for art acquisitions and collection conservation. There were about 350 members.[169]

Nelson Britt announced his retirement in 1997. We launched a national search for a new director. There was one candidate who caught everyone's attention: Lorne Render. He was the Director of the Charles M. Russell Museum of Art in Great Falls, Montana. With unanimous support from the search committee, Chuck Reagan offered Loren Render the job in November of 1998. After his call, Reagan told me that Lorne had turned us down.[170]

KSU WAS FORTUNATE TO HIRE LORNE RENDER

I was determined to hire Lorne Render. Chuck Reagan and I talked about a better offer. I called Lorne. I gave him "an offer he could not refuse." I told him we would pay his wife's way to fly to Manhattan for a visit. I offered him a much higher salary—and I threw in two excellent seats for football and basketball games.

Lorne Render accepted the position. Kansas State could not have found a more caring, thoughtful, and superb leader for the Beach Museum of Art. We had found an extraordinary Museum Director.

Lorne Render became the new director in April of 1999. From his first day, everyone working at the art museum bonded with the new director. The future was bright. The staff was dedicated, hard working, and committed to excellence. The three boards all had outstanding volunteers. The director reported to my chief of staff, Chuck Reagan. He did a great job working with Lorne Render, his staff, and the three boards right up to 2009.

In the next decade, Lorne Render was a superior leader for the Beach Museum of Art. During his tenure, the museum's art collection had increased from 2,000 works of art to 7,000; it was presenting about fourteen exhibitions and offering about 150 education programs annually; and it was attracting about 30,000 visitors.

In April of 2003, the American Association of Museums accredited the Beach Museum of Art. The staff now included eight professional staff, maintenance and security help, and fifteen part-time students. They served as receptionists, gallery attendants, interns, exhibit technicians, and collection management assistants.[171]

THE DECISION TO BUILD A NEW ADDITION

In 2001, an expansion of the museum was necessary. More gallery space was needed to "showcase" the permanent collections and the temporary exhibitions. Once again, the Moore/Andersson Architects of Austin, Texas were selected as the architect for a building expansion of 17,000 square feet.

The Beach Museum Advisory Board estimated the expansion would cost $9 million—$6.5 million for the building expansion and $2.5 million for an endowment. Lorne Render asked Ruth Ann Wefald to chair the fund-raising campaign.[172]

ROSS AND MARIANNA BEACH PROVIDE ANOTHER LEAD GIFT

Once again, Ross and Marianna Beach provided the lead gift. This special K-State couple continued their generous contributions. Ross made sure there would always be enough funds in the endowment. Ross became one of K-State's most selfless heroes ever.

Lorne Render pointed out some of the other incredibly generous donors: "Significant donations resulted in donor-named spaces in the new addition. They include the Mary and Morgan Jarvis Wing, the Hyle Family Gallery, the Marion Pelton Gallery, the Stolzer Family Foundation Bill and Eleanor Stolzer Gallery, the Lincoln and Dorothy Diehl entrance, and the Dan and Beth Bird Archway."[173]

In October of 2007, the new addition to the Marianna Kistler

Beach Museum of Art was dedicated. With the 17,000 additional square feet, the museum now totaled 43,000 square feet. It, too, was an architectural masterpiece. The contractors, Coonrod and Associates of Wichita, Kansas, did an outstanding job as well.

This new addition contained three new galleries, enlarged and new storage vaults, new workspaces, and additional offices. Inside and outside, the new addition was elegant, beautiful, and perfect. The Marianna Kistler Beach Museum of Art took its place as one of the nation's finest regional art museums. Linda Duke, the excellent new Director of the Beach Museum of Art since July of 2011, elegantly explained Ruth Ann's contributions to the Beach Museum of Art from 1986 to the present: "Along with countless others, I feel a personal debt to Ruth Ann Wefald for her vision and dedication in working to create an art museum at K-State."[174]

THE HISTORIC IMPORTANCE OF THESE TWO NEW BUILDINGS

The Beach Museum of Art in 1996 and the Hale Library in 1997 represented an "iconic shift" in the history of Kansas State. These two new buildings symbolized an historic and transformative shift for the entire university. The Beach Museum of Art and the Hale Library not only became two of the most iconic and celebrated buildings on campus, they helped diminish the notion of our school being in second place and always trying to catch up for thousands of K-Staters everywhere.

Chapter 6

Dramatically Expanding The Arts And Sciences, Beautifying The Campus, And Moving West

In my first State of the University presentation in the fall of 1986, I stressed that the College of Arts and Sciences had to be central to the entire university. In my inauguration speech on Thursday, October 30, 1986, I told the audience: "The goal of education here at Kansas State is to encourage the development of human potentialities; to allow our students to think for themselves; and to help our students to become what they want to be."[175]

In 1986, I did not realize until doing research on my manuscript in 2010 what the Chairman of the Board of Regents, Wendell Lady, had told the Manhattan Rotary Club on April 18, 1985. Regent Lady had declared that Kansas State should continue its academic emphasis on two programs: agriculture and engineering.

After all these years, the Chairman of the Kansas Board of Regents in 1985 still did not understand that the nation's best land-grant schools had been proclaiming for decades the importance of being comprehensive, modern, and diverse.

THE IMPORTANCE OF EMPHASIZING THE LIBERAL ARTS IN 1986

From 1943 to 1986, Milton Eisenhower, James McCain, and Duane Acker had elevated the importance of the liberal arts. All three had made good progress in promoting the arts and sciences.

But we still found it necessary to develop specific strategies to more properly fund the College of Arts and Sciences. The college had been off the school's radar screen for too long.

By 1986, Kansas State had fallen behind many of the other land grant universities—especially when you read the U.S. NEWS AND WORLD REPORT's rankings of colleges and universities.

The best land grants had been erecting first-class programs in the arts and sciences, promoting basic research, and creating stellar libraries for years.

These same superb land-grant universities had become members of the Association of American Universities (AAU) and the Association of Research Libraries (ARU). Kansas State failed to become a member of either one.

John Chalmers became the first dean of the College of Arts and Sciences in 1963. He served in that position until 1968 when he was chosen to be the academic vice president by President James McCain. Chalmers did an excellent job in both positions.

The College of Arts and Sciences Deans from 1968 to 2009, Bill Stamey, Tom Isenhour, Peter Nicholls, and Steve White, worked hard to enhance and improve the college.[176]

From 1986 to 1988, our leadership team determined that the College of Arts and Sciences was still horribly underfunded. The fiscal challenges facing us for this college were heightened by vastly increased enrollment. Keep in mind that most of the newly enrolled students were taking classes in the College of Arts and Sciences.

THE NEED TO FUND THE COLLEGE OF ARTS AND SCIENCES

Financial adjustments were imperative. Although it was hardly enough, our administration reallocated $6 million from virtually every cost center in the university to the College of Arts and Sciences from 1988 to 1993. This was blood money. It was blood money because every college and department at K-State badly needed new funds.

But we had no choice. K-State had received new funding for only about 1,000 of the additional 4,500 students enrolled between 1987 and 1991. Instead of the school receiving $11.3 million for those new students, Kansas State pocketed only $4.3 million.

If our school had received the additional $7 million, it would have been far easier to fund the starved programs in the humanities and social sciences.[177]

I decided there were some modest things I could do out of my office to support the College of Arts and Sciences—especially some of the underfunded departments in the arts, the social sciences, and the humanities.

THE ALLOCATION OF GRANTS TO THE ARTS AND HUMANITIES

Department heads in the arts, the social sciences and the humanities normally had tiny budgets—and little or no discretionary monies for faculty research and travel. From 1986 to 2009, we created a university reserve for the entire university in the spring of every year. It was never large enough. As you would expect, most major state universities over the years had reserves ranging from $5 million to $10 million annually.

The largest reserve our administration had for a fiscal year was about $700,000. For most years, it was about $600,000 a year or less. By the mid-1990's, I decided to use some of those monies to assist a number of departments in the humanities, the arts, and the social sciences with modest annual grants.

One of the first departments I assisted was the Department of English. On many college campuses, the English Department is unappreciated. I knew that our English major was exceptional. I knew many of their faculty members were recognized regionally and nationally as first-rate teachers and scholars.

I started allocating about $3,000 a year in 1995 to the English Department. I increased that figure to $10,000 a year by 2000 and to $25,000 a year by 2008. The English faculty members were delighted to receive expense money—many for the first time—to give a paper at a regional conference or a key national conference. They deserved every nickel.[178]

Karin Westman, who was the department head after 2008, knew the importance of these grants: "These funds primarily went towards supporting faculty conference travel during the academic year. The department also used these discretionary monies to support our faculty's research, scholarship, and creative activity."[179]

From 1996 to 2009, I distributed small grants from university reserves at the beginning of the academic year to departments in the humanities and social sciences. The department heads deployed much of this funding for faculty research projects and for faculty travel to attend academic conferences.

Some of the funds, however, were also used for computers, information technology, and office supplies. By 2005, I was providing grants in the arts and humanities of about $6,000 to $10,000 a year. For many of the department heads, these annual grants were literally like receiving a shipment of gold.[180]

For the first time ever, many of these departments had some discretionary funds. I wish I could have done more. A number of department heads in the social sciences and the humanities wrote memos to me indicating how these grants made a huge difference.

THE IMPACT OF THESE GRANTS: A TIPPING POINT!

Many of these department heads believed that these annual grants provided a "tipping point" for their departments. Steve White, who was a geography scholar and the Dean of the College of Arts and Sciences from 2002 to 2009, told me exactly that.

Dean White understood how much the grants provided hope and opportunities: "From 1986 to 2009, there truly was a renaissance in the arts and sciences. Indeed, the Wefald years launched a rebirth of the liberal arts at Kansas State University. The College of Arts and Sciences became for the first time a pivotal college for the entire university."[181]

The Department of Modern Languages, for example, was one of those departments that had been ignored for decades. Robert Corum, the department head, asked me in 2005 to allocate $20,000 for office and classroom renovations. In 2007, I sent Corum $10,000 so they could purchase additional IT systems and buy new faculty chairs for the department's seminar room.[182]

In the fall of 2008, I received an urgent call from Corum. He said his department badly needed a renovated seminar/multi-media room. I sent him the monies to do that. When it was finished, the students and faculty were using it from early morning to late at night.

Robert Corum explained how vital these funds were: "These improvements have had a huge effect on faculty and staff morale, and have greatly enhanced our ability to serve our students and the public. The 50 faculty and staff and the nearly 4,000 K-Staters who take our classes in 11 languages every year are grateful."[183]

The Geography Department had outstanding scholars and teachers long before I came to K-State. But Dick Marston, the department head and a UDP, told me several times in 2004 and 2005 that his department had little funds for faculty members and graduate students to travel to professional meetings. I provided some of that funding.

In 2005, I toured the department. I could not believe how bad their facilities were. The nagging problems included horrible lighting, peeling paint on the walls, missing ceiling tiles, and deteriorating ancient carpeting—just to name a few.[184]

After receiving these funds, Dick Marston reported the results: "These repairs were accomplished without delay. Our seminar room was formerly a trash heap of folding chairs and tables, plus old discarded metal bookshelves. The president equipped our seminar room with a table and matching bookshelves crafted by a local carpenter. Faculty morale has greatly improved and we now showcase our department to alumni and visiting scholars."[185]

Angela Powers became the Director of the A. Q. Miller School of Journalism and Mass Communication in 2004. She was a breath of fresh air. From 2005 to 2009, I sent Angela funding to help upgrade the conditions of Kedzie Hall. From my first year in 1986, I heard horror stories about Kedzie Hall.

I sent Angela Powers funds to create a suitable reading room on Kedzie's main floor for students. We provided funds to improve faculty offices and classrooms. Knowing that the main office and conference room had not been renovated for years, our facilities staff installed new carpeting and repainted the entire area."[186]

After Marcello Sabates became the Head of the Department of Philosophy in 2001, he asked for help. His department had been ignored forever. I started sending $5,000 a year. By 2008, I increased the department's funding to $6,000 a year. Sabates used these funds to set up a "World-Class Speakers Series."

Each year, the department invited four lecturers to deliver major presentations. Marcello wrote that the visting speakers "were some of the most important philosophers in America and Europe and that the series improved the national visibility of our department."[187]

In 2006, I sent Marcello $15,000 to improve the department's seminar room and a small lecture hall. Sabeto told me that the funds helped "provide an outstanding lecture hall for our Speakers Series, and an improved seminar room for our smaller classes. These funds helped our department become one of the best undergraduate-only programs in the country along with Dartmouth and Cal Tech."[188]

The Political Science Department represented another program that rarely received help from the central administration. In 1995, I started sending $10,000 annually to the department. Joe Aistrup, the department head from 2000 to 2009, told me that the department decided to use a large amount of the funds for junior faculty to travel to conferences to present their research.

Joe Aistrup defined the importance of these funds: "Over the course of my tenure as department head, we were able to build an excellent foundation for the department's large increase in publications in high visibility political science journals. These articles helped make the department's Security Studies program the 8th ranked program among international graduate programs."[189]

When Dale Herspring was the department head from 1993 to 2000, I allocated $5,000 a year to help launch a departmental lectures series called the Political, Military, and Diplomatic Lecture Series. I continued that funding until 2009. Under Dale's leadership, the lecture series became a huge success. He convinced a number of first-rate diplomats, scholars, political and military leaders to deliver lectures between 1995 and 2009.

The impressive list included speakers like General Wojciech Jaruzelski, the former President of Poland; Sergei Khrushchev, son of the late Soviet Party Secretary, Nikita Khrushchev; Admiral Dennis Blair, USN (ret), former Commander in Chief, U.S. Forces Pacific; Colonel Hans-Werner Weber, former officer in the East German Army who was in the East German military headquarters when the

Berlin Wall fell; and General David Petraeus, when he was the Commander at Ft. Leavenworth.

I doubt that any Department of Political Science has had a better lecture series in the past generation.[190]

The History Department was another academic program with limited discretionary monies. As an historian, I had reason enough to change that. Their department had been outstanding for years. Our mutual goal was to make it even better. From 1995 on, I sent the department annual grants.

Sue Zschoche, the excellent head of the History Department from 2003 to 2009, stated how she used their grants of $10,000 a year. The department used the monies for office supplies, phones, copying, and information technology. Some of the funds were set aside for her history colleagues to attend scholarly conferences. Sue said: "The result was that every faculty member had one conference a year heavily subsidized. This was very good for morale."[191]

For the history department and many other departments, I often asked Beth Unger to assist in the creation of technologically upgraded classrooms around the campus. From 1993 to 2009, Beth and her staff constructed 70 IT upgraded classrooms.

The history faculty were thrilled that two of their most highly used classrooms were upgraded for interactive learning. I also sent them funds to improve their highly used conference room with a new table, new chairs, and appropriate IT tools. This room became at once a virtual interactive classroom and conference room.[192]

Because the history department had placed a major emphasis on military history for years, it always had nationally ranked military historians. The military history program became its highest priority. After Jack Holl became the department head in 1999, a Military History Institute was organized. I allocated an additional $5,000 a year to the institute to enhance their military history program.

After 2000, the department found a way to hire several new military historians in European and American history. The new faculty helped the department gain more recognition as one of the nation's best military history programs.

This program had several vital advantages. One of the nation's largest U.S. Army bases, Ft. Riley, was only fifteen miles away. The Eisenhower Presidential Library and Museum was only fifty miles away. Ft. Leavenworth was only ninety miles away. The Truman Presidential Library and Museum was only 130 miles away.

THE CREATION OF A PARTNERSHIP WITH FT. LEAVENWORTH

From 2002 to 2009, we started talking about creating a partnership with Ft. Leavenworth. As the oldest active U.S. Army base west of Washington D.C., this historic army base has been known as the "Intellectual Center of the Army." The U.S. Army Command and General Staff College was the centerpiece of Ft. Leavenworth.

The army college trains most of the majors in the U.S. Army. George Marshall, Dwight Eisenhower, Douglas MacArthur, and Omar Bradley were some of the 5 Star Generals that passed through the General Staff College.

Chris King, the Dean of Academics for the General Staff College, agreed to form a partnership with our KSU Military History Institute. As a retired Brigadier General and a scholar, Chris King made our partnership possible. We agreed to add the Departments of Political Science and Educational Leadership in the College of Education to our evolving partnership with Ft. Leavenworth. The program became Security Studies.[193]

The academic partnership with the General Staff College would allow Kansas State to offer masters and doctoral degrees in Security Studies at the General Staff College and on our campus. We decided to ask our Congressional delegation about the possibility of getting federal grants to help us set up excellent graduate programs in security studies.

The state's two U.S. Senators, Pat Roberts and Sam Brownback and our Second District U.S. Congressman, Jim Ryun, were delighted to back this partnership between the "Intellectual Center of the U.S. Army" and Kansas State University. For the state's political leaders, this was a marriage made in heaven. They knew we had a great ally: the Ft. Leavenworth U.S. Army Command and General Staff College.

In 2006, our Security Studies program received our first $1 million grant from Congressman Jim Ryun. In 2007 and 2008, our new program received additional grants of $2 million through the good offices of our two U.S. Senators, Pat Roberts and Sam Brownback and Congressman Ryun. The newly elected 2nd district U.S. Representative, Nancy Boyda, with the help of Senators Brownback and Roberts, was able to find an additional $500,000 grant for Securities Studies fiscal in the 2009 budget.[194]

Before the era of earmarks basically ended in 2009 and 2010, the Democratic Representative Boyda and our two Republican U.S. Senators had secured an additional $1.6 million in new federal grant monies. From 2006 to 2010, K-State and its Security Studies program received total federal funding of $5.1 million.

Chuck Reagan and Sue Peterson did a superior job with our congressional delegation. Three new military historians and three new political scientists with specialities in Security Studies were hired. The history and political science departments were improved. About these federal grants, Chuck said with a touch of humor: "No history and political science departments in the history of the known world have ever received this kind of federal funding."[195]

According to David Stone, the Director of the Institute for Military History and a nationally ranked Russian historian, the Security Studies program launched "full-scale operations" in the fall of 2006. In the next four years, the program produced 74 MA graduates, with 50 of them from Ft. Leavenworth. By 2011, the MA program had 38 active students enrolled and the doctoral program had 28.

By 2009, Kansas State's new Security Studies program for Ft. Leavenworth army leaders had become a program that actually enhanced America's national security. With little red tape, K-State and Ft. Leavenworth implemented a masters and doctoral program in Security Studies—one that would benefit soldiers at Ft. Leavenworth and students at K-State for years to come.[196]

THE MODEST AMOUNTS SPENT ON ACADEMIC DEPARTMENTS

Using the academic year of 2008-09 as a guide, I allocated $251,700 during that school year to benefit a number of academic departments in the College of Arts and Sciences. This amount came out of the president's reserve of about $700,000.

Importantly, for every year, virtually the entire president's reserve was allocated to a variety of academic departments in a number of colleges. Some of it was allocated at the beginning of the school year. The rest was deployed to various departments in the entire university as necessary during the course of the year.

Compared to the huge funding available for our athletic teams, the $251,700 allocated to the academic departments in the arts, the social sciences and the humanities in 2008-09 was miniscule.[197]

THE IMPORTANCE OF K-STATE'S THEATRE, DEBATE AND SPEECH SQUADS, AND VARIOUS MUSICAL GROUPS

By the 1990's, I was resolved to assist our theatre program, debate and speech squads, and various musical groups. If Kansas State was going to be a modern and inclusive land grant university, these programs had to be outstanding. These programs were not only significant for the College of Arts and Sciences, they were important for the excellence of the university itself.

Ruth Ann and I became ardent supporters of the theatre program. The directors in theatre I worked most closely with were Charlotte MacFarland, an associate professor of theatre, and Marci Maullar, the managing director of the KSU Theatre program.

Ruth Ann and I started going to their plays and musicals in 1986-1987. We attended a multitude of them over the years. Ruth Ann and I saw many outstanding plays and musicals that had superb direction, brilliantly designed sets, and excellent student actors.

I soon noticed that the theatre chairs needed upholstering and the theatre carpeting was frayed. During my years, the theatre chairs were upholstered twice and the carpeting was replaced three times. Nichols Hall is a special place for the theatre and dance programs.

Then, I realized the interior halls, offices, studios, and the classrooms in Nichols needed repainting. Because this building was a showcase for the entire university, I made sure it was repainted at least twice.

Marci Maullar sent me a note in May of 2001: "I can honestly say that I would not have stayed at K-State if it were not for your support of the program. You and Ruth Ann have made the difference for so many of us in the arts."[198]

Starting in the late 1980's, I decided to host a nice reception after a spring play for the directors, the set designers, the audience, and especially the student actors. We did that up to 2009. Ruth Ann and I always liked mixing it up with the students. I was consistently impressed with their superior acting abilities. One of the student actors that I met at one of our receptions was Eric Stonestreet.

For four years, Eric caught everyone's attention as an excellent student actor. He was good in both dramatic plays and comedies. Even in 1995 and 1996, you could sense that Eric might be one of the lucky ones to make it to Hollywood some day. He graduated in 1996. After a great deal of hard work, Eric Stonestreet became a star on the weekly TV show called "Modern Family."

Charlotte MacFarland directed and produced many excellent plays for Kansas State over the years. After I retired, she sent me a touching note: "Before the Wefalds came to Manhattan, we were a small department that was often ignored. But all that changed. Every year, President Wefald gave us money to purchase new lights, to recarpet the Nichols Theatre, and to paint the walls when they began to fade. Every time I rehearse in one of the lovely studios in Nichols Hall, I remind myself of the difference they made. They have made this a golden time for all of us in Theatre, Music, and Dance. We shall not see their like again."[199]

Both the theatre and music programs used the McCain Auditorium for a variety of productions. The Music Department had its academic programs in McCain—including its faculty, music classrooms, and important space for Choral Studies, the K-State Singers and Glee Clubs, the KSU Symphony Orchestra, Jazz Ensembles, and the KSU Bands. McCain was a centerpiece building for the entire university.

I asked the facilities staff to upholster the seats and replace the carpeting in McCain three different times. I had them repaint the entire interior of the building at least twice and the public walkways surrounding the auditorium three times. There were people who noticed when Nichols, McCain, the Hale Library, and the Beach Art Museum needed work or repainting. I was one of those.

I supported the music department and its individual music groups with modest annual grants over my last 15 years. Even though these musical programs play a vibrant role in the life of Kansas State, there were few major donors standing in line to support them.

When I first came to K-State, I paid little attention to the marching band at the home football games. The football program had been out of sight and mind for years. Most fans ignored the marching band. Both programs aroused pity from 1986 to 1989. From World War II to 1986, the Kansas State Marching Band had seven directors. Phil Hewitt, the director from 1972 to 1982, was the most successful.

Under Phil Hewitt, the marching band got much bigger; it added many female members; and its formations became more complex. His band became competitive with many of the up-tempo Big 8 marching bands.

But under Stan Fink, the band director from 1983 to 1991, the marching band got much smaller and more invisible. Stan shunned the Big 10 up-tempo sound and style for a marching form of a softer drum and bugle marching approach. This style bored our fans.

THE INCREASING IMPORTANCE OF A BIG-TIME MARCHING BAND

With Bill Snyder and better football teams coming up, I saw that the Big 8 schools K-State played had superb marching bands. I came to see the need for a much better marching band. With the football team playing on national television from time to time after 1992, there was no choice. A really good marching band was compulsory.

The Big 8 had many excellent marching bands like Nebraska, Oklahoma, and Kansas in 1992. The K-State Marching Band was not one of those. Stan Fink, the marching band's director, retired in 1992 for health reasons. In the next year, I sensed that some music faculty members hoped the marching band might just disappear.

In 1992, the Department of Music had hired two marching band directors in a row. Because neither one saw any promise for a good marching band, both left abruptly after just a few months. The department turned to Stan Fink's assistant, Ben Rohr. He was the interim director for the next two school years. Then, Ben was hired as the band director at a Salina high school.

Early in the spring of 1993, a search committee in the Music Department was set up to find still another new director. Given the lack of enthusiasm in the Department of Music for a major marching band by 1992, I had to get involved. Just as we had to get the right football coach in 1988, we had to hire the right band director in 1993.

Because I doubted the department would get it right, I assembled an ex-officio group to make sure the right band director was hired this time. It included representatives of the alumni association, the foundation, and colleagues in Anderson Hall. Of the three finalists, there was just one who fit the bill—Frank Tracz, the Director of Bands at Morehead State University in Morehead, Kentucky.

In the first few minutes of the interview, all of us on the committee saw that Frank Tracz had exactly what was needed: enthusiasm, confidence, optimism, and a can-do attitude. He got the job easily.

Years later, Frank told me: "I personally believe you were the only one in the entire university to see the validity of having a first-rate marching band at the time. There were very few faculty members in the music department who saw the need for a terrific marching band. You stated to me, however, that you wanted a nationally top-rated marching band. You hit that nail on the head."[200]

In 1988 and 1989, hardly anyone believed the football team would ever win a conference championship. Certainly no one dreamed of a K-State Marching Band that would have over 400 members. No one, including Frank and me, believed that one day the school's marching band would receive the Sudler Award—an award given every two years to the nation's best big-time university marching band.

From 1988 to 1993, someone had to say that these two programs could be turned around. I knew that American history was all about hope. I knew K-State could have both a good football team and a good marching band. The challenge was difficult. But as William James once said: "The greatest discovery of my generation is that man can alter his life simply by altering his attitude of mind."

The state of our marching band in 1993 was bad. Frank Tracz told me how horrible everything was for the band that summer: "The cupboards over here are bare." He spelled out how the band uniforms were ancient and moth-eaten; how the instruments were old and in disrepair; how the facilities were dismal; and how the band members were dispirited.

Frank also told me that the marching band was down to 120 members. The band budget was next to zero. The director had no secretary and only 1.5 graduate assistants. He put it this way: "The structure, format, and system of the band was weak or even non-existent. The marching form was one of more "soft corps style" with little 'entertainment' and 'spirit' value. Enter Jon Wefald. I provided him with a list of needs and I asked for assistance—I got it."[201]

I had to help Frank Tracz and the marching band. No one else would. If I had not stepped in to help, Frank would have departed years ago. From 1993 to 2009, I provided the funds so he could do the following: hire a new assistant band director; hire talented graduate assistants; hire an administrative assistant; purchase new silver instruments for everyone in the band; and find the funds from a variety of sources to buy new band uniforms.

In November of 2011, Frank evaluated the progress of the KSU Marching Band: "In looking back at the Wefald years and my 18 years at K-State I am adamant in stating that none of the band success would have been possible without the backing of the K-State

President. His ability to help us with the 'physical' needs is dwarfed by his enthusiastic support of the band and me. Jon Wefald was and is the reason we now average close to 400 students in the marching band and also why the K-State Band job is the best in the nation."[202]

THE IMPORTANCE OF THE SPEECH AND DEBATE SQUADS

The K-State Debate and Speech Squads required some central support as well. I wanted to have All-American students in speech and debate. With some additional funding, I thought we could do exactly that. Craig Brown was our Director of Forensics.

In 1990, we started providing funds for the Kansas State speech and debate squads. It included monies for scholarship money, coaching staff, and especially travel funds.

Coach Craig Brown understood the sigificance of these funds: "Starting in 1991-1992 and for the next 18 years of the Wefald Presidency, the K-State Individual Events team placed in the Top 20 at the AFA-NIET every year. Fourteen times the team placed in the Top Ten."

From 1991 to 2009, 24 K-Staters became national champions in oratory, impromptu, extemporaneous, critical analysis, and after dinner speaking. Few universities in America won 24 individual championships over those 18 years.[203]

Each year, the AFA-NIET selects the best overall speaker of the year in the nation. This award is analogous to winning the Heisman Trophy. Three K-State speakers from 1990 to 2009 were selected as the overall national speaking champion—Tim Schultz, Chris McLemore, and Jessy Ohl. All three were brilliant speakers.

I always wondered why these three national champions did not receive front-page stories. They normally received a story on Part B, page 2. When a student is voted the best college speaker in the nation, this means they could become another Henry Clay, Daniel Webster, Abraham Lincoln, FDR, John Kennedy, or Ronald Reagan.

In 1989, the K-State Debate Team needed support. It had little state funds. No debate team can win national honors unless they have the funds to travel to prestigious debate tournaments. I added base budget funds to the debate team so they could do exactly that. I also allocated funds for an additional assistant debate coach and monies for additional graduate students to help coach the team.

In 1991, the Debate Team led by two superb debaters, Rich McCollum and David Filippi, won the Cross Examination National Debate Association Debate Championship (CEDA). The debate team, the coaches, and Ruth Ann and I were fortunate to meet with President George H.W. Bush in the White House in April of 1991.

In 1992, the Kansas State Debate Team, led by Jill Baisinger and K.J. Wall, finished 2nd in the nation. Led by Baisinger and Wall, Kansas State won the Cross Examination National Debate Championship in 1993. This time, we all had the opportunity to visit with Vice President Al Gore in the White House.

In 2005, the Department of Speech Communication, Theatre, and Dance hired an impressive new debate coach, Justin Green. After meeting him, my instinct was it would not take long for our Debate Team to win another national championship. Under the recruiting and coaching of Justin Green, our debate team started winning tournaments again throughout the nation.

One day, Green invited me over to see the room the debate team used. It was a former professor's office. I thought, how in the world could anyone recruit excellent student debaters to a small faculty office in McCain. This had to change. The size of the debate squad had grown to 25 students and five coaches by 2005.

Meanwhile, I was informed the facilities office was intending to renovate the basement area of Kedzie Hall to build a new classroom and add several conference rooms in the fall of 2006.

When I heard about their plans to renovate the basement of Kedzie, I asked the facilities staff if they would be willing to carve out a nice space for the debate team at the same time. With a sense of urgency, they tore down two concrete walls and constructed a brand new, spacious, and excellent debate room.[204]

When we dedicated the new Debate Center in Kedzie Room 007 in the spring of 2007, the coaches and students were overjoyed.

Kedzie 007 was perfect. It had the necessary furniture. It was equipped with wireless Internet access, video cameras and projecter, storage and work places. For the first time, the team had a special room for squad meetings, practice, a room to gather together and have a cup of coffee. The cost for this new Debate Center was $50,000.

During my last three years, I spent some funds to purchase purple and white sweatsuits for both the Debate and Speech teams. They were thrilled to wear them. They wore them everywhere with incredible pride. Coach Green told me Northwestern, Michigan State, KU, and Wake Forest followed suit. Justin truly appreciated my support.

After the KSU debate team won the 2011 CEDA National Debate Championship in April of 2011, Green sent me an email. "You have done more to support our debate team than any other President of a major university. Your support in recruiting, obtaining quality coaching, facilities, and travel funds has helped K-State become a debate powerhouse for the past 20 years. This championship would not have happened without you."[205]

THE GOAL: WIN THE ELITE NATIONAL STUDENT SCHOLARSHIP

In July of 1986, I met Nancy Twiss. She was the Pre-Law Advisor in the College of Arts and Sciences. With Nancy advising students for the Truman scholarship, K-State had its first Truman in 1980 and two more in 1982. By 1986, she was the major advisor for students applying for the Rhodes, Marshall, and Truman scholarships.

I asked Nancy if we could make K-State a national leader in winning the elite academic scholarships. Indeed, I hoped to execute a strategic plan to win more Rhodes, Marshalls, Trumans, and Goldwaters than any public university in America.

Step by step, Twiss, her successors, and I set up a process that you could call the "K-State Way." Nancy and I recruited deans and department heads to help us find students who had "the right stuff."

When they were identified, Nancy met them to see if they had the right work ethic, dedication, and determination.

The student applicants had to spend six months perfecting their applications. They had to write a 'perfect' essay for our scholarship advisor. This took four or five drafts. Ordinarily, I never saw them. But I did see the essay of our 2008 Rhodes winner, Vincent Hofer, of tiny Franklin, Kansas. After reading it, I understood why Hofer won a Rhodes scholarship—it was perfect. I wondered if any Harvard applicant had ever written a finer essay.

The students' grades had to be almost straight A's. The students needed excellent letters of recommendations from distinguished faculty members. They had to appear before a heavyweight campus scholarship committee made of K-State's best faculty. They had to meet often with our scholarship advisor. They had to read numerous magazine and newspaper articles on many topics.

In 1996, we put together a search committee to find a good replacement for Nancy Twiss. Beth Powers got the job. She was an excellent scholarship advisor from 1996 to 2000. K-State continued to rack up more than our fair share of scholarship winners. In 2000, Beth left for a similar position at the University of Illinois, Chicago.

Chuck Reagan and I interviewed the finalists to replace Beth. We hired Jim Hohenbary. He was smart. He worked around the clock. For him, it was always about doing good things for K-State. In 2006, Dean White promoted Jim to the position of assistant dean for scholarships and head scholar coach. We provided Jim the funds for travel, luncheons, and the very latest IT equipment.

K-STATE AND THE RHODES SCHOLARSHIP

The brightest university students in America knew that the Rhodes scholarship was the ultimate award. If you won one, your resume was complete. Only 32 Rhodes are offered nationally every year. This scholarship was a full-ride worth over $75,000 for two years to attend Oxford University in England.

In my 23 years, eight students won the Rhodes—including Virgil

Wiebe of Garden City in 1986, Kelly Welch of Moran in 1987, Janelle Larson of Hiawatha and Mary Hale of Topeka in 1990, Kristy Parker of Valley Center in 1991, Jonathan Winkler of Wichita in 1998, Ben Champion of Olathe in 2003, and Vincent Hofer of Franklin in 2008.[206]

Most universities in America have never had one student win a Rhodes. With 12 Rhodes Scholars, North Carolina was first of all public universities. With eight Rhodes from 1986 to 2009, K-State ranked 2nd of all of the nation's 500 public universities. This meant KSU students had won more Rhodes than Michigan, Wisconsin, UCLA, Kansas, and Texas.[207]

K-STATE AND THE MARSHALL SCHOLARSHIP

K-State student scholars also competed well for America's second most prestigious scholarship: the Marshall scholarship. About 40 students are selected each year to receive it. The finest private colleges like Harvard, Yale, Princeton, and Stanford win more than their fair share of Rhodes and Marshalls every year.

This happens mainly because Ivy League schools have brilliant students with near perfect ACT scores from all over the nation. Established in 1953, the British government funded this full-ride scholarship as a gesture of thanks for the Marshall Plan after WWII.

This $35,000 scholarship was awarded for one to three years of study at any university in the United Kingdom. From 1986 to 2009, 11 KSU students won the Marshall. Kansas State was third in the nation among the 500 public universities. The University of California-Berkeley was first with 16 Marshalls and Arizona State was second with 13. But K-State had more Marshalls than schools like Wisconsin, Penn State, Kansas, and UCLA.[208]

The Rhodes and Marshalls are selected regionally. Because the best universities have students from most of the 50 states, they have a greater opportunity to win the nation's top scholarships. At KSU, our students are largely from Kansas. Using the metaphor of a bowling alley with 20 lanes, our students normally bowl on only one lane.

The best private universities bowl on all 20 lanes. Elite public schools like Michigan and UCLA bowl on ten to fifteen lanes.

In his popular Monday through Friday noon national radio broadcasts for years, Paul Harvey mentioned the success of K-State students in winning the Rhodes, Marshalls, Trumans, Goldwaters, and Udalls at least five times between 1993 and 2008. In 1993, Paul Harvey declared: "Kansas State has become the student scholar capital of the nation for the 500 public universities."[209]

People have asked me how I connected with Paul Harvey. I knew that he identified with underdogs. We were that and more. Whenever K-State won several of these scholarships, I wrote Paul a short handwritten note. I explained many of our winners were either from the farm or a small Kansas town. Out of seven letters I wrote to Paul from 1993 to 2007, he used five.

K-STATE AND THE TRUMAN SCHOLARSHIPS

The Truman Scholarship is the third most important national scholarship for undergraduates. About 65 students are selected each year to receive these $30,000 scholarships for graduate study. The criteria included academic achievement and leadership in public service. K-State had 23 Truman scholarship winners from 1986 to 2009. About half of them came from small towns like Welda, Hoxie, Beloit, Lyons, Arkansas City, Ellsworth, and Altoona.[210]

From 1986 to 2009, Kansas State was the Number 1 public university in America with 23 Truman scholarship winners. When our students won these elite scholarships, I hosted a lunch for the winners and their parents. The deans, the faculty senate president, the student body president, and faculty members were invited as well. After a brief talk, I introduced the winners and presented them with a handsome embroidered K-State sweatshirt and an engraved pewter mug. These lunches were always fun and good celebrations.

K-STATE AND THE GOLDWATER SCHOLARSHIPS

Inaugurated in 1989, the Barry M. Goldwater scholarship provided up to $15,000 for two years. These Goldwater scholarships were for science, math, and engineering students. K-State led all 500 public universities from 1989 to 2009 in America with 64 winners.

With 60 winners, Penn State was in second place and Illinois was in third place with 58 winners. Of the nation's 1500 private colleges and universities, only Harvard and Princeton had more Goldwater scholarship winners than K-State. Four of our students won the Goldwater scholarship in 1991, 1992, 1993, 1994, 1995, 1996, 2000, 2005, and 2006. No other public university was close.[211]

K-STATE AND THE UDALL SCHOLARSHIPS

The Udall scholarship was started in 1996. This scholarship provides $5,000 for students preparing for careers related to the environment or the well being of Native Americans. With 23 Udall scholarship winners, K-State had the second highest number of Udalls for the nation's 500 public universities from 1996 to 2009.[212]

KSU'S RECORD IN WINNING THESE FIVE SCHOLARSHIPS

From 1986 to 2009, K-State was ranked Number 1 out of 500 public universities in America in winning the Rhodes, Marshall, Truman, Goldwater, and Udall scholarships. Our students won 129 of these five scholarships over 23 years. In 2009, Arizona State University was Number 2 in the nation with 94 winners. Penn State and North Carolina were tied for Number 3 with 91 winners. KSU students won 53 more of these scholarships than Michigan.[213]

OUR FACULTY WON MANY NATIONAL AWARDS TOO

None of these student successes would have been possible without an excellent faculty. K-State faculty members have won numerous national awards over the years. The CASE/Carnegie Foundation sponsors one of the most prestigious national awards—when it selects one National Professor of the Year every year.

In 1996, Dean Zollman, a KSU physics professor, was selected as the CASE/Carnegie Foundation National Professor of the Year from many applicants at America's premier research universities. In 2007, Kansas State hit the equivalent of a World Series-winning double when Chris Sorensen, a physics professor, was picked for the CASE/Carnegie National Professor of the Year and Robert Littrell, a music professor, was chosen as the Kansas Professor of the Year.[214]

In 2008, I was surprised to receive another call from the Carnegie Foundation president. He said: "I am sure you will be shocked to know that we have selected another Kansas State faculty member as the 2008 CASE/Carnegie National Professor of the Year." It was Michael Wesch, a professor of anthropology. Only a few land-grant universities from 1986 to 2009 have had three faculty members selected for the CASE/Carnegie National Professor of the Year.[215]

The CASE/Carnegie Foundation also selects a Professor of the Year for all 50 states. Every private university and all six state universities in the state can submit faculty for the CASE/CARNEGIE Kansas professor of the year award. From 1990 to 2009, Kansas State faculty members won seven of these prestigious Kansas Professor of the Year awards. No school in Kansas has done better.

The seven faculty members and the year they were selected for the Kansas Professor of the Year include: In 1990, Miles McKee, a professor of animal science and industry, was chosen as the KANSAS Professor of the Year; in 1991, Deborah Canter, in hospitality; in 1992, Melvin Hunt, in animal science and industry; in 1993, Andrew Barkley, in agricultural economics; in 2000, Bryan Schurle, in agricultural economics; in 2006, Harald Prins, in anthropology; and, in 2007, Robert Littrell, in music.[216]

POINTED QUESTIONS FOR U.S. NEWS AND WORLD REPORT

Jim Coffman and I always wondered why the U.S NEWS AND WORLD REPORT in their annual rankings of the nation's colleges and universities never included how many prestigious academic scholarships our students won every year. And why they never included the number of our faculty who were selected as CASE/CARNEGIE Professors of the Year every year.

We had a conference call in 2002 with several top staff members of U.S. NEWS AND WORLD REPORT. We asked them to consider including these accomplishments in their university evaluations. We argued that these awards were easy to verify. Although every university in America hopes that their students and faculty are selected for these scholarships and awards, the magazine's staff retorted their rating analysis only included input criteria—like the ACT and SAT scores of entering freshmen, the level of faculty salaries, the number of volumes in the school's library, and extramural funding.

WHY KSU LAGGED IN NATIONAL RANKINGS

Jim and I asked the magazine's staff this question: Would it be possible for its ratings to include value-added criteria? Using the number of our student scholarship winners, we argued K-State did a good job of adding value to our students between their freshman years and graduation.

The ratings staff of U.S. NEWS AND WORLD REPORT did not budge. They had zero interest in including value-added criteria. We might as well have been talking to second-level bureaucrats in the former USSR.

The bottom line, however, for Kansas State is this—the two of us found out in talking with the staff of U.S. NEWS AND WORLD REPORT that we were still paying a heavy price for the first 75 years of our history as a vocational institute.

THE IMPORTANCE OF BEAUTIFYING OUR CAMPUS

I did want to spend some time on cleaning up and beautifying the campus. I saw too many weeds and too much trash. There seemed to be few flowerbeds and niche gardens. Because there were too many other challenges, I did not focus on campus beautification right away.

In my 23 years, I really only micro-managed one thing at Kansas State—namely, to keep the campus clean and beautiful. I have always been a fanatic about trash. I hated trash as a kid; I hated seeing trash on the highway or anywhere else; whenever I saw trash, I had to pick it up. Period. At K-State, I became even more aware of trash. I became determined to do everything I could to have the cleanest, nicest, and most beautiful campus in the nation. I know that I increasingly drove the facilities workers crazy.

Sometimes, I would see newspapers or other trash swirling around the green space in front of Anderson Hall. I would call the facilities office and ask if they could please send someone over to pick up the trash. Often, I just told the people in my office that I would be right back. I did not want them to know that I was just going out the front door and across the street to pick up the trash myself. Walking from the president's house to work, I picked up trash wherever I saw it. The facilities workers gave me two pickers over my 23 years. I still have one of them.

In my first year or two, I started going out for a walk on a Sunday afternoon to pick up trash with a grocery bag. Most people with normal eyesight never see trash anywhere. I do. It drives me nuts. Shortly, Ruth Ann joined me in picking stuff up. We switched to the bigger plastic bags.

I soon realized this was not a good way to run the railroad. In 1987, we took eight of our custodial positions and reassigned them to exact zones for trash pickup. These eight pickers were soon seen everywhere. They became superb. They would even go deep into the bushes and shrubs to retrieve trash. They all knew that I was a fanatic about trash.

I also wanted to have a trash barrel in front of every door of every building on campus. Our carpenters were soon crafting hundreds of trash barrels. Made of wood, they were handsome. We wanted everyone to know that there was no reason whatsoever to throw a pop can or any paper on the ground. Although it took several years, we had trash barrels everywhere and, of course, we soon had the cleanest campus anywhere.

THE VITAL ROLE OF K-STATE'S FACILITIES WORKERS

I got to know many of our facilities workers. Whether they were custodians, carpenters, plumbers, mowers, or street sweepers, I showed them respect. I was happy to provide them football and basketball tickets for various games. Often when I ran into a custodian, I would say: "Please stop by my office so I could give you some KSU memorabilia—like a coffee mug and a paperweight."

In the fall of 1999, I noticed that one of our masons was redoing the cement work on the south side steps of Anderson Hall. I came out to give him a KSU coffee mug and a paperweight. I ran into him later and he said: "I have been working for K-State for many years. Your gifts are about the nicest thing that anybody has ever done for me." I recalled a quote from William Wordsworth: "The best portion of a good man's life are his little unremembered acts of kindness."

In 2002, I started a Thanksgiving lunch for the facilities staff. All of them were invited to the lunch. I will always remember the first one. The Student Union food staff went all out to have a first-class Thanksgiving lunch with all of the trimmings, including turkey, stuffing, mashed potatoes, vegetables, rolls, and pies with ice cream.

At 11:30 a.m., I saw a line stretching from the entry doors on to the second floor ballroom down the stairs. Because there were four lines, everyone was served quickly. Anyone could have second helpings. I thanked everyone at the lunch. From 2002 to 2009, these Thanksgiving lunches were held in the middle of November.

K-STATE NEVER HAD ENTRANCE GATES BEFORE 1986

Over the years, the associate director of the Office of Facilities Planning, Mark Taussig, and I partnered on three projects: the construction of the Higinbotham Gate in 1989, the building of the Peine Gate in 2002, and the construction of a World War II Memorial from 2004 to 2009. All three added to the beauty of the campus.

In the summer of 1986, I wondered why Kansas State did not have one handsome entrance gate anywhere. Mark and I needed to find the right place for our first major entrance gate. In 1989, the Higinbotham Gate was built at the end of Bluemont Avenue and North Manhattan.

This beautiful new gate became the primary linkage between Aggieville and the campus. Today, graduating seniors still flock to this lovely gate for classic photos.[217]

Mark and I soon agreed that our campus needed a second major entrance gate. By 1995, 17th Street at Anderson Avenue had become a primary entrance to the campus. But we needed to find a major donor. Ironically, the donor for this entrance gate was right in our midst—Caroline Peine.

Caroline Peine, our long-time assistant dean of students, asked her brother, Perry and his wife, Virginia, to join her. The result was stunning. The handsome limestone Peine Gate was dedicated in the fall of 2002. The new entrance gate had huge pillars on each side of 17th Street. The pillars provided a connection between the beautiful Alumni Building and the handsome new K-State parking garage. Our school now had two beautiful entrance gates.[218]

After 2000, many people believed that K-State should honor its World War II veterans. In the summer of 2004, Mark and I met with the KSU veteran's committee—including Burke Bayer, Jack Goldstein, Cecil Eyestone, Dick Jepsen, Dick Bergen, and Phil Finley.

One day, Taussig told me how he had designed a plan in 1987 for a new driveway at McCain Auditorium. The strategy now became something that we always tried to keep in mind—namely, to try and get two good results for the price of one.

We decided to put the WWII Memorial smack dab in the middle of the new access driveway. Presto, the new memorial would be located front and center in the middle of the new access driveway. It would include new sidewalks, shrubs, and benches around the driveway.[219]

By putting the new memorial right in front of McCain, there were several nice outcomes: it would soften the plain functional lines of McCain; and it would make the entire building more inviting and accessible.

The driveway construction was completed in September of 2008. The groundbreaking ceremony was on October 25, 2008. We named the circle drive after a great business leader, a WWII veteran, and a superb K-State supporter, Jack Goldstein. Many K-Staters and veterans were at the ceremony. It was completed in April of 2009. The unique sculpture design was unveiled on May 20, 2011.[220]

THE CREATION OF THE UNIVERSITY GARDENS

In 1991, Tom Warner was selected as the new head of the Department of Horticulture, Forestry, and Recreation Resources. He released design plans for the construction of the "new" University Gardens along Denison Avenue.

The first project for the university gardens involved the conversion of 'the old dairy barn' into a new "Garden's Visitor Center." Tom Warner told me that the roof of the barn was falling apart. We replaced it in two weeks.[221] Tom knew he had a reliable sidekick. Then, he called me about a 'hay barn' that blocked a parking lot for the garden's visitor center. It was removed shortly.[222]

In the mid-1990's, K-State was annexed into the city of Manhattan. The additional city sales tax revenue generated by entities like the Student Union and the athletic department would flow to university projects that benefited both the city and the university.

I found out that the new city-university fund would generate over $200,000 for university projects annually. I was able to ask the University Advisory Committee to help fund the new Gardens.[223]

Over the next five years, about $250,000 of this new fund was directed to the gardens. Phase I of the gardens would take seven years to complete. Tom strategically used these funds to help complete the gardens' visitor center, the gateway, the cottage garden, the butterfly garden, and the All-American garden with its annual flowers and vegetables.

One day, Tom called me: "I have good news. The beautiful Phase I Fountain and Pergola have now been finished." It remains the centerpiece of the gardens today.[224]

From 1986 to 2009, I often walked by the century-old lovely limestone walls that surrounded the central campus. I told Tom how fitting it would be to have a similar limestone wall along Denison Avenue—especially if the new wall was coupled with an elegant "Limestone Entrance Gate."

Today, all visitors walk under the gate to see the beautiful gardens and the visitor center. In the spring of 2000 when the new wall and gate entrance was dedicated, Tom said: "The University Gardens would not exist today without the help of the Wefalds and their 23 years of excellent work."[225]

For years, the Department of Entomology had kept butterfies in the old historic glass greenhouse until the winter. Two K-State entomologists, Ralph Charlton and Sonny Ramaswamy, were determined to build an insect zoo.

It would hold a variety of butterflies, dangerous spiders, a singular collection of leaf cutting ants, and insects from all over the world. I allocated $5,000 annually to help the insect zoo over five years.

In the fall of 2002, many people attended the dedication of Kansas State's first Insect Zoo. The original colony of leaf cutting ants became one of the most popular exhibits. Visitors to the Insect Zoo wanted to see spiders like the Brown Recluse, the Black Widow, and the Tarantula.

By 2009, the Director of the Zoo, Kiffnie Holt, was reporting that 8,000 people were coming through the entrance every year. The Gardens and its insect zoo became a hit for many visitors and buses of school children from all over the state.[226]

THE MERGER WITH THE KANSAS COLLEGE OF TECHNOLOGY

In 1989, we were surprised to learn that the College of Technology in Salina, Kansas in 1989 might be merged with a state university. Started in 1965, the Schilling Institute was a two-year engineering technology school in Salina.

In 1969, the legislature changed the school's name to the Kansas Technical Institute (KTI). It was placed under the Kansas State Board of Education.[227]

In 1976, the state legislature transferred the control of KTI from the Board of Education to the Kansas Board of Regents—which increased the number of institutions under the Board of Regents from six schools to seven.

In 1986, Anthony L. Tillmans was selected as the new President. In 1988, the school's name was changed to the Kansas College of Technology.[228]

By 1988, KCT was appearing often on the Board of Regent's radar screen because of declining enrollment. The Regents claimed that KCT had two major problems: a small enrollment and a top-heavy administrative structure.

In 1989, the Kansas College of Technology had a total of 95.25 FTE positions—which included one president, four vice-presidents, five deans, and six department heads.

In 1989, the Regents set up a "Task Force on the Future Direction of the Kansas College of Technology." Chaired by Regent Don Slawson, the task force considered options that ranged from closing KCT down to a merger with either Pittsburg State or Kansas State. Between January 11, 1990 and May 30, 1990, the task force met four times. After reviewing over 500 pages of testimony, it recommended that KCT be merged with Kansas State on June 1, 1990.[229]

Chuck Reagan had been to the Salina campus a number of times. After one visit to the Aviation Technology program in 1990, Reagan wrote: "What I found was appalling. The five aircraft were military surplus or very old airplanes that had been rebuilt by the Aviation

Technology program. Students took the planes whenever they wanted to. It resembled more of an apprentice program than an academic training program."[230]

On April 18, 1990, Provost Jim Coffman presented a plan to the Board of Regents explaining what K-State needed for a merger. First, he argued that the old KCT campus built on a former air base had to be abandoned. Second, he insisted that a new north campus would have to be built.

Coffman's letter of April 18, 1990 to the Board of Regents was very specific: "The merger would require the construction of a new residence hall to accommodate 300 students ($3.0 million), a student center/cafeteria building ($1.9 million), and recreational facilities ($1.6 million)."

Coffman also argued that the new campus would need $2.0 million from the state for an Aeronautical Center, $1.5 million from the city and county for 6,500 net assignable square feet for the Technology Center, and $2.0 million from the city or the county for a new entrance to the campus, new sidewalks and streets, and new landscaping for the new north side campus.

These projects would cost about $12 million. The funds would come from the state of Kansas, Salina, Saline County, student fees, and user fees.[231]

The leaders for KCT and K-State truly believed that the citizens of Saline County would vote for a half-cent sales tax to help finance the merger. In September of 1990, that happened. The sales tax passed by the voters generated about $5.3 million for the new KSU, Salina campus.

We will always be grateful to the citizens of Salina and Saline County for their generosity. During the 1991 session, the legislature approved the merger. Governor Joan Finney signed the legislation on May 2, 1991 for the new KSU, Salina campus.[232]

The new school would place primary emphasis on its technology and aviation programs. In 1992, Anthony Tillman stepped down as president. For the first time, the school was under the leadership of a Dean, Jack Henry.

During the five years of Dean Henry, enrollment improved; the college added a handsome new KSU, Salina granite entrance to the campus; and the entrance was complemented with newly designed streets and sidewalks.

In 1994, a 100-bed Residence Hall was dedicated. In 1995, a Salina business leader, Bill Harbin, donated $2 million for the construction of a second residence hall. Named Harbin Hall, it would be opened in the fall of 1997.[233]

From June 20, 1990 to April 6, 1992, Chuck Reagan had 27 meetings with his colleagues at KSU, Salina to find ways to improve the college's aviation program. In late 1992, Chuck Reagan and Ken Barnard, the aviation department head, prepared a major federal grant proposal for a fleet of new training aircraft

Their joint proposal was submitted to the Air Force Office of Scientific Research for a $7.7 million grant. Senator Bob Dole announced in the late spring of 1993 that the Air Force Office of Scientific Research had funded the joint proposal.[234]

The grant provided for 24 aircraft. It included: one Beech C-90 King Air, four twin engine Beech B-58 Barons, and six single engine high performance F-33A Bonanzas. The used aircraft included one Beech F-33C Aerobatic Bonanza and 12 Beech C-23 Sundowners. Three simulators were included for ground training, engines, and equipment; three maintenance aircraft were added to the aviation maintenance program; and an Avionics, Composite Fabrication and Non-Destructive Testing Laboratory was completed with this grant.

This $7.7 million grant proved to be of vital importance for KSU, Salina and its aviation program for years to come. It soon became one of the best aviation programs in America.[235]

In late 1996, Dean Henry announced that he was retiring after the spring semester in 1997. A search committee was set up. Although a number of candidates applied, Dennis Kuhlman came to my mind. He was a K-State extension agricultural engineer; he was a pilot; and he had been the president of the K-State Faculty Senate in 1994-1995. Most everyone concluded that Dennis was a great choice to be the new dean for KSU, Salina.[236]

Dennis Kuhlman became a superb manager and leader. The staff, the faculty, and the students liked his leadership skills. Student numbers increased nicely. In 2006, KSU, Salina broke ground for a new Student Life Center. By 2009, KSU, Salina had become a handsome and unique campus.

The planned new Student Life Center would prove to be a game-changer. After 1991, we knew that the Salina campus needed a student union. It would be a center where students could meet for coffee, lunch, and provide space for recreational opportunities as well. The 20-year dream of having a special Student Life Center was realized in a dedication ceremony on November 6, 2009.[237]

By June of 2009, the Kansas State campus in Salina had excellent programs in engineering technology and aviation. The graduates were getting good jobs in both program areas. By 2009, the students could take courses in the arts and sciences at K-State, get a four-year degree at KSU, Salina, or transfer to Kansas State in Manhattan to obtain a BA or BS degree.

When the people of Salina and Saline County look back today at their support for a tax increase for a new campus in 1990, I know that they are pleased with the excellent growth and progress of KSU, Salina over the past two decades.

AFTER 1990, THE LIBERAL ARTS AT KSU WERE ENHANCED AND OUR CAMPUS MOVED WEST

The nation's finest land grant universities had been promoting excellence in the arts and sciences from the early 20th century on. For decades, Iowa State, Purdue, Michigan State, and Texas A&M had been aiming to be modern, inclusive, and major research schools.

These land grant schools had long sought a balance between solid technical programs and superb offerings in the arts, humanities, and science. All four schools demanded excellence in teaching and research. All four land grants became members of the AAU.

I supported the College of Arts and Sciences more than any other Kansas State President. If K-State was to become a more modern, diverse, and comprehensive land-grant school, it was imperative to enhance our arts and sciences.

By 2009, the departments in the arts, humanities, and social sciences were showing extraordinary intellectual growth and vibrancy. Their faculty members were publishing more, giving more papers at national conferences, and enjoying their jobs more.

Science departments like physics and biology were leading the way for the entire university in generating peer-driven research grants. Moreover, they were winning far more than their fair share of University Distinguished Professorships and the Coffman Chairs for University Distinghished Teaching.

After 1986, our programs in theatre, debate, and speech were revitalized. Our university theatre program was putting on outstanding productions. Our debate and speech squads had become nationally competitive. The K-State Marching Band became one of the nation's elite marching bands from 1993 to 2009.

From 1986 to 2009, K-State students won 129 Rhodes, Marshall, Truman, Goldwater, and Udall scholarships. Out of 500 public universities in America, Kansas State University was No. 1 in winning these nationally elite academic scholarships. K-State students had won 35 more of these five scholarships than any other public university in the nation.

By 2009, there was no question that our administration had revitalized the College of Arts and Sciences, beautified the entire campus, and reinvigorated the campus to the west now called KSU, Salina.

Chapter 7

Restoring Hope On The Field: A Football Renaissance At Kansas State, 1989-1999

When I became President of K-State on July 1, 1986, the football program was seldom mentioned. When I spoke to the Downtown Kansas City Rotary Club in October 1986, I covered the topics our alums were most concerned about: the need to increase the enrollment; the importance of hiring a new leadership team; the challenge of building a new library and art museum; and the need to make our school more modern and comprehensive.

At the end of my talk, I briefly mentioned there was no reason that K-State could not have a competitive Big 8 football team. Rick Harmon, an All-American basketball player at Kansas State from 1946 to 1950 and a well-known business leader, was present.

In the June 2008 edition of POWERCAT ILLUSTRATED, the Associate Editor, Becky Fitzgerald, explained how Harmon came up to me after my speech: "Young man, don't ever talk about football again because it can't be turned around. People have said in the past that they are going to turn football around and it never has been."

Rick Harmon reflected the views of every K-State fan in the world. When I said K-State could have a decent football team in the future, I was talking about three wins a year and maybe six wins every five years. No one believed that K-State could ever win 11 games in the future.

Most college presidents would not choose to write a chapter on football if they were writing their memoirs. If I had been president of Florida, Alabama, Oklahoma, Nebraska, or Ohio State, there would be no need. For me, a chapter on football was required. Kansas State had been a long-time member of the Big 8 Conference. After July 1, 1986, I learned our membership in the Big 8 was in question.

There were serious challenges for K-State's membership in the Big 8 in 1986. First, our football program had been the worst in the nation since 1945. Second, Oklahoma and Nebraska were fed up playing in front of 15,000 fans. Third, Arkansas and its AD, Frank Broyles, had made it clear in 1978 they would leave the Southwest Conference and replace K-State in the Big 8. Fourth, the NCAA had a rule every school had to average at least 19,000 fans per game to maintain its standing in Division I football. Fifth, our football facilities were absolutely the worst of any Division I school.

DOUG LOONEY'S S.I. ARTICLE IN FALL OF 1989

I did not have to wait too long to find out how our football team was viewed nationally. On September 4, 1989, the senior football writer for SPORTS ILLUSTRATED, Doug Looney, wrote a story about the history of K-State football. The title of Looney's article was brutal: "FUTILITY U—KANSAS STATE, WINLESS SINCE 1986, HAS ONE CLAIM TO FAME: IT IS AMERICA'S MOST HAPLESS TEAM."[238]

Doug's first paragraph was riveting: "When it comes to college football, nobody does it worse than Kansas State. After 93 years of trying to play the game, the Wildcats' record is 299-509-41—dead last among the 106 schools in Division I-A. . .Kansas State has been looking for its 300th win since October 18, 1986: the Wildcats have failed 21 straight times—the longest nonwinning streak in the land (they forged a 17-17 tie with Kansas in 1987)."

Although I knew Looney was correct, it was the title of the September 1989 S.I. article that got my attention—FUTILITY U. This headline for the September 4, 1989 S.I. article on K-State football indicated that the university itself was in a state of futility.[239]

I knew football had to be upgraded. There was no choice. From World War II to the early 1990's, there was no "Avis mind-set" for our football team sitting in second place. Second place was only in our dreams. For most K-State fans, the words hope and football were seldom mentioned in the same sentence.

After World War II, Kansas State was known for having great basketball teams. Some of the nation's finest basketball coaches in the history of the game coached at Kansas State: Jack Gardner, Tex Winter, Cotton Fitzsimmons, Jack Hartman, and Lon Kruger.

Under these five superb coaches from 1948 to 1989, Kansas State basketball teams played in four Final Fours, 11 Elite Eights, 15 Sweet Sixteens, and 19 NCAA Tournaments. These coaches won 15 regular season Big 7/8 Championships from 1948 to 1977.[240]

FROM 1935 TO 1986, FOOTBALL WAS NEVER A PRIORITY

From 1935 to 1986, football at Kansas State never was a priority. Indeed, it was clearly on the back burner. Although there was no serious administrative opposition to good football teams, the necessary willpower was missing. The prevailing attitude for the school's leaders might best be summed up like this: if you had a winning football program, that was fine; if not, that was fine as well.

During this era, having a good football team was analogous to the challenge of having a good library. With the library constructions of 1927, 1954, and 1969, the refrain for the library was "half was good enough." The metaphor of "half was good enough" epitomized the Kansas State football program as well.

If a similar September 1989 S.I. article had been published in the 1960's or 1970's, maybe more of the school's leaders would have appreciated the importance of a competitive football program. While Kansas State became a big-time basketball school after 1945, the football program was neglected.

Doug Looney talked to Dev Nelson in the spring of 1988 about the school's bad football program since 1945. The great Wildcat sports announcer told Looney that all of the Big 8 universities spent far more money on football than Kansas State. Dev declared, for example, that decent coaching salaries, a good training staff, sufficient football scholarships, and major renovations for the two stadiums were seldom considered by any administration.[241]

THE SCHOOL'S BEST FOOTBALL COACHES ALLOWED TO LEAVE

Over its early football history, Kansas State had two excellent football coaches—Lynn "Pappy" Waldorf in 1934 and Bill Meek from 1951 to 1954. Both were allowed to leave without a fight. Both had the potential to be the equivalent of a Bud Wilkinson at Oklahoma or a Bob Devaney at Nebraska.

Kansas State built a nice stadium in 1922-23 that seated 23,000 fans. But, from 1923 to 1967, it was never completed the way the architects had planned it. Moreover, stadium renovations were mainly non-existent. After a new stadium was built in 1967, no major improvements were made in that stadium either for 25 years.

Kevin Haskins, a sports writer for the TOPEKA CAPITAL JOURNAL, wrote an excellent book in 2009 titled KANSAS STATE UNIVERSITY-FOOTBALL VAULT. He writes about one coach that many K-Staters still fondly remember: Bill Meek. He was hired at the age of 30 in 1951. After two rebuilding years, Coach Meek led his team in 1953 to an overall record of six wins, three losses, and one tie. For the first time in history, the Kansas State football team was ranked—reaching 18th in the United Press Poll in 1953.

Haskins used a clever quote from Bill Schroeder, a football writer for the FOOTBALL DIGEST, at the end of the 1953 season about Meek's success: "Oregon's Len Casanova did the mostest with the leastest. Notre Dame's Frank Leahy did the mostest with the mostest. Bill Meek did the mostest."[242]

In a well-written book entitled WILDCAT GRIDIRON GUIDE, Tim Fitzgerald writes how lucky Kansas State was to have a coach like Bill Meek. In 1954, Coach Meek had his best team in four years. The Wildcats finished the season with seven wins and three losses. In the last game of the season, Kansas State had a shot at the Orange Bowl before losing to Colorado 38 to 14.

After four years as the school's best football coach since Pappy Waldorf in 1934, Meek asked for modest raises for himself and his assistant coaches at the end of the 1954 season. Although Meek's salary was raised modestly, they refused to raise the salaries for his assistants.

The University of Houston agreed to raise the salaries of both his assistant coaches and Coach Meek. Fitzgerald analyzed the meaning of Meek's departure in 1954: "Kansas State got what it paid for. Not just bad football, but wretched football arrived in Manhattan. Kansas State turned a chance for a postwar boom on the gridiron into a bust of historic proportions."[243]

Before Bill Meek left town in 1954, he had an interview with the MANHATTAN MERCURY. He told the paper: "This place was the greatest mess I had ever seen. They asked me what I thought was wrong with the program. My response was, 'Do you have that much time? The field has no grass, there was no living area for the players, no training table, no shoes for the players, old jerseys were tattered and torn, and the practice field wasn't regulation length.'"

Unable to contain himself, Meek said: "As it ended up, when we wanted to work on pass plays, we had to change direction and run plays toward the street. Half the time, the football would end up in the street." Meek even recalled a conversation where he "once was asked by President James McCain what difference it would make if the football field was plowed under."[244]

The low point of Kansas State football's history after 1945 is the era of Coach Doug Weaver. As the head football coach from 1960 to 1966, Weaver's record was eight wins, 60 losses, and one tie. In seven years, he had "two" of the nation's longest losing streaks in college football history. In 1965, Weaver was hung in effigy in front of the library. His response was classic: "I am glad it happened in front of the library. I've always emphasized scholarship."

On October 29, 1966, Weaver's tenure was defined in the annual match-up between KU and KSU. KSU was ahead 3 to 0 with less than one minute to play. Because KU had no timeouts left, everyone expected the KSU quarterback to run out the clock. Weaver called several running plays and naturally the tailback fumbled the ball.

Although KU's kicker had never kicked a field goal, he made this one to tie the game. Both coaches were fired after the game. One Kansas State cheer came to embody Weaver's standing with the fans in 1965 and 1966: "Give 'em hell Doug Weaver, give 'em hell," "Give 'em hell Doug Weaver, give 'em hell." The fans changed the cheer: "Give 'em hell Doug Weaver, give 'em hell," "Oh Hell, give 'em Doug Weaver."

In his informative book on Bill Snyder, Mark Janssen talked about Coach Jim Dickey. As head coach from 1978 to 1985, he became one of K-State's best football coaches. His 1982 football team was our first football team in history to go to a bowl game. K-State played Wisconsin in the Independence Bowl on December 11, 1982.

Janssen summed up the huge challenges that Coach Jim Dickey inherited in 1978: "He was saddled by the previous probation, facilities that were falling apart, financial woes, and a severe lack of administrative support." When asked about the school's support, Dickey replied curtly: "It was non-existent."[245]

From 1935 to the 1980's, even if several of Notre Dame's most famous football coaches—including Elmer Layden, Frank Leahy, and Ara Parseghian—had been hired at Kansas State, how long would they have stayed? Two of our most successful football coaches during that era, Bill Meek and Jim Dickey, answered that very question. The answer: Not long, not very long.

Bill Meek told the MERCURY after he announced that he was leaving for Houston in 1954: "This place was the greatest mess I had ever seen." When the paper asked him what was wrong with the program, Meek retorted: "My response was, 'Do you have that much time?'" Almost exactly 30 years later, the MERCURY'S Mark Janssen asked Coach Jim Dickey in 1985 about the administration's support for his football program. Dickey replied: "It was non-existent."

AFTER 1945, OU AND NEBRASKA SHOWED HOW TO DO IT

The key leaders at Oklahoma and Nebraska decided to follow a much different strategy after 1945. Excellent academic and athletic programs do not just happen. They are part of a strategic plan—a plan that takes focus, willpower, and calculated risks.

Oklahoma and Nebraska administrators were determined to have outstanding football teams. Both universities seemed to have a bevy of academic and athletic leaders who set priorities, made timely decisions, took risks, and allocated the necessary funds to get the job done to have a winning football program.

Oklahoma became one of the most successful football programs in the nation after 1945. As President from 1943 to 1968, George Lynn Cross was a key figure in OU's rise to both academic and athletic excellence. After he retired in 1968, he wrote a book entitled THE OU FOOTBALL TRADITION: PRESIDENTS CAN'T PUNT.[246]

President Cross decided that Oklahoma could be recognized nationally if the school fielded a great football team. You might say that George Cross kept his eye on the ball. He made sure that OU's stadium improvements were made on a timely basis.

In 1925, the football stadium had less than 20,000 seats. The stadium was expanded to 55,000 seats from 1949 to 1952. By 1957, it was increased to 62,000 seats. By 2009, it had seating for 82,000 fans.[247]

George Cross hired Bud Wilkinson in 1946. With President Cross' backing for 15 years, Bud went on to win three national championships, 14 Conference Championships, and won 47 games in a row from the third game of 1953 to November of 1957. Bud almost accepted a job in Texas in private business in 1951. But Cross would not let that happen. He invited Bud Wilkinson and his wife to the president's home for dinner to seal the deal.

George Cross might be the first college president to see that winning sports could become the window through which many alums and fans would view the university itself. But he also greatly enhanced the school's academic excellence. George Lynn Cross became one of Oklahoma's best Presidents.[248]

From the 1940's to the late 1950's, Nebraska had a number of average football teams. Cornhusker fans were restless. Nebraska's Board of Regents hired a new Chancellor in the summer of 1954, Clifford M. Hardin. He was chancellor from 1954 to 1968. He had been the Dean of the College of Agriculture at Michigan State. Hardin was a fan of Michigan State's football coach, Duffy Daugherty. He wanted Duffy to be NU's next head football coach. But Coach Daugherty recommended Bob Devaney at Wyoming.

In a book on Nebraska football edited by Rob Doster, it explains how Chancellor Hardin hired Coach Bob Devaney away from Wyoming in 1962. Bill Jennings was fired in 1961 after Nebraska won only three games and lost six. Developing NU into an immediate winner, Bob Devaney won eight Big 8 Conference championships and two national championships in the next ten years.[249]

The Hardin administration backed the Nebraska football program. The first NU stadium built in 1923 had 31,000 seats. Under Hardin, Nebraska's stadium was expanded two times. In 1964, it was increased to 48,000 seats. By 1966, it was upgraded to 65,000 seats.

By 1972, Nebraska's stadium had become one of the nation's largest with a seating capacity of 73,650. In 2010, the NU Chancellor, Harvey Perlman, wrote that Cliff Hardin was not only a founder of the modern University of Nebraska, but a pivotal leader in making Cornhusker football into one of the nation's elite programs.[250]

THE HUGE FOOTBALL CHALLENGES WE FACED AFTER 1986

When I became president of Kansas State in the summer of 1986, Larry Travis was the athletic director and Stan Parrish was the head football coach. Travis had fired Coach Jim Dickey after the second game of the 1985 season when K-State lost to Northern Iowa 10 to 6. Travis replaced him with an interim coach, Lee Moon. Parrish was hired away from Marshall University.

After Coach Parrish was hired in December of 1985, he declared that he would win right away. His teams had won 13 games and lost eight games at Marshall. To make up for the team's lack of talent, Coach Parrish's plan was to throw the ball all over the field. He won his first game over Western Illinois 35 to 7 on August 30, 1986. On October 18, K-State beat KU 29 to 12.

From late October of 1986 to the end of the 1988 season, however, Stan Parrish's teams would not win another game. In 1988, his team had a record of 0 wins and 11 losses.[251]

Many high schools in Texas and Oklahoma had more up-to-date

and better football facilities than Kansas State. The stadium press box was literally a joke—a very bad joke. To enter the press box, you had to climb a medieval spiral ladder. You needed to be an Olympic gymnast. Once you got up there, the windows were mainly fogged over. The president's box had five or six folding chairs.

The artificial turf was ancient. The weight room, the training room, and the locker room areas were antiquated. The artificial turf was quite dangerous. The stadium itself was surrounded by gravel parking lots. The entire stadium complex was the worst in the Big 8—and probably the entire nation.

Larry Travis never mentioned a strategy for transforming the football program. He never articulated the need for any major stadium renovations. He had no sense of urgency. He seemed indifferent to the concern that the Big 8 might kick us out.

The attendance for the 1987 season was below the NCAA standard of 19,000 fans a game. How long would Oklahoma and Nebraska want to play in front of a small crowd? Not long. In 1987, I must have been out of my mind to believe that our school could field a good football team.

Before the Big 12 was organized in 1994, the old Big 8 Conference hosted the Orange Bowl in Miami, Florida every year. The Big 8 Conference invited every president, athletic director, and its faculty representative to attend the Orange Bowl. Most of us were happy to accept two first class airline tickets and nice hotel rooms at the historic Seaview Hotel in Miami Beach. You can imagine what bowl game I attended.

I actually looked forward to the Orange Bowl every year. It was great fun to take your family to Miami Beach for a week of good meals, interesting meetings, and nice trips in the Miami metropolitan area. One of the special events for everyone involved a short trip on a cruise ship with the two teams playing in the Orange Bowl. In 1987, it was Arkansas and Oklahoma.

It was on this cruise ship at the 1987 Orange Bowl when I first met OU's head coach, Barry Switzer. Years later, Mark Janssen talked to Coach Switzer about our encounter on the ship. I went out to the deck to get some fresh air. I saw Barry Switzer. I walked over to meet him. I had no idea what Barry thought about meeting some little guy who happened to be the new Kansas State president.

After some small talk, I said to Barry: "Someday, I hope that Kansas State might be playing in a bowl game like the Orange Bowl." In Janssen's interview with Switzer years later, Mark asked him about my comments in 1987? Switzer laughed and told Janssen: "I was stunned, literally stunned. K-State was a team that OU would run up half-a-hundred points by halftime, so our other guys, who only got to practice, would actually play in a game."

If I had remembered our homecoming game with OU on October 17, 1987, I would have been more guarded. I might have told Switzer what a nice night it was and let it go at that. After all, in the 1987 game, OU had scored seven touchdowns by halftime. After halftime, the 22 OU starters had come onto the field without their jerseys and shoulder pads so they could just lollygag around.

After asking his AD, Donnie Duncan, to join our talk, Switzer told Janssen: "I remember saying, 'Donnie, this is Dr. Wefald, and he says he is going to have a team like ours and play in the Orange Bowl.' Well, I've had quite a few by then, and I am laughing even harder, which I think embarrassed Donnie, but then Wefald repeated it. 'I can't wait to bring a team to the Orange Bowl.' I was rude. I couldn't help laughing. I'm not sure how it came out, but I tried to say, "President, I admire you, and I hope it happens."

Eleven years later, Coach Switzer talked to Janssen about watching Texas A&M playing K-State for the Big 12 Championship on December 5, 1998. He told Janssen that he had waited too long to apologize. Barry actually called me shortly before the game and said: "Well, Jon, I am calling to apologize for my comments to you at the 1987 Orange Bowl. I know Bill is a helluva coach, but I also know he didn't do this by himself. It starts at the top and you should be commended." I said there was no need to apologize because I often exaggerated.

THE HIRING OF A SUPERB NEW ATHLETIC DIRECTOR IN 1988

By 1987, I sensed that Kansas State had only a few years to change the calculus in football. I needed new allies. No one had ever heard of Bill Snyder. K-State needed a confident and positive athletic director. Larry Travis was a perfect gentleman after Bob Krause and I met with him on a Saturday morning in April of 1988. The interviews were in Kansas City. Four good candidates were interviewed, including Northern Iowa's AD, Bob Bowlsby.

One candidate captured our imagination—Steve Miller. He was a visionary, a doer, and a risk-taker. He had irrepressible optimism, energy, and unbridled confidence. I saw somebody who would be a crackerjack ally in turning our football team around.

Steve Miller was hired as K-State's next athletic director on June 27, 1988. At the press conference, I affirmed that Steve was the right person at the right time at the right place. K-Staters had waited for an eternity to have an AD like Steve Miller.

The K-State football program could never have been transformed without the vision and risk-taking mentality of Steve Miller. Without Steve Miller, there is no Bill Snyder. Steve was the difference-maker.

Near the end of the 1988 season, Steve and I met with Coach Stan Parrish at the president's house. Parrish became quite agitated and asked if he could have at least another year. I thought back to Coach Doug Weaver. He, too, was livid when he was fired after the 1966 season. Parrish continued as coach for the rest of the 1988 season.

FROM 1935 TO 1986, 11 COACHES, NINE AD'S AND FOUR PRESIDENTS COULD NOT SOLVE THE PROBLEM OF LOSING FOOTBALL

The challenge of turning our football program around after 1986 was still another intractable challenge for me that had to be unraveled. It was all of this and more because Kansas State from 1935 to 1986 had no president, no athletic director, and no football coach who had ever come close to solving the intractable problem of our school's perennially losing football program.

In those 50 years of losing football at Kansas State, no major university in the entire nation had ever matched this sorry record. After all, Kansas State's football record was singular—over more than 5 decades, our school had a total of 14 coaches, 9 athletic directors, and four presidents who simply could not unravel our history of losing football.

Equally troubling as the 50-year drought of losing football, the vexing problems of Kansas State football were made even worse by the school's entire football complex. How bad was it in 1986? It was the worst in America. When I use the word "worst" in the nation, I have to repeat the following words because our modern-day fans have no idea of how bad our football facilities were in 1986: It includes the worst of everything—namely, the press box, the weight room, the training room, the football turf, the practice fields, the stadium seats, the gravel parking lot, and the low salaries of the coaches.

Indeed, it was hard to name anything right about the state of football and its facilities at K-State in 1986. To untangle this football Rubik's Cube, everything would have to go just right. Even with all that, we still needed a huge amount of luck.

WE KNEW IT ALL STARTED WITH GETTING THE RIGHT COACH

Steve Miller, Bob Krause, and I knew that this new hire would be the most important hiring of a head football coach in the history of Kansas State. Tim Fitzgerald was spot-on: "In the wake of Parrish's departure from Kansas State, there was serious talk of surrendering the football fight. President Jon Wefald would not have it. Instead of dropping football and leaving the Big Eight Conference, Wefald and Miller hired little-known offensive coordinator Bill Snyder from Iowa to piece together the wreckage."[252]

In his SPORTS ILLUSTRATED article of September 4, 1989, Doug Looney had a number of colorful anecdotes that accurately depicted the state of the Wildcat football team in the 1960's, 1970's, and 1980's. Will Cokeley, who was a Kansas State linebacker from 1980 to 1982, said: "The problem is every time we think we are good, we remember we are Kansas State." Lynn Dickey, who became a superb NFL quarterback, was equally blunt: "The thing about tradition at Kansas State is there is none."

Damian Johnson, who was good enough to play for the New York Giants in the 1980's, said simply: "The problem is, they don't get good players." Steve Willis, a kicker, was even more candid: "I was like all the other players who came here. This was our last resort." A safety under Coach Stan Parrish, Eric Harper, told Looney: "I look at Oklahoma and I see only three differences—they look bigger, they look faster, and they look better."[253]

Steve Miller and his associate athletic director, Jim Epps, had the onerous job of finding exactly the right coach who was the right fit. They started interviewing potential candidates right after the 1988 season. How tough was it? How many athletic directors in a Power 5 Conference today have had to talk with 18 football coaches in order to find their next new head coach?

Many of them were outstanding head coaches or associate head coaches. They included Jack Bicknell of Boston College, John Fox of Pittsburgh University, Bill Thornton of TCU, Milan Vooletich of Navy, Frank Solich of Nebraska, Charlie Bailey of Memphis, and many others. Bill Snyder was not one of them. Most of the coaches Miller talked with were either flabbergasted or even angry that we would even ask them if they were interested. There were no major head coaches anywhere thirsting for our job.[254]

Near the end of the search, Steve Miller was leaning toward Weber State's head coach, Mike Price. The word serendipity comes to my mind. Jim Epps told Tim Fitzgerald what happened: "I was sitting in this very office and happened to have an Iowa media guide lying around. I started reading about all of the offensive records that had been set under their offensive coordinator, Bill Snyder. I thought, 'What the hell. We've already called 50 others. Why not one more?'"

Epps called Coach Snyder. Although the Iowa coach seemed to have little interest, Snyder asked about the school's academic programs, administrative support, and the city of Manhattan. Steve Miller immediately flew to Iowa City.[255]

THE HIRING OF BILL SNYDER IN 1988

Before deciding to visit K-State in November of 1988, Bill Snyder asked his Iowa boss, Hayden Fry, what to look for. Fry told Bill to find out if the school's president and athletic director were on board. Bill was told by Hayden to probe deeply into whether the top leaders would rebuild K-State's football facilities and whether they would upgrade the salaries of the assistant coaches.

In his visit to Manhattan, Steve and I assured Bill he would have our support. After talking with Bill for 45 minutes, I remember certain things: his keen mind; his work ethic; his attention to detail; his confidence; and his common sense. All of these factors were vital for Bill's future success as our football coach. But there is no coach in the next 20 years that would pay such extraordinary attention to detail as Bill Snyder. After our talk, Bill responded: "I think I can do this."[256]

Still, I felt that the odds were stacked against us. Many Kansas State administrators from 1935 to 1986 believed they had hired the right football coach. I actually wondered for weeks if there was anyone on the planet who could elevate our football program.

Coach Snyder signed a five-year contract for $90,000 a year on November 30, 1988. With other benefits, Snyder would be making about $200,000. Doug Looney used a priceless quote from Bill: "There is only one school in the nation that has lost 500 games. This is it and I get to coach it." At the November 1988 press conference, Steve Miller was candid about the task ahead: "Kansas State is flat on its back. You may have heard it's one of the toughest jobs in America. It's not. It's the toughest."[257]

HOW WE TURNED THE FOOTBALL PROGRAM AROUND

Because Snyder and Miller knew that K-State could not win without superb assistant coaches, Steve allocated funds raising assistant coaching salaries from a 1988 scale of $29,000 to $42,000 to a 1989 scale of $32,000 to $64,000—which was near the salary levels at most Big 8 schools. The football budget was increased from $2.3 million in 1988 to $3 million in 1989. The recruiting budget was raised from $175,000 to over $300,000.

By 1989, it was vital to invest millions in our facilities. The football stadium was 20 years old. Nothing of consequence had been done to modernize either the football stadium or the football facilities. More private funds were needed immediately. Sometimes in life, there are certain people that come into your life and make a real difference. I immediately think of Jack Vanier and Ernie Barrett.

Jack Vanier and the Vanier family came to our support with countless gifts. Moreover, I had the good sense to hire back a legendary K-Stater in early 1989—Ernie Barrett. He had been let go by the Acker administration in 1976. Ernie Barrett became the best athletic fundraiser in the history of the school.

OUR NEW TEAM HAD TO TAKE HUGE RISKS

Our entire athletic team realized the limits of private giving—meaning we had to take the risk of issuing bonds to raise the necessary capital for the new projects. In the game of issuing bonds, Steve Miller, Bob Krause, and I were replaying the theme of a later movie, FIELD OF DREAMS: "If you build it, they will come."

We had to build it and hope for the best. If we did build it, K-State would have to field winning football teams. In the movie, the main character, Kevin Costner, is a farmer whose mortgage is due. He bet his farm. He risked everything by building his homemade baseball field. Like Costner, we were also betting the farm.

In building a new pressbox, a new football indoor facility, three new practice fields, and a remodeled football office, we took major risks. Issuing bonds was calculated risk. K-State would have to field a winning football program or else. If that did not happen, all of us would have been fired. And Kansas State probably would have been dropped from the Big 8 Conference.

If we had not raised the funds to build these new facilities, many of our excellent assistant coaches would have left. Our recruiting would have suffered. By 1991, Bill Snyder could tell both our coaches and our recruits that one new facility had been completed and the next one is on the way.[258]

THE COMPLETE REBUILDING OF THE FOOTBALL COMPLEX

From 1989 to 1993, under the leadership of Ernie Barrett, the department raised $3 million to revamp the football offices. In just a few years, K-State football had excellent new locker rooms, a 6,500 square foot weight room, state of the art classrooms with new video equipment, a new training room, a player's lounge, and a Big Eight Room. For all the right reasons, this facility was called the "Vanier Football Complex." In 1991, Dave Wagner of Dodge City, Kansas contributed $1 million for a "new Astroturf" for the football field.

In 1993, we built a state of the art $2.2 million indoor facility. It stunned our Big 8 rivals. This new indoor facility became one of the seven wonders of the Division I football world. This facility measured 230 by 400 feet and included a full-length 100-yard playing field.

By 1993, with funds from private giving and a key bond issue, the athletic department was able to complete an excellent $4+ million five-level press box with 24 luxury suites. The suites were quickly sold out.[259] After the five-level press box with 24 luxury suites was completed, one was reserved for the president.

From 1986 to 2009, Ruth Ann and I never missed a game. Our suite had 18 seats and a lot of standing room. The five stools behind the regular seats were reserved for five people: Senator Pat Roberts, Bob Krause, Marty Vanier, Ruth Ann and me.

From 1993 to 2009, Pat Roberts and I agreed on one main goal in our suite—to win. Because this was serious business, Pat, Bob, and I stood for the entire game. Over those 16 years, many political leaders visited my suite—including Governors Joan Finney, Bill Graves, and Kathleen Sebelius, Senators Sam Brownback, Nancy Kassebaum, Bob Dole, Congressmen Jerry Moran, and many Republican and Democratic legislators.

Most of them had a hot dog and a coke. But most of them were at the game to talk about the political affairs of the state and nation. Pat and I never joined in. We mainly 'shushed' them. They paid no attention. Pat, Bob, and I remained totally glued to the game.

Governor Kathleen Sebelius and her spouse, Gary, visited our suite for many games from 2003 to 2009. Pat Roberts had been an aide to Gary's father, Keith, who was the lst District Congressman for years. Pat later replaced Keith Sebelius in the Big First. While Kathleen was Governor, everyone got along well. Pat, Kathleen, and Gary had always been close friends. After 2011, when Kathleen joined the Obama administration, it seems everything changed.

There were several tense situations in my suite over the years. One of those moments came in a game against Nebraska on October 15, 1994. Everyone wanted tickets for this game. Pat Roberts called and said a Nebraska congressman, who was the Chairman of a key House Committee, wanted eight tickets for the game.

In a weak moment, I agreed. These eight Cornhusker fans showed up in bright red sports coats. They became breathtakingly obnoxious. By the middle of the fourth quarter, they were doing high fives in my suite. When Chad May threw an interception early in the fourth quarter, K-State lost 19 to 7. After the game, I told Pat and Ruth Ann anyone visiting our suite in the future had to wear purple.

Another tense moment came when K-State was playing KU at home on November 8, 1997. Bill Graves had been Governor since 1995. Bill was there because he liked football. But he was also there to present the Governor's Trophy to the winning team.

For this game, Governor Graves came with an assistant who was a Jayhawk fan. That was fine with me. But I got irritated after KU scored in the first half and the aide did the 'wheat wave.' Pat Roberts was irked too. I told the aide he would have to step out into the hall to do his 'wheat wave.' I never saw it in my suite again.

WE KNEW THE FOOTBALL IMPROVEMENTS HAD TO CONTINUE

The litany for football success was quite simple: hire good coaches, invest in the appropriate facilities, and continue to improve those facilities over time. With the exception of Oklahoma and Nebraska, K-State football had some of the best football facilities in the Big 8 by 1993. K-State had come a long way since 1986.[260]

In 1996, Ernie Barrett was able to raise $1 million to build a much-needed Academic Learning Facility attached to the Vanier Football Complex. This facility contained the academic support services for all of our student athletes. We also added a $2.6 million 20x26-foot Jumbotron scoreboard.

After the 1998 season, we allocated $17 million to add a massive three-tiered deck on the east side through another bond issue. Designed by the HOK architectural firm of Kansas City, this superb addition boosted seating capacity from 39,000 seats to 51,000 seats. It also added a "club section" that featured purple chairback seats that stretched the length of the field and an upper deck with aluminum bench seats.

After the 2000 season, the final work on the popular "club section" was completed at a cost of $1.5 million. In 2002, a new $850,000 Field Turf playing field was installed.[261]

From 2003 through 2006, Ernie Barrett and his staff went to work on renovating the Vanier Football Complex. Jack and Donna Vanier stepped up to the plate again. As the lead donors on this football project, the Vanier Football Complex received a complete $8 million makeover. It included a new training facility, weight room, equipment room, coaches' offices, meeting rooms, locker rooms, and permanent seating in the north end zone.[262]

In 2006, at a cost of $1.7 million dollars, the athletic department installed new video and message boards at the north and south ends of the stadium—which included on the south end of the stadium a huge 23 x 61 foot fully integrated ProStar VideoPlus display system.

In 2007, the seating in the lower bowl of the football stadium was completely upgraded. It included new chairbacks below the press box on the west side of the stadium and new aluminum benches throughout the balance of the lower bowl. A new stadium sound system was installed.

I offer thanks to all of our athletic directors from Steve Miller to Max Urick to Tim Weiser. I also want to thank Ernie Barrett for his superb fund-raising ability. All of these individuals and many more helped transform K-State's completely inferior football complex of 1986 to one of the best football stadiums in the nation for a school of our size in less than 15 years.

Bob Krause and I had been great friends and partners since we got together at Southwest State in 1977. From 1988 to 2009, Bob and I worked together to support Bill Snyder. Coach Snyder told me often that Bob Krause and I were the two guys who always had his back no matter what—meaning that we had Bill's back in planning new facilities, freeing up funds for better salaries for his coaches, and supporting the way he ran the K-State football program.

OUR FOOTBALL TEAM GOT BETTER AND BETTER AFTER 1989

When Doug Looney wrote his S.I. article in September of 1989, he concluded his piece by quoting Coach Bill Snyder: "We will be as good as we can be and we will not be 0-11." Mentioning my unbridled optimism as well, Looney concluded his article with two simple words: "Stay tuned." Looney was hardly convinced that we could transform the program.

Doug was shocked when I called him several days after his critical 1989 article. I called Doug for several reasons. First, I said he had written an accurate story about K-State's horrible football program. Second, I wanted to ask Looney this question: "When we turn around our football program, Doug, will you promise to come back and write an update?" Quickly, he said, "Of course, I will come back." Years later, he told me: "I knew I was making a promise that I would never have to keep."

In Snyder's first year, the football team won only one game. But it was a big game because we beat North Texas State 20 to 17 on the last play of the game on September 30, 1989. We acted like we had won the league championship. Knowing Doug had a sense of humor, I called him. I told him K-State won a football game. In 1990, K-State ended the season with five wins and six losses. I did not call him.

1991, K-State won seven games and lost four—including winning the last three games. For the first time since 1954, K-State won seven games. After the game, I called Doug. I told him he had to come back. Looney brushed me off. He told me that he had no time for that. I reminded him of his promise. No, I actually begged him to please come back.

Within several days, Doug called back. Thank goodness, he relented. I knew that Doug Looney and SPORTS ILLUSTRATED had never done a mulligan for any college football program. To this day, I think it was Doug's sense of humor that allowed him to return.

In the spring of 1992, Looney returned to Manhattan with a photographer in hand. For K-State and its image, this was a big deal. Very few schools ever get an opportunity for a redo—especially in a national magazine like SPORTS ILLUSTRATED. Whether it is in 1989 or 2015, many people read this magazine. With the article on August 31, 1992, this time our school was on the magazine's cover with a positive title: "Kansas State Is Reborn."

Doug's story headline was also sweet—"The Power of Positive Thinking: A charismatic coach and a savvy school president joined forces to resurrect Kansas State." After I saw the headline, I called Looney for a small correction: I related that Snyder is the one who is "savvy" and I am the one who is "charismatic."

As Doug Looney thought about our 1991 record of seven wins, he penned: "What was happening was that ineptitude on the gridiron was clouding the future of a major university. Now, only six autumns later, a miracle is occurring in Manhattan." In his 1992 article, Doug wrote about football programs at places like K-State and other under-achieving programs around America where "football usually doesn't get turned around if the president doesn't care."[263]

WE ALWAYS BALANCED ATHLETICS AND ACADEMICS

Provost Coffman and I always agreed that the faculty would support our athletic programs if we had the right balance between athletics and academics. We continually reminded the school's faculty from 1990 to 1997 our administration was building a new $30 million library and a $10 million museum of art.

Faculty members also knew that Kansas State was in the midst of the Essential Edge Campaign to raise $125 million. We explained that 80 per cent of the monies raised in the campaign would be allocated to new academic buildings, endowed chairs, and academic scholarships. From 1986 to 2009, 80 per cent of all private funds raised at K-State went to academic programs and buildings.

THE IMPORTANCE OF HIRING SUPERB ASSISTANT COACHES

To change the football dynamic after 1989, we knew the vital need of hiring top-notch assistant coaches. Their salaries had been increased. After 1989, Coach Snyder put together a first-rate group of assistant coaches. In his book on Bill Snyder and K-State football, Stan Weber writes about the sterling quality of these coaches.

In Stan's book, he talks about the great assistant coaches Coach Snyder hired between 1989 and 2003—Bob Stoops, Mike Stoops, Mark Mangino, Jim Leavitt, Del Miller, Nick Quartaro, John Latina, Brent Venables, Bob Cope, Dana Dimel, Ron Hudson, Mo Lattimore, Phil Bennett, Bobby Elliott, Greg Peterson, Bob Fello, and Bret Bielema. Eight of them became Division I Head Coaches. Our success would never have happened without them![264]

Early in 1989, Bill Snyder told Mark Janssen: "I think that ten years down the road, we can be winning four, five, six games a year, and every once in a while get to a bowl game." As Bill looked at that team, he realized there were only 49 players on scholarship.

K-State had not won a Big 8 football game in four years. In 1990, K-State defeated Oklahoma State 23 to 17 on October 13 and Iowa State 28 to 14 on November 3. We ended the year with a record of five wins and six losses. Not one fan complained about losing six games in 1990. Today, of course, our fans would be very unhappy.

THE RESIGNATION OF STEVE MILLER

As the greatest turnaround in college football was taking place, Steve Miller shocked us by taking a job with the Nike Company in Portland, Oregon in 1991. Because Steve had hired Bill Snyder, I believed he owed us five years.

But Steve Miller was the visionary that provided K-Staters hope for our football program. He was the leader who helped our school have a once in a lifetime turnaround in college football. Without Miller, our football turnaround would never have happened.

Kansas State was also in the midst of a major rebuilding program of our school's football facilities. The department faced a big deficit. After Steve left as our athletic director on June 13, 1991, we hired the associate athletic director at Temple University, Milt Richards. He was viewed as a solid budget and financial leader at Temple. The department's number one priority was to have a balanced budget.

Richards did that in the next year and a half. The department's budget went from a $6 million deficit to a balanced budget. During Milt's tenure, our football building and improvement projects progressed without a hitch. But Milt was not ready to lead a Big 8 Conference athletic department. On January 5, 1993, months after coming to K-State, Milt Richards resigned.

THE IMPORTANCE OF HIRING MAX URICK AS THE NEW A.D.

A search committee was set up. After an extensive search, we hired Max Urick on June 28, 1993. He was the perfect choice. Max had been Iowa State's athletic director for 19 years. He knew exactly how the Big 8 Conference worked and how to win friends for the department. Bob Frederick, the Kansas AD, agreed: "I'm absolutely ecstatic for Kansas State, for the state of Kansas, and for the Big 8 Conference. Max Urick is a true professional." Max became one of K-State's best athletic directors.[265]

WINNING STARTS IN FOOTBALL IN 1993

Kansas State had not won nine football games in a season since before World War I. In 1993, the football team won nine games, lost two, and tied Colorado 16 to 16. Kansas State finished 20th in the final Associated Press Poll. K-State was invited to the 1993 Copper Bowl in Tuscon, Arizona to play Wyoming on December 29, 1993.

This bowl game was extraordinarily important and much fun. Ruth Ann and I and our two sons stayed at the team hotel with the coaches and players. I enjoyed all of our 11 bowl games. For me, the Copper Bowl will always be "The Magical Bowl." We won the game 52 to 17. The 1993 season and the Copper Bowl victory represents one of K-State's most special and unforgettable seasons.

I remember the first alumni-sponsored rally the night before the game. Because this was our first one, no one knew how many fans would come. It was held in the team's hotel ballroom. It was packed. You could hardly move. The atmosphere was electric. At least three thousand fans were jammed together.

Max Urick's quote stole the show: "As the sun begins to set on Tucson tonight, you're going to see a purple haze on the horizon because they're coming and they're coming by the thousands." Urick was prophetic. Over 25,000 K-Staters came to the game. This game was our version of the movie HOOSIERS.[266]

With the Copper Bowl victory, the K-State football program turned a corner. In 1994, season ticket sales increased from 10,000 to 20,000 in 1994. The football team finished the 1994 season with a record of nine wins and three losses. The Wildcats were invited to the Aloha Bowl in Honolulu, Hawaii where they played a tough Boston

College team and lost a close game 12 to 7.

The 1995 season was the best in decades. K-State's football team accomplished a record of ten wins and two losses. We were invited to the Holiday Bowl game in San Diego, California. K-State beat Colorado State 54 to 21. In 1995, the K-State football team finished seventh in the final AP poll. Life was good.

Many people have wondered how we kept Bill Snyder for so many years. First, our athletic directors, Bob Krause, and I firmly backed Snyder and his teams. Second, we made sure Coach Snyder had assistant coaches with competitive salaries and benefits. Third, we always made sure the school's football facilities stayed competitive. I will say this: I never worried about Bill Snyder leaving on my watch.

THE 1996 TEAM AND THE COTTON BOWL

The new Big 12 Conference started officially in the fall of 1996. Kansas State and Texas Tech played the first Big 12 game ever in Manhattan, Kansas. K-State defeated Texas Tech in a thrilling finish. The Wildcats finished the 1996 season with a record of nine and two. We were invited to play Brigham Young in the Cotton Bowl in Dallas.

Our fans had become believers. Dallas was an easy ride. About 45,000 Wildcat fans attended the game. On the afternoon before the game, we had a rally that no K-Stater will ever forget. On a cold and icy afternoon with the temperatures in the low 30's, over 20,000 fans came to the Cotton Bowl amphitheater for our first major rally.

The dignitaries sitting on the cold stage included Governor Bill Graves, the two U.S. Senators, Pat Roberts and Sam Brownback, and Congressman Jerry Moran. Pat Roberts introduced me as the "Moses from Minnesota."

In my rally speech and with a few tears shed, I could not stop thinking of the many years where our fans could only cheer for first downs and an occasional touchdown. Now we were playing in the legendary Cotton Bowl. Rick Baker, the president of the Cotton Bowl, said: "I give Coach Bill Snyder and their administration a lot of credit for helping save the future of the Cotton Bowl. K-State brought along a wave of 45,000 fans. It was a watershed moment."[267]

HOW VITAL IT WAS TO GET K-STATE INTO THE BIG 12

The Big 8 Conference had existed from 1958 to 1996. If I could have waved a magic wand, the Big 8 Conference would have lasted forever. Our fans loved it. All of the presidents and chancellors knew one another well. We met four or five times a year in Kansas City, Missouri. It was the conference headquarters for years. The Commissioner, Carl James, was excellent.

But the world was changing. It was hard to forget the old adage—you either get bigger or you get smaller. I started worrying about the future of the Big 8 Conference in 1990. Huge changes were taking place in big-time college football. If everything fell apart, there was one school that had the most to lose: Kansas State.

More than any Big 8 president, I worried about the future of our conference. Our football program had been the worst team in Division I football. Our football facilities had been the worst. And our state had no television value for the TV networks.

More important, the key factor for any school aspiring to be a member of a realigned conference was football, football, and more football. A good men's basketball team was not a deciding factor. KSU did have one big advantage—our membership in the Big 8.

By 1990, the Southwest Conference looked like it might break up. If that happened, I had one conclusion: the University of Texas would bolt straight to the PAC 10 Conference. In August of 1990, the first shoe to drop came when Arkansas left the SWC to join the SEC.

In September of 1990, Florida State joined the Atlantic Coast Conference. Another shock came when Penn State joined the Big 10 in June of 1990. The Commissioner of the Big 10, Jim Delaney, seemed to be replicating the expansion plans of Julius Caesar during the Roman Empire from 58 B.C. to 44 B.C.[268]

The world of major college football was seemingly coming apart. Dominoes were flying everywhere. At the very least, I had to try and keep K-State in a major conference. I was elected to be the chairman of the Association of Big 8 schools in 1990 and re-elected in June of 1991. I served in that position until 1993.

After Arkansas left the SWC in 1990, I started working hard to convince my colleagues that our Big 8 Conference should consider merging with all of the eight Southwest Conference schools.

But there was one key to a merger. For me, it was always the University of Texas. By hook or crook, I had to find a way to get UT on board. The state of Texas had more people than all of the Big 8 states put together—meaning that it had a zillion TV sets.

I never ever wavered from my feeling that the game-changer for the Big 8 and its future was the University of Texas—period. As we found out many times from 1994 to the summers of 2010 and 2011, UT was the difference maker. It was a school that could literally make a conference. And it did.

At first, I felt like the Lone Ranger—mainly because our school had the most to lose. But I soon had some good allies. From 1990 to 1994, I worked closely on a possible merger with Chancellor Gene Budig of KU, who became one of my best friends, President Martin Jischke of Iowa State, and Chancellor Jim Corbridge of Colorado.

The Chancellor of Missouri, Haskell Monroe, and the President of Oklahoma State, John Campbell, basically sat on the sidelines waiting for others to act. The President of Oklahoma, Richard Van Horn, and the Chancellor of Nebraska, Graham Spanier, were largely indifferent—mainly because their schools would end up in a major conference no matter what.

The story of how the Big 12 was put together is incredibly complicated. My story mainly involves the role played by the Big 8 CEO's. Of course, I certainly understand that the Big 8 and SWC athletic directors played an instrumental role in the final merger between the two conferences.

No Big 8 CEO or SWC CEO could ignore the huge role that Texas and its athletic director played in the final outcome. DeLoss Dodds was UT's AD from 1981 to 2014. He became arguably the school's best athletic director. From 1990 to 1994 and beyond, the Texas presidents always listened to Dodds' advice not only on the issues involving a possible merger, but also on the entire athletic program.

My first attempt to get a conversation going between the Big 8 and the SWC CEO's came in November of 1990. The National Association of Land Grant Colleges and Universities had its annual meeting on November 12-14, 1990 in Kansas City, Missouri. As the chair of the Big 8 schools, I requested a meeting of the 16 CEO's of the Big 8 and the SWC.

It was like whistling in the dark. Why would Texas listen to a president from a weak football school like K-State? About 12 CEO's from the two leagues attended this informal meeting. Thirty minutes into the meeting, I saw how much clout UT had. After a brief conversation on a possible merger, its President, Bill Cunningham, took charge. Looking out at the group, he declared that the SWC and its presidents were not interested in any merger. None of them said a word. The meeting was over.

Sometime later, I learned President Cunningham would have only considered one move in 1990—that move would have UT sliding right into the PAC 10 Conference. After all, the PAC 10 was loaded with some of the elite academic schools in the nation—namely, Stanford, USC, UCLA, Washington, and California, Berkeley.

In the next two years, I realized that Bill Cunningham was not speaking for the SWC schools. In the fall of 1992, many of the Big 8 CEO's and their AD's heard reports the SWC might break up. In the HOUSTON POST on September 20, 1992, Jim Molony wrote that the SWC might not last much beyond 1995.[269] Everyone in the Big 8 was concerned about the plans of the Big 10.

Commissioner Delaney's major target for the Big 10 in 1992 and 1993 was Notre Dame. Ed Sherman reported in the CHICAGO TRIBUNE on December 16, 1993 that the Big 10 was also looking at Missouri and Kansas from the Big 8 and Texas from the SWC. In 1992 and 1993, the PAC 10 was targeting both Texas and Colorado. In his CHICAGO TRIBUNE story, Sherman quoted one top league official: "It's all in the Big 10's hands." All of this sounds much like the conference discussions from the summer of 2010.[270]

Timing is so important in sports. In 1992, Bill Cunningham had moved up to the system position of Texas Chancellor. Bob Berdahl became the next President of Texas. In 1993, Jim Corbridge, the Colorado Chancellor, succeeded me as the chairman of the association of Big Eight Universities. Thank goodness, Jim was a Big 8 partisan. He made a major difference in 1993 and 1994.

In early January of 1994, I asked Chancellor Corbridge to set up a meeting in Dallas, Texas with the 16 Big 8 and SWC CEO's to discuss a potential merger between the two conferences. This time, the idea of a merger had some momentum. Every Big 8 CEO favored the meeting.

THE FEBRUARY 1994 MEETING IN DALLAS TO FORM THE BIG 12

On Friday, February 11, 1994, the important meeting of the two conferences took place at a Dallas-Ft. Worth airport hotel. Fourteen of the sixteen Big 8 and SWC CEO's were at the meeting.

For Kansas State University, this February 11, 1994 meeting was arguably the most historic and important athletic meeting in our school's history.

After having coffee, we all took seats around the conference room. Tension was in the air. I was a bundle of nerves. At least 14 of the athletic directors, including the Big 8 Commissioner, Carl James, and the SWC Commissioner, Steve Hatchel, were standing out in the hallway.

After 30 minutes of discussion, I asked each Big 8 and SWC CEO to indicate if they backed a merger. In moving around the conference room, each president and chancellor signaled their views. The first 13 CEO's in a row raised their hands for a merger.

Ironically, UT's Bob Berdahl just happened to be the last CEO to speak. His comments still ring in my ears: "On behalf of Texas, I cannot make a decision today. I will have to take this decision to my Board of Regents." Under my breath, I uttered a few cuss words. But Bob stated that Texas would make a decision soon.

Then, after taking a breath, the normally reserved Texas CEO decided to belittle the SWC. For me, it was an out-of-body experience. Bob Berdahl explained why Texas despised the SWC: one, UT hated playing most of its games in the state of Texas; two, the SWC was hurting UT's recruiting of the best athletes in the state; three, UT's attendance at football and basketball games was lagging; and four, Berdahl declared that he favored UT joining the PAC 10.

The room temperature soared. Berdahl's SWC colleagues were stunned and even angry. Baylor's President, Herb Reynolds, was the first SWC CEO to respond. He reminded Bob that the Governor of Texas, Ann Richards, was a Baylor graduate. As an ordained Baptist minister, "Pastor" Reynolds did not sound like a loving minister when he warned about bloodshed in the state if UT left the SWC for the PAC 10. The shoot-out at the OK Corral crossed my mind.

Bob Lawless, the Texas Tech President, heated up the room by ten more degrees. He declared that his school had powerful leaders in both houses of the state legislature, including Robert Junell, the Chair of the House Appropriations Committee, Pete Laney, the Speaker of the House, and John Montford, the President pro-tempore of the State Senate.

President Lawless announced that his three Texas Tech legislators would be furious if UT willy-nilly left SWC. At that point, Berdahl meekly responded: "Look, I know that Texas cannot leave the SWC without spilling considerable blood on the floor."

Shortly after this exchange, our Dallas meeting adjourned. None of the Big 8 CEO's knew what would happen next. But I was pleased that 13 Big 8 and SWC CEO's backed a complete merger. After the meeting, I asked Jim Corbridge to set up a conference call with the SWC CEO's A.S.A.P. We knew time was of the essence. About ten days later, we had scheduled a conference call.

All eight of us were on the call. After a few minutes, I asked gently what the SWC presidents wanted us to do. I was not surprised that Bob Berdahl was the first SWC CEO to speak up: "Here is what we have decided. We encourage the Big 8 Conference to invite Texas A&M, Texas Tech, Baylor, and Texas to form a new conference."

For four years, I had hoped we could convince Texas to join the

Big 8. I did not want to ask Bob Berdahl any questions about the fate of Rice, Houston, SMU, and TCU. I knew there was only one difference between K-State and them: we were in the Big 8. After the Big 8 CEO's agreed with UT's proposal, Bob quipped: "Will it not be better for all of us to split the money 12 ways instead of 16 ways?"

The presidents of Texas, Texas A&M, Baylor, and Texas Tech rapidly notified us of their acceptance into the new athletic conference. After naming the new conference the Big 12, we had to set up a search committee to hire a new Commissioner.

I was selected to chair the search committee for the new Big 12 Commissioner. It was made up of several presidents, athletic directors, faculty representatives, and staff from the old Big 8 and SWC. There were a number of applicants. We interviewed four finalists. But the choice came down to Steve Hatchell, the former SWC Commissioner, and Bob Frederick, the KU Director of Athletics.

I liked them both. I had known Bob for years. He was an outstanding AD and a classy person. I was hoping he would be chosen. I knew there might be a split between the old Big 8 and SWC schools—and that OU and OSU would lean towards the state of Texas.

But I was shocked to find out that Charles Kiesler, the Missouri Chancellor, would not vote for any KU candidate. If Kiesler had set aside his pettiness, Bob Frederick would have been the new Big 12 Commissioner. Steve Hatchell narrowly got the job.

THE SERIOUS DEMANDS OF TEXAS TO JOIN THE BIG 12

When the Big 12 CEO's had our first organizational meeting in Dallas, Texas in the spring of 1994, there was agreement on most of the new rules and procedures. But the meeting soon turned south after Bob Berdahl outlined UT's absolute priorities—meaning that the rest of us had to support their proposed new rules or else. My position was easy: I would support all of them.

Berdahl listed three issues of vital importance to UT. All of them were dealbreakers. The first issue involved home football gate receipts. Texas wanted to maintain the old SWC rule that each school would keep all their home football gate receipts. The Big 8 rule allowed for the division of gate receipts for conference games. This rule passed easily.

The second issue was far more contentious. Bob Berdahl and DeLoss Dodds wanted serious changes in the Proposition 48 rules for the new Big 12. The SWC schools had never followed Prop 48 rules. The Big 8 schools had. The Prop 48 rules allowed a student athlete—who had recorded a below-average test score as defined by the NCAA but who had at least a C grade average—to enroll in a Big 8 school and still have three years to play three.

Those players became so-called Prop 48's. All of the Big 8 schools had some Prop 48 student athletes, especially in football. But DeLoss Dodds and his football coach believed that Nebraska had been loading up on Prop 48's for years.

The Nebraska football program often had 20 or more Prop 48's on their teams for years. They were frequently NU's best football players—including a ton of future NFL'ers. Reminding everyone that the SWC forbade the playing of Prop 48 players, this proposal was a conference buster for UT.

Indeed, Berdahl demanded a huge reduction in the number of Prop 48's from unlimited to just one for football and one for men's basketball. The vote was 11 to 1 in favor. One school was furious over this new rule—Nebraska and its CEO, Graham Spanier. It still is.

HOW A TEXAS PRESIDENT HURT NEBRASKA TWICE

From 1994 to forever, Nebraska hated the new rule. It was aimed directly at the power of Cornhusker football. By the late 1990's, this new Big 12 rule had seriously damaged the quality of Nebraska football. In fact, you could say that it brought the era of Bob Devaney and Tom Osborne to a close.

Fast forward to the summer of 2010 when NU left the Big 12 for the Big 10. In 2010, Nebraska saw its chance to leave the Big 12 behind. The Big 10 chose NU for two reasons: it was a national football program with a huge football stadium; and it was a member of the Association of American Universities (AAU).

Bob Berdahl proved to be a major nemesis for the Cornhuskers twice. He was the Texas CEO that forced through the new Big 12 Prop 48 rule in 1994. It is difficult to overestimate the damage this new rule did to the fortunes of Cornhusker football after 1996.[271]

As history would have it, Nebraska would again face Bob Berdahl in 2011. Bob was now the President of the Association of American Universities (AAU). In April of 2011, Nebraska was voted out of the AAU. Harvey Perlman, the superb Nebraska Chancellor, was shocked by this decision. The school's academic prestige took a huge hit. This action was far more serious than the 1994 Big 12 decision on the Prop 48's. After years as a member, Nebraska was kicked out of the AAU by a mere two votes.

Chancellor Perlman believed that Berdahl could have used his influence to keep Nebraska in this elite academic organization. Bob could have claimed that the vote was so close that Nebraska should have been allowed to continue as a member.

The truth is that no outside academic leader has dented Nebraska's athletic and academic standing over the years more than Bob Berdahl.

In another irony, if Nebraska had not been a member of the AAU in 2010 when the Big 10 was adding a new school, the University of Missouri, an AAU school, would likely be a member of the Big 10 Conference today.[272]

THE THIRD ISSUE FACING THE BIG 12 IN 1994

In our 1994 meeting, the third issue also generated a spirited debate that divided the Big 12 members until 2010. It involved how the Big 12 would split up future football television revenues. The Big 8 divided up all football TV revenues evenly.

Bob Berdahl argued that only 50 per cent of the TV revenues should be divided equally. The other 50 per cent would be based on television appearances. The four huge stadium football schools loved that plan because they were on national TV every week.

Allthough the eight other Big 12 members wanted the television revenues divided equally, Texas won the day on that issue as well. The question surrounding the division of football television revenues lingered as a thorny issue right up to 2010 and 2011.

CHALLENGES OF KEEPING THE BIG 12 TOGETHER IN 2010-2011

If our fans did not understand the vital role of Texas in the Big 12 in 1994 or 2004, they certainly did by the summer of 2010. By that summer, Kansas, Kansas State, Missouri, Iowa State, Oklahoma State, Texas Tech, and Baylor knew how crucial it was for Texas to be the lead school in the Big 12. In 2010, both the Big 10 and the PAC 12 were recruiting schools from the Big 12.

In the summer of 2010, the Big 10 focused on adding Nebraska. When Colorado signaled its willingness to join the PAC 10 that summer, Nebraska jumped ship early and joined the Big 10. The leaders of Iowa State, Missouri, Kansas State, Kansas, and Baylor were now praying that Texas would stick with the Big 12.[273]

What would happen to schools like K-State, KU, and Missouri if the Big 12 Conference fell apart? Those schools and its fans were worried sick. The Big 12 was the only good option. The Mountain West and the Big East Conferences were underfunded. If the Big 12 disappeared, TV revenues for KU and K-State would plummet overnight. K-State's athletic future was at stake.

Sam Mellinger, a KANSAS CITY STAR sports columnist, summed up how bad this it would be in a story on June 11, 2010. It was a column for the ages: "We've dealt with sports disappointments before, but not like this. The Royals always have hope in the minor leagues. The Chiefs always have next year. Kansas City didn't have the ties to those lost pro teams that it has to its beloved colleges. If today is when the Big 12 ends, this is something bigger, something scarier, something more permanent. It's quite possible that Kansas

City's college sports scene will never fully recover. . .Barring a miracle save to keep Kansas, Kansas State, and Missouri in a financially competitive conference, June 11, 2010, could be remembered as our darkest sports hour."[274]

IN ITS DARKEST HOUR, DAN BEEBE THROWS A HAIL MARY

Just when things looked dire for the Big 12's future in June of 2010, Dan Beebe, the Big 12 Commissioner, threw a "Hail Mary pass." He has never received enough credit for that last-second pass. Dan knew how ESPN and ABC would react to his offer: the conference could survive if they guaranteed the Big 12 the same revenues for ten schools in the future that the 12 universities were receiving in 2010.

ESPN and ABC agreed. Beebe informed Texas that the Big 12 would permit it to have its own Longhorn TV network. His strategies worked. Texas announced that they were staying with the Big 12. Texas Tech, Oklahoma, Oklahoma State and Texas A&M proclaimed that they would remain with the Big 12.

Iowa State, Kansas State, Kansas, Baylor, and Missouri could breathe a sigh of relief. They no longer had to worry about joining the Mountain West or the Big East. Without the Big 12, their television revenues would have dropped off the face of the earth.[275]

But there would be another shoe to drop in the late summer and early fall of 2011. Texas A&M and Missouri announced publicly that they were leaving the Big 12 for the SEC for different reasons. But under the brilliant leadership of the interim Big 12 Commissioner, Chuck Neinas, the remaining schools in the Big 12 stayed united. Acting quickly, the Big 12 added Texas Christian and West Virginia. They became the ninth and tenth members of the Big 12.[276]

BY THE END OF 2011, THE BIG 12 IS HERE TO STAY

All ten universities now believed that the Big 12 Conference was here to stay. I agree. With new football TV contracts from FOX,

ESPN, and ABC in August of 2012, the Big 12 Conference would see their revenues go up dramatically in the next five years. Indeed, on July 1, 2014, each of the Big 12 schools received about $25 million in base funding from ESPN, ABC, and FOX.

Today, there are 65 universities that belong to Power 5 Conferences. If fans did not know how much revenue would be channeled to every one of these schools before 2013-14, they do now. In the years ahead, those 65 schools will receive the bulk of their revenues from ESPN, ABC, FOX, and CBS.

Those same Power 5 Conferences, moreover, will receive additional millions from the new football Final Four Team Playoffs initiated in January of 2015. Each one of the 65 schools received a check of $5 million on July 1, 2015. When you add this $5 million check to the $25 million that each school in the Big 12 received from their football TV contracts, it is easy to grasp why every athletic budget in the Big 12 soared.

In 2008, the K-State athletic department was receiving roughly $8 million from those same TV football contracts. Today, KSU is receiving about $30 million in TV revenues—mainly for football. These TV revenues will only go up in the future.

With the 65 Power 5 Conference schools getting richer and richer in the future, there will be few limits either for coaching salaries or new athletic buildings. The salaries for head coaches in football and basketball will continue to skyrocket and many splendid athletic edifices will be constructed from coast to coast. After the summers of 2010 and 2011, our fans now understand for sure how vital it is for K-State to belong to a Power 5 Conference.[277]

K-STATE FOOTBALL AND HOW IT FARED IN THE BIG 12

In 1994, Bill Snyder and I had no idea how successful the football team would be in the new Big 12. Neither one of us ever considered that Kansas State would go to seven more bowl games and two BCS bowl games from 1997 to 2003—or that Kansas State would be one of just four schools in the nation to win 11 games in six of those seven years.

All of these teams could clearly compete with any of the nation's Top Ten football programs in America on any given week. From 1996 to 2009, K-State would rank fourth all-time in the Big 12 with a total of 66 wins. Snyder's teams would rank fourth in the Big 12 in all-time road wins with 26 wins.[278]

In 1997, K-State had a record of 11 wins and one loss. Except for a loss to a great Nebraska team, we finished the Big 12 season with a record of seven wins and one loss. The Wildcats were chosen for our first pre-eminent bowl game when K-State played an excellent Syracuse football game on December 31, 1997 in the Fiesta Bowl.

With over 40,000 plus K-State fans traveling to the Fiesta Bowl game in Phoenix, Arizona, John Junker, the executive director of the Fiesta Bowl, gave this colorful quote: "I can think of two things that have lived up to their billing. They are Kansas State football fans and Michael Jordan. You cannot sell either of them short and they both get it done."[279]

The 1997 football team became a great K-State football team. Normally, Coach Bill Snyder recruited solid high school players and some community college transfers. For the 1997 season, Snyder and his assistants recruited 12 junior college transfers and 14 high school players. One of the 12 community college transfers, Michael Bishop, became arguably the best and most valuable player to ever play football for the Wildcats.

K-State football has never had a more brilliant community college class—and it probably never will. With ten wins and one loss, K-State played Syracuse University in the Fiesta Bowl on December 31, 1997. At a reception before the game with all of the K-State and Syracuse coaches, one of their coaches told me how shocked he was to see what K-State players were starting for the game.

The Orange coach said he and his colleagues were floored to find out that ten of the Wildcat's 22 starters for the Fiesta Bowl were community college transfers who had just showed up at K-State in early August. Against a team loaded with talent and four first-round NFL players, including Donavan McNabb at quarterback, K-State played its finest game of the year by beating Syracuse 35 to 18. K-State was making national waves in football. It finished the season as the eighth-ranked team in the final AP Poll.[280]

THE 1998 FOOTBALL TEAM IS THE BEST KSU TEAM EVER

Because our 1997 team had very few seniors, the Wildcats were loaded for 1998. This team had at least 15 future NFL players. Coaches nationally talked about what a great team K-State would have in 1998. This was a team that could absolutely face any college team in America. Indeed, this team was as good, if not better, than any team in the Big 12, PAC 12, Big Ten, SEC, and ACC.

Consider the 20 great players on this 1998 football team. Most of them played in the NFL. The defensive players included Darren Howard, Mark Simoneau, Jeff Kelly, Damion McIntosh, Andre Rowe, Lamar Chapman, Jared Cooper, Keith Black, Gerald Neasman, and Travis Ochs. The offensive players included Michael Bishop, Eric Hickson, David Allen, Ryan Young, Brian Henley, Justin Swift, Darnell McDonald, Everett Burdette, and Martin Gramatica. My conclusion is simple—this is the best team in the history of Kansas State![281]

For the first time in history, Kansas State was ranked as the No.1 team in the final regular season AP Poll and No. 2 in the final Coaches' Poll. All we had to do was beat the tenth-ranked Texas A&M Aggies in St. Louis, Missouri for the Big 12 Championship. If K-State won, our school would play in the national championship game.

For the first time in college football, there was a new formula in place called the Bowl Championship Series formula. The final poll had Tennessee ranked first, UCLA second, and K-State third. One of those two teams would have to lose their last game. Tennessee was playing an average Mississippi State team and UCLA was going on the road to play Miami University. Miami won.

THE DEVASTATING LOSS IN ST. LOUIS IN DECEMBER, 1998

When your favorite team plays such a pivotal game, you tend to remember key plays—especially if you lose a game that you should have won. The Wildcats controlled the game in the first half and for much of the second half. By the middle of the third quarter, K-State was playing a more conservative game and taking fewer chances. Still, early in the fourth quarter, K-State led Texas A&M 27 to 12.

With a 15-point lead and about ten minutes to play, K-State might have been playing not to lose. Texas A&M scored a touchdown with five minutes to play. But the Wildcats still led by eight points. After getting the kick-off, we had the ball on the 25-yard line. Michael Bishop was running the ball on every play for five yards a carry.

Tim Fitzgerald reminded me K-State was just one play away from the National Championship game. On third down with three yards for a first down on the 45-yard line and a few minutes left on the clock, everyone knew the next play. On a play none of us would ever forget, Bishop ran an off-tackle play to his left and picked up the first down. By trying for a few more yards, however, an Aggie defender stripped the ball from Bishop. With a first down, K-State would have run out the clock and played for the National Championship.[282]

Instead, Texas A&M scored another touchdown and made the two points. In a double-overtime game, K-State was defeated by Texas A&M 36 to 33. Our school had lost the most heart-breaking game in any sport in our entire history. The coaches and the players were heartsick. We all were. It was a loss no K-Stater will ever forget.

I still remember flying to San Antonio on a university-chartered flight full of administrators and staff members for the December 29, 1998 Alamo Bowl. One of the stewardesses asked me minutes into the flight: "Why are all of you K-State fans so sad when you are flying to San Antonio to have a great time and play in a bowl game?" I tried to tell her. But she could not see how heartsick we all were.

During the great run of Bill Snyder's football teams going to 11 bowl games in a row from 1993 to 2003, I still sensed that many K-State fans felt our winning football program could end at any moment—and that we were always one game, one season, or one coach away from a return to football mediocrity. For many fans, our confidence level often was like the Platte River in Nebraska—a mile wide and an inch deep.

After our loss to Texas A&M on December 5, 1998 for the Big 12 Championship in St. Louis, Missouri, I knew some fans believed the football program might be headed for a precipitous decline.

I could see that attitude myself when a K-State fan from Kansas City called me at home on the Sunday night right after we learned that KSU had fallen all the way down to the Alamo Bowl. Already angry over our loss to Texas A&M, this K-Stater blamed me for failing to convince the Sugar Bowl Committee to select K-State.

This so-called fan was furious with Bill Snyder, the football team, and me. In many ways, this K-Stater could just as well told me that our school was headed back to the days of "Futility U."

Making things even worse, the new head coach at OU, Bob Stoops, had convinced his brother, Mike Stoops, to leave K-State. That move was inevitable. But the news got worse. K-State fans were unhappy to hear that Mark Mangino, our superb recruiting coordinator, and Brent Venables, a terrific defensive coach, were also leaving to join the Sooners. A season that had gone all the way to a record of 11 and 0 record ended on a depressing note—when Kansas State lost the Alamo Bowl game to Purdue.

If we know anything about Bill Snyder, we know he does not normally dwell on the past. Although the football team had ended the 1998 season with two depressing losses, it is nice to prove the pundits wrong. For the third year in a row in 1999, the Wildcats won 11 games. The only 1999 loss was to a talented Nebraska team. But K-State beat Iowa State, Missouri, Kansas, Oklahoma State, Colorado, Baylor, and Texas.

Although K-State had a chance for the Orange Bowl, its bowl committee opted for Alabama and Michigan. In 1999, Bill Snyder had a choice between the Cotton Bowl and the Holiday Bowl. The coaches and players chose the Holiday Bowl. The Holiday Bowl had become Snyder's favorite bowl. With over 25,000 K-State fans in attendance, K-State beat Washington 24 to 20. As Mitch Holthus, our greatest and legendary K-State sports announcer, said after the game, "This was a big, big, big win."[283]

THE BRILLIANT SUCCESSES OF K-STATE FOOTBALL: 1989 TO 1999

The Bill Snyder program had been in business for ten years. From 1993 to 1999, we had been to seven bowl games in a row. The Wildcats had ended the season in four of those years ranked in the Top Ten.

In 1989, we had no choice: the football program had to become more competitive or else. Some good fortune and luck were necessary. Bill Snyder might have done too good a job. Maybe, he made winning ten or 11 games every year seem too easy.

Today, if a football coach wins only five or six games a year in the Big 10, Big 12, or SEC, his job is in jeopardy. Even after years of losing football from 1935 to 1989, it would not be good enough at K-State either.

Between 1989 and 1999, Coach Bill Snyder had engineered the greatest turnaround in the history of Division I football. The former head coach of the Oklahoma Sooners, Barry Switzer, said: "Bill Snyder isn't the coach of the year, and he isn't the coach of the decade. He's the coach of the century." Doug Looney agreed: "I think you have to say it is the greatest turnaround in college football history."

Coach Bill Snyder and his football teams had given K-Staters a shot in the arm of renewed confidence and optimism. From 1989 to 1999, I appreciated how important it was for Kansas State to finally have a successful football team. By 1999, Kansas State's academic programs, academic stature, and the football program had come a long way. We had turned the entire university around—and we had transformed the football team as well.

Alumni Building

Anderson Hall

Beach Art Museum

Leadership Studies

Bioscience Research Building/Pat Roberts Hall

Peine Entrance Gate at 17th and Anderson

Former President Bill Clinton's Landon Lecture

June 2008 Tornado

Hale Library

From 1990 to 2005, Jon Wefald played a touch football game with the varsity. He played quarterback for the purples. This pass is thrown to Yamon Figurs who ran the 40 in 4.3 seconds. His record was 15 and 0 and he threw many touchdowns over the years.

Jon and Ruth Ann Wefald

Andy and Skipp Wefald, Manhattan HS Students

Wefald Grandchildren: Cassie, Jonathan, Kaeli and Halle

Jan. 30, 2008 K-State Beats KU

President George Bush's Landon Lecture

Jardine Apartments

Kansas State University Gardens

Kansas State Football

Kansas State Campus

Kansas State University
Founded 1863

Football Complex

President's House

Fiedler Hall & Library

Higinbotham Gate

Hale Library

Hale Library

Up!
Up!

Chapter 8

Winning Three Big 12 Trophies In 2003-04; The Turnarounds In Volleyball, Women's And Men's Basketball; And Leaving Behind Great Coaches

By the year 2000, college sports were becoming even more important. Sports fans could see their favorite teams play frequently on cable TV and the traditional national networks. With increasingly huge TV revenues from ESPN, FOX, and the national networks, the BCS/Power 5 Conference schools were able to pay their coaches exorbitant salaries and build more expensive football facilities.

All of this coincided with the meteoric rise of media technology in the next decade such as personal computers, smartphones, tablet computers, and the ubiquitous high-bandwidth networks to support the flow of information between all of these devices.

Those devices were able to give people the ability to exchange information instantaneously via social media websites such as Facebook, Twitter, and YouTube. These websites and the IT infrastructure that support them allowed anyone with a cell phone to communicate anything to anybody anytime.

As sports talk radio, cell phones, personal computers, emailing, text messaging, Twitter, YouTube, and Facebook mushroomed all over America, fans found out how easy it was to weigh in on how well their college teams and their coaches were performing.

From the 1990's to about 2005, most coaches hired at the Division I level received five-year contracts. After 2005, salaries were dramatically skyrocketing at major football and basketball schools to extreme levels. Now those same coaches, with five-year contracts, would only have three years to prove they were the right coaches for that job. By 2009 and beyond, coaches might only have two years to prove their value.

IN THE BCS CONFERENCES: IT BECAME WIN OR ELSE

If most sports fans overlooked the short leash BCS/Power 5 Conference head football coaches were on before, they knew it on the morning of Monday, November 26, 2012 when they read the USA

TODAY sports section. They read that five head coaches were fired over the weekend.

After two years as Colorado's head football coach, Jon Embree was fired after winning four games and losing 21. Two years after Auburn won the National Championship in 2010, Gene Chizek was fired and walked away with $7.55 million. After three years, Coach Derek Dooley was fired by Tennessee and was paid $5 million. North Carolina State fired Tom O'Brien after a 7-5 season and Purdue released Danny Hope after a 6-6 season.[284]

BCS/POWER 5 COACHES AND THEIR OUTRAGEOUS SALARIES

On April 17, 2013, Coach Bill Snyder did an interview with a Kansas City radio station. He said: "College athletics are in a bad place now." Always on target, he suggested that major college sports were out of control; that athletic prowess had become more important than academic excellence; that college sports had become the 'tail that wags the dog;' and that salaries for major football and men's basketball coaches had reached absurd levels.

In December of 2013, Nick Saban, the head football coach at Alabama, became the first ever $7 million coach. A number of head football coaches were making well over $5 million a year in 2015—with no end in sight.

Indeed, in a USA TODAY article on December 10, 2015, there is a detailed article on the salaries of assistant football coaches. Maybe, the real story of outrageous salaries in major universities today are the salaries paid to unknown and invisible assistant coaches in the Power 5 Conferences. By 2015, it looks like successful football teams are much more important than the enhancement of academic excellence in all of those 65 universities.

As the 2015 article points out, there were now at least five defensive and offensive coordinators making over $1.5 million dollars a year; ten or more were making well over $1 million a year; there were another 20 making over $700,000 a year; and there were 25 more making $500,000 to $700,000 a year. The USA TODAY article does not include a listing of salaries for coaches with the rank of assistant. By definition, many of them at our 65 Power 5 Conference schools were making upwards of $300,000 to $400,000 a year.

You know the world has changed when you see head coaches, coordinators, and many assistant football coaches making more money than almost all major public university presidents, deans, and its most brilliant scholars and teachers. Today, at virtually every Power 5 Conference schools, the top seven or eight highest paid people in the entire university are head coaches, coordinators, assistant coaches and athletic directors.

With the Power 5 Conference schools and their future, the result will be increasingly outrageous—their athletic departments will get richer and richer and their academic programs will get poorer and poorer. In a number of Power 5 schools, the athletic department had more money on hand than all of the academic departments and colleges put together. Head coaches in football and basketball and their many assistants will be part of the elite rich and the football and basketball facilities of the 65 Power 5 schools will resemble the luxury of Louis XIV's Versailles.[285]

The emphasis on big-time sports and huge salaries for coaches will not stop anytime soon. There is no law that the Congress can pass and there is no rule that the NCAA can enact that can reverse the law of supply and demand. As the nation's top 65 schools receive higher and higher television revenues, the "arms" race will persist and head coaches in football and men's basketball will keep making ten times more money than all other employees at their schools.

In one of his columns for the KANSAS CITY STAR on November 7, 2011, Sam Mellinger wrote: "Nothing brings out self-serving hallucinations like college sports."[286] In 1939, Robert Hutchins, the president of the University of Chicago, said: "We Americans are the only people in history who ever got sports mixed up with higher education." William C. Friday, a former president of North Carolina, was quoted on December 11, 2011 by THE CHRONICLE OF HIGHER EDUCATION: "Big-time college sports today bears only slight resemblance to the goals and objectives for which intercollegiate athletics were begun in America."[287]

TIM WEISER'S SUCCESSES AS THE NEW ATHLETIC DIRECTOR

Max Urick, who had been our athletic director from 1993 to 2001, retired on July 1. For eight years, Max had been an outstanding athletic director for Kansas State. K-State was fortunate again when Tim Weiser was hired as the new athletic director in July of 2001. Having been at Colorado State from 1998 to 2001, Weiser came to K-State with impeccable academic and administrative qualifications.

Tim represented a new breed of young athletic directors. He was an advocate of fiduciary responsibility. He insisted on a balanced budget—which we had in all of his years. He was determined that the school, the department, its staff, coaches, and players follow the rules and regulations of the NCAA.

Tim fought hard to have excellent teams in all of our sports. Of all the AD's I worked with over 23 years, Weiser had the best instincts for evaluating head coaches. Long before I did, he understood that Jim Wooldridge was not the right coach for basketball and that Ron Prince was not the right coach or the right fit for football. He did hire superb new coaches in men's basketball, baseball, and volleyball.

Under Tim Weiser, the amount of private funds from donors and corporate support increased sharply. From 1990 to 2008, the athletic department raised well over $300 million to make upgrades in all 16 intercollegiate athletic programs. Tim played an important role in improving many of our facilities—including upgrades to the Vanier Football Complex, the football stadium, and the building of premium loge seating in Bramlage Coliseum.

Tim also added new volleyball offices and a new volleyball floor. During his watch, the department constructed an outstanding new Big 12 track and field facility. Bob and Betty Tointon, two of the most generous K-Staters in our school's history, donated the lead funds so we could construct a spectacular new Tointon Family baseball stadium. With Ruth Ann's help, the department built a new rowing house for our women's crew team.

K-STATE'S BIG 12 CHAMPIONSHIPS IN FOOTBALL, VOLLEYBALL, AND WOMEN'S BASKETBALL IN 2003-04

A significant milestone for Tim Weiser and everyone at Kansas State University was accomplished in 2003-2004 when our school became the first Big 12 institution to win conference championships in three top tier sports—football, volleyball, and women's basketball. Kansas State had come a long way since the Big 12 conference was inauguarated in 1996.

THE FOOTBALL TEAM KEEPS WINNING AFTER 2000

In 2000, K-State football had another great year. For the fourth year in a row, K-State won 11 games. On January 1, 2001, led by another great quarterback, Jonathan Beasley, the Wildcats easily beat a Tennessee team loaded with future NFL players 35 to 21 in the Cotton Bowl.

In 2001, K-State fell back to a record of six wins and six losses, losing to Syracuse in the Insight.com Bowl 26 to 3. But Ell Roberson led the team to a special win on September 8, 2001 by beating Coach Pete Carroll's USC team 10 to 6 in the LA Coliseum. This USC team—like all of Carroll's USC teams—had a ton of NFL players.

USC came to Manhattan on September 21, 2002. In front of maybe the loudest crowd in history, Roberson and Sproles led K-State to three straight touchdowns and two field goals to beat USC for the second straight year 27 to 20. In his first four years as USC's head coach, Carroll's Trojan's teams had not lost to any team two years in a row. In 2002, KSU won 11 games and lost two and went on to San Diego to beat Arizona State in the Holiday Bowl 34 to 27.[288]

Most of Kansas State's star and future NFL players were returning for the 2003 season. The team had outstanding players and future NFL'ers everywhere. With Ell Roberson at quarterback and Darren

Sproles at tailback, these two became the most lethal K-State backs in years. As superb runners, both could take it to the house on any play. Ell became the best option quarterback in college football in 2003.

Bill and his first-rate assistant coaches from 1993 to 2003 not only recruited three of the best quarterbacks in the history of Kansas State, they landed players who became future National Football League draft choices at every position. From 1997 to 2003, K-State won 11 games in six out of seven years for several reasons: one, because Bill Snyder was a great head coach who had terrific assistant coaches; and two, because each one of those teams had anywhere from 12 to 15 future NFL players. It was an unbeatable combination.

From 1997 to 2003, K-State had three of the most elite option quarterbacks in college football. Michael Bishop, Jonathan Beasley and Ell Roberson became quintessential experts in running this singular "shotgun" offense. Snyder was one of the first coaches to implement "shotgun football."

He explained its potency: "The shotgun offense was incredibly beneficial to our running game. No matter the play, the shotgun quarterback was always a threat—as opposed to when he was under the center and could only run sneaks or the option. When quarterbacks like Michael, Jonathan, or Ell lined up deep, they had access to every single play in our play book."[289]

In Bill's return as head coach for 2009, with his next line of quarterbacks, he added the "pop pass" to his unique shotgun arsenal. This gave our quarterback another option in the shotgun—fake a run into the line of scrimmage, stop, and quickly "pop" a short pass to either a wide-open tight end or the fullback. It usually resulted in either a long run or a touchdown.

K-STATE BEATS OU FOR BIG 12 CHAMPIONSHIP

The Wildcats started the 2003 season with four straight wins over the University of California, Berkeley, Troy State, McNeese State, and Massachusetts. With Ell Roberson out with an injury, Marshall edged K-State 27 to 20 on September 20, 2003. In the next two games, Kansas State lost close games to Texas and Oklahoma State.

With Ell Roberson and Darren Sproles leading the way, K-State got on a roll. The Wildcats won six games in a row with wins over Colorado, Baylor, Kansas, Iowa State, Nebraska, and Missouri. Once again, K-State would play OU for the Big 12 Championship.[290]

Having worked with Bill since 1989, I knew that he never got too high or too low. Oklahoma was undefeated and ranked No. 1 in the nation. Many football experts were calling the 2003 OU team one of the best football teams ever. Still, Coach Snyder exuded cautious optimism. In fact, it might have been one of the very few times in his coaching career where he was actually euphoric.

Bill's optimism was based on decisive wins in the last six games of the 2003 season. K-State had beaten Colorado by 29, Kansas by 36, Iowa State by 45, and Nebraska by 29 points in Lincoln—a game that cost the Cornhusker head coach, Frank Solich, his job. Before the game, Mark Janssen got a telling comment from Snyder: "Our attitude was great, and we had two weeks of great practice. I was almost to the point of cautioning the players about being over-confident." These comments were almost un-Snyderlike.[291]

On December 6, 2003, the Wildcats won arguably our biggest victory in history by beating a great No. 1 ranked Oklahoma team 35 to 7. The players were in heaven. So was I. Everyone was very joyful—except Bill Snyder. Janssen quoted him: "It was a resounding victory, and I understand why our fans felt it was the biggest ever. But, in my opinion, we had others just as important."[292]

Ironically, Bill was in a better mood before the game. After his win over OU, Snyder was unable to forget about the three losses to Marshall, Texas, and OSU. He knew this 2003 team might have won the National Championship if they had come together a month earlier.[293]

I had been in the dressing room after games since 1989. Whatever happened, Snyder was all business. He never allowed his players to disrespect the other team. He was seldom wont to criticize any of his players. One philosophical word that defines Snyder might be stoicism. The literal definition of a stoic is someone who shows little emotion. The word that comes to my mind is—calmness.

Kansas State would now play the eighth-ranked Ohio State football team at the Fiesta Bowl on January 2, 2004. The Fiesta Bowl executives estimated that K-State had at least 45,000 fans. Our fans were overjoyed to be in Phoenix for a big game once again.

All of that changed about 3:00 a.m. on January 1, 2004 when Ell Roberson was accused of sexual assault by a female acquaintance at the team hotel. We went from the mountaintop of exhilaration to the valley of despair in one night.[294]

Bill Snyder and Tim Weiser worked together to gather the facts on Ell Roberson's situation. Bill wanted to make a rational decision when that was impossible. He believed the entire team should not be penalized for one player's mistake.

Snyder had handled "mistakes" by former players in exactly the same way. Roberson played the entire game. The drama with Ell actually overshadowed the game itself: Ohio State edged K-State 35 to 28 to win the Fiesta Bowl on January 2, 2004. Coach Snyder was hardly prepared for the national media criticism that poured forth in the next two or three days from sports columnists all over America.

MY ROLE IN WORKING WITH FOUR SPORTS: FOOTBALL, VOLLEYBALL, AND WOMEN'S AND MEN'S BASKETBALL

By definition, the role of a university president is seldom talked about when it comes to recruiting student athletes. For one thing, most presidents have no interest in recruiting student athletes. For another thing, most would feel like a duck out of the water if they even tried to do that. If I had been the president of Oklahoma, Michigan, Ohio State, or Alabama, I probably would have been mainly a fan.

When I came to K-State in 1986, I never envisioned I would be recruiting football players—let alone recruiting players for volleyball, women's basketball, and men's basketball as well. It just evolved. By 1990 and 1991, I was mainly involved in the recruiting of football players. By the mid-1990's, I was recruiting players in the three other sports.

Given my leadership style of empowerment and the delegation of authority to a multitude of leaders on campus, I had the time to do exactly that. I actually took the time over the years to help the marching band, the debate team, the speech squad, the theatre program, and coaches in four different sports.

Most presidents in major universities were too busy trying to micro-manage the entire school to even consider recruiting athletes. Even if the thought crossed their minds, most did not know the first thing about the whole process. Most lacked the confidence to even try it.

Few Power 5 Conference CEO's developed knowledge or insights about the ins and outs of the game of football, let alone the games of volleyball, women's basketball, and men's basketball—mainly because they had little or no interest. For me, however, in just a few years, I became a pretty good recruiter in all four sports.

After all, once again, from 1935 to 1986, 14 coaches, nine athletic directors, and four presidents never came close to solving the challenge of the losing football program. Because I had the time, I thought I should at least try to change that equation.

A number of coaches who had been at Kansas State from 1989 to 2009 in those four sports provide their analysis of the role I played in recruiting. The coaches that I reconnected with after 2011 had won a ton of games in those sports.

They knew I was the only president they had ever worked with who made a difference in recruiting good players. Presidents who got involved in recruiting for four sports in any of the BCS/Power 5 Conferences over the years did not exist.

Over two decades, I hosted Saturday lunches for over 1,300 recruits in those four sports. Using football as an example from 1989 to 2005, I hosted at least five to six lunches every year over the late fall and early winter recruiting period. At each lunch, there would be ten to 15 recruits—often accompanied by their parents.

With Coach Snyder and his nine assistant coaches at every lunch, we met at noon sharp at a nice campus location. Although I talked with the players before the lunch, I spent most of that time recruiting their moms and dads. At the lunch, Bill usually had me sitting by the best two or three recruits. After the lunch, he introduced me and I gave a 15-minute pep talk on why the recruits should commit to K-State.

Most of the coaches I worked with in recruiting had Kansas State in their rear view mirror for years. I had only reconnected with many of them after I retired. Each one uniquely explains how our partnership worked and how it succeeded.

Those coaches that weighed in on my role in recruiting for football, volleyball, women's basketball, and men's basketball include 14 head coaches and seven assistant coaches. Their views speak for themselves.

I spent about 5% of my time during the academic year in recruiting student athletes during my 23 years—which included attending all of the home games in the four sports. My recruiting was essentially on my own time and normally on weekends.

Before I explain the comments of many coaches on my role in recruiting, I want to start by mentioning an article written by Doug Tucker, the well-known and long-time Associated Press sports columnist in Kansas. One of Tucker's AP columns appeared in the MANHATTAN MERCURY on December 19, 1993. K-State had achieved their best football record in decades. The 1993 team won nine games and lost two. It finished 20th in the AP final poll.[295]

In Doug Tucker's December 19, 1993 AP story, he wanted his readers to better understand the role I played in helping turn our football team into a winner: "If Bill Snyder is the Big 8 coach of the year, what does that make Jon Wefald?" Doug quoted an assistant football coach at another Big 8 university about the success of our football team in 1993: "Jon Wefald should be the Big Eight President of the year. Kansas State never would have done it without Wefald."

Tucker offered his assessment about my overall backing of K-State football from 1989 to 1993: "Without the unflagging support and fund-raising ability of Kansas State's dapper president, there wouldn't be 10,000 Kansas Staters headed for Tucson, Arizona and the Copper Bowl. Without Wefald, it's quite likely K-State still would have one of the most unsuccessful programs in collegiate history."[296]

In the December 19 AP column, Tucker asked Bill Snyder for his views on our partnership from 1988 to 1993: "When we came here in 1988, we were promised the full backing of the administration. Nothing that we have accomplished could have been done without the administration."

On September 24, 2000, Mark Janssen wrote a story for the MANHATTAN MERCURY about Coach Snyder's record from 1990 to 2000. He quoted three rival Big 12 head coaches praising Snyder as a superior football coach. But the Texas A&M coach, R.C. Slocum, also talked about my support for Snyder: "At K-State, they've given Bill the total control of the program. A lot of presidents are afraid to give that freedom, but Bill has total commitment by the university. Jon Wefald is leading the charge. When your president is willing to do that, a lot can get done. I admire what he's done for KSU."[297]

When I announced my retirement on May 12, 2008, Jason Whitlock, the well-known sports columnist for the KANSAS CITY STAR, wrote a column on May 13 about my years as K-State's President. Of course, I probably had read well over a hundred of Jason's columns since he came to Kansas City in 1994 to write about college and professional sports.

I knew that Jason had written a multitude of columns about the Kansas City Royals, the Kansas City Chiefs, the University of Missouri, the University of Kansas, and Kansas State University over the years. Very few sports analysts and columnists for any daily paper wrote more powerful, and often more controversial, columns than Jason Whitlock. I also came to recognize that very few general managers or coaches for the Royals and the Chiefs or presidents, athletic directors, or head coaches in football or men's basketball at KU, K-State, or Missouri ever wanted to face Jason's wrath or penetrating critiques. I was one of those.

But on May 13, 2008, Jason Whitlock wrote a nice column about my years at K-State: "Jon Wefald is the sports person I respect the most since moving here. Kansas State fans might find that hard to believe, considering what I have written over the past year about the hiring of basketball coaches Bob Huggins and Frank Martin. Wefald, president of Kansas State, is as good as it gets. Wefald's shortcomings are irrelevant once he retires. You don't judge a man by his failures. You judge him by the integrity and doggedness of his pursuit of success. He's smart, passionate, goofy, and genuine. He's everything that a sports fan would want in a school president. There would be no Bill Snyder era without Jon Wefald. No K-State proud. No Powercat. I just hope when I reach my career finish line, my victories stack anywhere close to as high as Wefald's. He raised the bar at Kansas State."

On April 2, 2016, Dolph Simons, the editor of the LAWRENCE JOURNAL WORLD, a KU alum, and a three year letterman in football, wrote a column about the future of KU and K-State. On my 23 years, he wrote: "Former KSU president Jon Wefald turned the school around during his 20-plus years as its leader. Enrollment numbers were dropping, fiscal support was lagging, faculty morale was poor, the football program was so poor it could easily have affected KSU's membership in the Big Eight conference, and alumni support was not good. Wefald, in many respects, saved KSU."

Sid Hartman, the well-known national sports columnist for the MINNEAPOLIS TRIBUNE who has covered college football and men's basketball teams since 1946, wrote about my role in recruiting athletes for K-State on July 15, 2010: "Jon Wefald is the most well-informed college president I have ever met when it comes to judging athletes."[298]

The late John Kadlec spent fifty years at Missouri as an assistant coach and associate athletic director. In the 1960's and 1970's, John spent several years at K-State as an assistant football coach and a fundraiser. In 2012, Kadlec claimed: "Jon Wefald helped Bill Snyder in every way. He worked very hard to help Snyder recruit and get championship players to Wildcat-land. You could say that Jon Wefald was not only President of Kansas State, but he also performed like an 'assistant coach' recruiting here, there, and everywhere."[299]

In his 2000 book, Professor Bob Shoop asked Coach Snyder about my role with the football program: "President Wefald has set the national standard regarding a president's support for athletic programs. I want you to know that he is one of the few presidents and chancellors in the nation to get involved in recruiting student athletes and we appreciate his involvement."[300]

A writer for the K-State COLLEGIAN in 2001, Chris McLemore, weighed in with this quote from Bill Snyder on how the two of us worked together: "Wefald has set the precedent. I've been blessed to have what I consider to be the finest president any coach could have. At other institutions, this just isn't happening."[301]

What kind of partnership did Coach Snyder and I develop over the years? The answer to that question came on Friday, September 26, 2008 when the Kansas State Athletic Department inducted Bill Snyder and I together into our Department of Athletics Hall of Fame. That is one night I will never forget.

COMMENTS FROM A NUMBER OF FOOTBALL COACHES

The head football coach at Oklahoma, Bob Stoops, has been one of the best coaches in college football for years. In a note to me in April of 2012, Bob detailed how bad the KSU football program was when he arrived as an assistant coach in 1989. He remembered that the facilities were the worst he had ever seen. And he was shocked by the fans' indifference to the football program.

Coach Stoops penned this about my role: "Jon Wefald realized the importance of a successful football program. Just as President George Cross did at OU by hiring Bud Wilkinson in 1946, Wefald and Steve Miller hired Bill Snyder. Like Cross at Oklahoma, the Wefald administration allocated more funds to increase the salaries of assistant coaches and to secure funds for much-needed facility improvements, locker rooms, training and weight rooms, a great press box, and a tremendous indoor facility."[302]

In April of 2013, Coach Bret Bielema, who is now the head football coach at Arkansas, wrote about our partnership when he was the Kansas State defensive and recruiting coordinator for the seasons of 2002 and 2003. In 2006, Bret became Wisconsin's head coach. His teams won the Big 10 Championship in 2010 and 2011.

Although Bielema left KSU in 2003, he recalled the role I played in recruiting: "Meeting Jon for the first time, it was easy to see what he believed in. In the world of college recruiting, often a decision hinges on a weekend visit to a university. One of the biggest assets at Kansas State was the uniqueness of the school president. Jon would know every recruit by name, his parent's names, key statistics, hometown, high school, and what they wanted to study in college. Jon Wefald was a key element for K-State that helped separate them from the rest of college football."[303]

Until May of 2012, I had not talked with Mark Mangino in years. Mark had been a terrific assistant coach at K-State from 1991 to 1998. After coaching for Bob Stoops at OU for three years, he became KU's head coach in 2002. His KU team won three out of four bowl games. In 2007, KU had a record of 12-1 and won the Orange Bowl.

Mark recalled our recruiting partnership: "As the KSU recruiting coordinator for seven years, I had hundreds of detailed discussions with Jon Wefald about recruiting. His keen knowledge of recruiting made him a valuable asset to me. He knew the background of top recruits as well as any member of the coaching staff. Few, if any, head coaches in college football ever received the type of support that Jon Wefald provided Bill Snyder. It wasn't until I became a head football coach that I truly appreciated how valuable President Jon Wefald was to Kansas State University."[304]

Phil Bennett was K-State's excellent defensive coordinator from 1999 to 2001. After serving as SMU's head coach from 2002 to 2007, he became Baylor's defensive coordinator. On April 18, 2012, Phil said: "During my tenure at K-State, Jon Wefald was instrumental in many Texas players choosing the Wildcats. Terry Pierce, from Western Hills High School in Ft. Worth, and DeMarcus 'Petey' Faggins from Navarro JC, came for a visit. Wefald played a key role in convincing them to play football at K-State. Both were NFL picks. Wefald had great knowledge of the process. He was awesome in a room full of recruits. In a nutshell with parents and recruits, Jon became our biggest Closer."[305]

I also heard from Ron Hudson, who now lives in South Carolina.

He was our quarterback coach from 1995 to 2002. He coached at California, Oregon, Notre Dame, Illinois, Ohio State, Kansas State, and Kentucky. In April of 2012, Coach Ron Hudson analyzed how we teamed up on recruiting: "As I reflect on various approaches taken by the different schools I coached at, K-State was the most unique because of the commitment from the president. The fact that he took so much of his personal time to visit with all of the recruits and their parents was a great recruiting tool for the football program. That was not the case with the other schools I coached at."

Remembering his years from 1995 to 2002, Coach Hudson wrote: "I appreciated Wefald's involvement with the recruitment of the athletes. He was a tremendous help in convincing the best players to select Kansas State. To have success, it takes a commitment from the highest administrative level. Without Jon Wefald, I can honestly say that the Kansas State University football program would have not been able to have the success it had over the years."[306]

Mike Leach, who was the head football coach at Texas Tech from 2000 to 2009 and is now the head coach at Washington State, wrote me on January 13, 2014 about K-State's success in football under Bill Snyder. At TTU for nine years, Leach won nine, ten, and 11 games a year. In 2015, Mike was selected as the PAC 12 football coach of the year and his WSU team won nine games and the Sun Bowl.

Mike talked about the partnership between Bill and me: "In the organization of my program at Texas Tech and now Washington State, I often reference what Bill Snyder and Jon Wefald got done at K-State over two decades. I am not the only football coach who has learned from their example of leadership and their commitment to excellence. I am still amazed that these two guys could accomplish great things at a place where everyone else thought it couldn't be done. I remain astounded by what they created at KSU and their example has helped me on my path throughout my career."[307]

Dale Brown, the head basketball coach at LSU from 1972 to 1997, wrote a letter to the editor of the MANHATTAN MERCURY on November 8, 2012. Brown had two Final Four teams at LSU and recruited players like Chris Jackson, Stanley Roberts, and Shaquille O'Neal. In August of 1989, he read Doug Looney's article on K-State's losing football program.

In his 2012 letter, Coach Brown wrote: "When Jon Wefald became President at KSU things slowly started to change for the good when he hired Coach Bill Snyder. To watch Coach Snyder and President Wefald work together to build the football program into one of the elite teams is something our politicians should catch on to. Jon and Bill realized that the 'best potential of me is we' and look at what a powerhouse had developed. There has never been a better pair working together than these two men."[308]

What would these two outside coaches know about how things worked with K-State football? First, Leach and Brown understand that Bill Snyder is one of America's greatest football coaches ever. Second, they realized that the success of K-State football does not happen without Bill Snyder. Third, both of them had read Doug Looney's S.I. article in August of 1989—meaning they knew how bad Kansas State's record was for 50 years under a bevy of football coaches, AD's, and presidents.

MY ROLE IN RECRUITING FOR VOLLEYBALL

I did not become a huge volleyball fan until we were fortunate enough to hire Jim McLaughlin as our volleyball coach in 1997. Jim was a successful coach for the USC men's volleyball program. One of his USC teams won the NCAA Championship. Believing that men's volleyball was becoming mainly a West Coast sport, he left USC to become an assistant women's volleyball coach at Notre Dame.

After six months, Jim heard that the K-State volleyball job was open. Max Urick invited him for an interview. After taking Jim to dinner, Max was extremely impressed. After lunch with Jim the next day, I liked him too. I readily agreed with Max that Jim McLaughlin would be the right coach for the KSU volleyball team.

From our first home game of the McLaughlin era on September

3, 1997 against the University of Texas, Arlington to the last game of the 2009 volleyball season against Colorado, Ruth Ann and I attended almost every home volleyball game. For 13 successive seasons, Ruth Ann and I sat on the front row of the Ahearn south side bleachers. All of those volleyball games were fun.

Under Jim McLaughlin and his successor, Suzie Fritz, Ruth Ann and I hosted lunches for many of their greatest players over the years. We knew them all. There were many great players that became All Big 12 and All America players. After 1997, Jim McLaughlin's volleyball team went to four straight NCAA Tournaments. Frank Tracz had a pep band and the cheerleaders for every game. With the stands on both sides filling up, the excitement became contagious.[309]

Coach Jim McLaughlin kick-started our volleyball team into a winning national orbit. He did for volleyball exactly what Bill Snyder did for football. Suzie Fritz, the associate head coach, who succeeded McLaughlin in 2001, continued the winning ways for volleyball.

Our program became a national power under Jim McLaughlin and Suzie Fritz. In his first year, Coach McLaughlin coached the team to a record of 20 wins and 13 losses and went to the NCAA Tournament. He inherited some superb players from the former coach, Jim Moore. In Jim McLaughlin's four years, I helped him recruit some outstanding volleyball players—including Liz Wegner, Kelle Branting, Lisa Mimmick, Disney Bronnenberg, Lauren Goehring, Cari Jensen, Kris Jensen, Jayne Christian, and Laura Downey.[310]

In April of 2012, Coach McLaughlin recounted how we teamed up on many of the best recruits: "I don't think we would have landed some of our top recruits without Jon Wefald's help. How often does that happen—a president actually helps get a top volleyball recruit? I went to see a prime Texas recruit named Lauren Goehring. At the recruit's home, I pulled out a phone (not a cell phone because few people had one at that point) and they gave me a jack so I could plug it in. I said, 'I want you to hear from our president. He understands success at all levels better than anyone I have ever been around.'"

Jim concluded our conversation this way: "I turned the phone on speaker and dialed his home number early in the evening, and Wefald answered, 'Coach, how are you doing?' While he was talking, the look on Lauren's face was unbelievable. Twenty-four hours after that phone conversation, I called Dr. Wefald again. This time I said: 'Lauren has committed to Kansas State.' I wanted him to know this could not have happened without him." Lauren Goehring became an All-American and the best middle blocker in K-State history.[311]

Coach McLaughlin recalled another recruit, Liz Wegner. He badly wanted Liz to becomed a Wildcat. Jim said: "We needed Wefald's help on this one. I thought she could become an All-American if we could teach her. Jon Wefald had lunch with her and her family. Just listening to Wefald talk to Liz, made me want to attend K-State. Keep in mind, this is the guy who is in charge of the university, and he put so much energy and time into a volleyball recruit. I wanted to play for him." Liz Wegner twice became an All-American outside hitter in 1999 and 2000.[312]

In August of 2001, Jim McLaughlin got an offer from Washington to be their head coach. Tim Weiser and I tried to keep him. We knew that Washington had a tradition of great volleyball. Under Jim McLaughlin, the Huskies won the NCAA championship in 2005.

Thankfully, McLaughlin had hired first-rate assistant volleyball coaches. He told Tim Weiser and me Suzie Fritz would carry on his success. Tim appointed her as our interim head coach. That did not last long. Three weeks into the season, we appointed Suzie as our volleyball coach.

From 2001 to 2009, Coach Suzie Fritz became one of America's elite college volleyball coaches. Suzie led the Wildcats to seven NCAA Tournament appearances from 2001 to 2010. Her 2003 volleyball team won the Big 12 Championship—including two wins over the Big 12 heavyweight team, Nebraska. During this nine-year period, Fritz had a winning record of 195 wins and 113 losses.

As an assistant coach and head coach, Suzie Fritz coached nine All-Americans, 16 All-Region performers, and 37 All-Big 12 players. Ruth Ann and I hosted lunches to help recruit every one of them—including great players like Lauren Goehring, Gabby Guerre, Vali Hejjas, Nataly Korobkova, Angie Lastra, Kelsey Chipman,

Megan Farr, Rita Liliom, JuliAnne Chisholm, Sandy Werner, and Agata Rezende.[313]

Suzie Fritz's volleyball teams won over 20 games in 2001, 2002, 2003, 2004, 2005, 2007, and 2008. There was no team that we wanted to beat more than Kansas. From October 1, 1997 to October 5, 2005, our volleyball team beat KU and its head coach, Ray Bechard, sixteen straight times. In 2002 and 2003, Coach Fritz was picked the Big 12 Coach of the Year.

Suzie recounted how Ruth Ann and I often visited the players in the locker room: "I remember Jon Wefald coming into the locker room after a big win and how he stopped to tell me to give the team his praises and he said: 'You guys just kicked their #&*@.' This is when I knew that we would be lifelong friends. This was the president telling me: 'You guys just kicked their #&*@.' Now he was speaking my language. President Wefald always helped me with our very best recruits. What he meant to me, to volleyball, and to K-State is truly magnificent and extraordinary—and those words don't even come close."[314]

MY ROLE IN RECRUITING FOR WOMEN'S BASKETBALL

In 1996, Kansas State was fortunate Max Urick hired Deb Patterson as the head coach for our women's basketball team. Deb hired a great associate head coach, Kamie Ethridge. They became the best coaching duo for women's basketball in the history of K-State.

Between 1996 and 2009, Coach Deb Patterson did for women's basketball team exactly what Bill Snyder did for the football team. She turned it around completely. She was a great coach and a superb recruiter.

From 1985 to 1996, the Kansas State women's basketball team had five different head coaches. The program's progress had slowed down. Fewer people attended the games. There seemed to be little enthusiasm for women's basketball. In 1996, Max Urick had found exactly the right coach who was the right fit for our school.

Coach Deb Patterson and Kamie Ethridge were determined to

find the best players in Kansas and the region. They were dedicated to building a contender in the Big 12 Conference. Similar to the football team under Bill Snyder after 1989, it would take Coach Patterson and her staff several years to get over the hump. In the next four seasons, the Lady Cats competed hard but struggled.[315]

The season of 2000-2001 was the one that launched the paradigm shift for women's basketball. In 1999 and 2000, Coach Deb Patterson, Kamie Ethridge, and I knew there were some great high school basketball prospects in nearby small towns. Within a short drive of 25 miles, 50 miles and 90 miles from Manhattan, three of the greatest high school girl's basketball players in the state's history were starring on their high school teams—Nicole Ohlde, Laurie Koehn, and Kendra Wecker.

One of the three players lived in nearby Clay Center. She was the 6'5" phenom and future center, Nicole Ohlde. There was a superb 5'8" three-point shooting guard in Moundridge about 90 miles south of Manhattan, Laurie Koehn. Even more amazing, about 50 miles north in Marysville, there was an all-world high school player who would graduate in 2001, Kendra Wecker. She was a 5'11" power forward who was first team All Big 12 in basketball—and she could have been first team All Big 12 in volleyball, softball, track, and even Ping-Pong.[316]

Recruiting is an art and not a science. Every coach knows that if you want to sign an excellent player, you have to cover everything: including how the recruit likes the coaches, the quality of the team, the future teammates, the adequacy of the gym, the academic quality of the school, the beauty of the campus, the fan attendance, and the support of the students. You have to hit every single point.

In Bob Shoop's book, he quotes Coach Patterson on how I did exactly that: "In my fifteen years as an assistant coach at several universities, the door to the president's office was never open. Here at K-State, that door is never shut. His role in recruiting is virtually unbelievable. He hosts lunches, writes letters, and fields phone calls from recruits. He spends time with parents, discusses academics, and sells K-State in every area. He has made himself available a month in advance, a week in advance, or a day in advance, if that's what we needed."[317]

In the fall of 1998, I got an invitation to speak to the Clay Center Rotary Club. I called the club's president and said I would attend if they made sure Nicole Ohlde's mom and dad could sit at my table. Although I could not mention Nicole's name in my talk, I told her Mom and Dad at the lunch how much she would love K-State. In October of 1999, the Marysville Rotary Club wanted me to speak at their club as well. Again, I said I would do that if they made sure that Kendra Wecker's folks could sit at my table.

Some people might wonder if any Big 12 or Power 5 president can play an important role in recruiting. In April of 2012, Deb Patterson answered this question: "President Wefald was directly responsible for helping us sign many of our best recruits over the years. High school girl's basketball in Kansas produced three of the best players in the country in 2000 and 2001. We signed these three great players because of Jon Wefald. He followed Kendra Wecker since she was in the ninth grade. There is no distance he would not travel to attract tremendous young players to K-State."[318]

Coach Kamie Ethridge reminded me that I hosted lunches for a multitude of elite basketball players from 2001 to 2009. In May of 2012, Kamie talked about the role I played: "So many of our players would tell us one of the best things we did in recruiting was introduce them to President Wefald. He hosted luncheons and impressed recruit after recruit—including some of our greatest recruits between 2001 and 2008 in Nicole Ohlde, Laurie Koehn, Kendra Wecker, Shalee Lehning, Claire Coggins, Kimberly Dietz, Ashley Sweat, Marlies Gipson, Kari Kincaid, Amy Dutmer, and Danielle Zanotti. These players led K-State to the 2004 and the 2008 Big 12 championships. President Wefald was one of a kind."[319]

These years represent the "Golden Age" of women's basketball in the history of Kansas State. Seven of these athletes played in the WNBA. Nine of these players were Associated Press All-Americans. Under Coach Patterson, the Lady Cats recruited the best players in the state and in the region. And she coached them up.

From January of 2002 to February of 2012, Coach Patterson's record against KU was 23 wins and two losses. From 2001 to 2009, her teams were consistently ranked in the top 25 nationally in major polls. Deb Patterson was the first Kansas State coach to win two Big 12 championships—in 2004 and 2008. Her Lady Cats won the 2006 WNIT Championship and finished in the Final Four of the 2007 WNIT tournament. In my years, there was only one coach who won three championships for K-State: Deb Patterson.[320]

Whether it is football, volleyball, women's basketball, or men's basketball, you have to have the right coach who is the right fit. Deb Patterson was that. On May 4, 2012, she defined the meaning of our partnership: "In athletics, when we speak of a co-worker, it means they are your friend and supporter in good times and bad times. It is difficult to understand the uniqueness of the demands and dynamics that are required in building a successful athletic team. Jon Wefald understood! He was the ultimate co-worker, leader, and teammate. He made our program! There has never been a university president like K-State's Jon Wefald."[321]

FROM 1946 TO 1990, KSU HAS WINNING MEN'S BASKETBALL

In contrast to the losing Kansas State football program from 1945 to 1986, the men's basketball program at Kansas State was outstanding from Jack Gardner's basketball team in 1946 all the way up to Lon Kruger in 1986. From Jack Gardner to Tex Winter to Cotton Fitzsimmons to Jack Hartman to Lon Kruger, Kansas State basketball was fortunate to have five outstanding coaches in a row. From 1946 to 1990, Kansas State men's basketball was a constant power in the Big 7/Big 8 Conference and nationally.

MEN'S BASKETBALL FALLS OFF: 1991-2006

Winning teams can sometimes disappear. From 1991 to 2006, that happened with three different coaches. There is no question that this 16-year period of men's basketball at K-State from 1990 to 2006 was a big drop-off from the generation before. Under three different athletic directors and me, we hired three coaches in a row who failed to restore our basketball program to its earlier standard.

I was very surprised to get a call from Steve Miller, who was in attendance at the April 1990 NCAA Final Four in Denver, Colorado. Steve told me that Coach Lon Kruger had taken a new job at Florida and that he had taken Kruger's advice to hire Dana Altman as our new coach. Altman had been Kruger's top assistant. He was the head basketball coach at Marshall in 1990.

Although lacking in experience, Dana Altman had the potential to become an excellent coach. With limited talent, Coach Altman's first two years were difficult. After years of Kansas State basketball excellence, the fans got restless. In going to Catbacker events from Dodge City to Kansas City, there was a growing chorus of criticism.

During his tenure as head coach, however, Altman's basketball teams were 28 wins and 13 losses in games decided by six points or less over his four years. In 1993-94, his team had a record of 20 wins and 14 losses. Dana's team reached the NIT Final Four. Max Urick and I should have given Dana Altman more time. Dana went on to become an excellent head coach first at Creighton and now at Oregon.[322]

Tom Asbury was our next basketball coach. He had been a very successful head coach at Pepperdine University. From 1988 to 1994, Asbury's teams had been to two NIT tournaments and three NCAA tournaments. Invited by Max Urick, Tom Asbury came to Manhattan for a visit. The search committee was very impressed with his record at Pepperdine. I was too.

In his six years at Kansas State, Coach Asbury won 85 games and lost 88 games, including one NCAA tournament and two NIT's. Sometime after Asbury's third year, he seemed to be losing interest in the job. Tom was never eager to reach out to our fans in the state. He even seemed uninterested in the job of recruiting top athletes.

If you are a head coach at K-State in any major sport, there is a simple truth. You have to work at it. You have to get around the state. By the end of Tom's fourth year, the fans were unhappy. Although Tom was a very good basketball coach at Pepperdine and K-State, he was never a good fit. When Asbury was leaving Manhattan in the spring of 2000, he quipped to a reporter that he "had been getting tired of working with K-State's bib-overalled fans."[323]

Kansas State needed to find a new coach. Heading up the search, Max Urick interviewed a number of different candidates. Max consulted with Tex Winter, the associate head coach with the Chicago Bulls and K-State's most successful basketball coach. Tex strongly recommended a Bulls assistant coach, Jim Wooldridge. Urick recommended Wooldridge. I agreed.

Max and I, however, should have studied in greater detail Coach Wooldridge's record as a head basketball coach. Over his career, Wooldridge was a 50-50 coach. In his six years, I felt that Jim was a very good basketball coach. But somewhat similar to Tom Asbury, Jim showed little interest in the task of recruiting.

Charles Baker, an assistant coach, was Jim's best recruiter. Charles carried the load. I might have been Charles' top recruiter. I worked more with him than any of the other basketball coaches. Charles sent me a letter on April 15, 2012 on that subject: "In 2003 HoopScoop Magazine rated the K-State basketball recruiting class one of the best classes in the nation. What very few knew at the time is that Jon Wefald had as much to do with signing that recruiting class—which included Cartier Martin, Lance Harris, and Jeremiah Massey—as any of the coaches did. He knew as much about the visiting players as any of the coaches recruiting them."[324]

Soon after Tim Weiser became our new AD in July of 2001, he told me that Wooldridge was not the answer for our basketball team. Tim's instincts were always on target for coaches who were the right fit and the right coach for K-State. Tim rightly questioned whether Coach Wooldridge could transform our basketball program.

After the NIT Tournament failed to pick Kansas State in 2005, Tim Weiser said that we should let Coach Wooldridge go. We talked it over. Tim and I disagreed on giving Wooldridge a sixth year. I felt that the Wildcat basketball team had improved. The team had some good young players in Cartier Martin, Lance Harris, Fred Peete, and a new freshman point guard, Clent Stewart.

I was completely wrong about that. Today, very few coaches ever get six years without producing a winning record. I have kidded Tim Weiser several times since 2006. If K-State had fired Wooldridge at the end of the 2005 season, we would not have been able to hire Bob Huggins. By waiting until the end of the 2006 season, Bob Huggins could become the head coach at K-State.[325]

If K-State fans 12 years ago had been like today's fans, Jim Wooldridge would have been our coach for only three years. Because coaches like Bill Snyder won so many games after 1993 and Bob Huggins and Frank Martin won so many games in basketball after 2006, K-State fans today have little patience in these two sports—mainly because they know our school can win a ton of games if we have the right head coach who is the right fit.

Many college sports fans today have no clue how difficult it is for their schools to hire the right coaches. For example, at least three BCS/Power 5 universities in three different conferences have found it daunting to field winning men's basketball teams in the past generation—including Auburn in the SEC, Northwestern in the Big 10, and Oregon State in the PAC 12.

From 1963 to 2011, the Auburn basketball program has had seven coaches in a row with losing records in SEC conference play. From 1950 to 2012, Northwestern has had 11 coaches in a row with overall losing records in men's basketball. From 1990 to 2011, Oregon State has had six basketball coaches in a row with losing records.[326]

THE HIRING OF BOB HUGGINS AND FRANK MARTIN

Tim Weiser always seemed to know what a winning coach looked like. In 2006, he hired a former Wichita State basketball coach, Eddie Fogler, to be our consultant. Shortly after that, Tim told me that he and Eddie had a surprise coach in mind. Several weeks later, Weiser asked me what I thought about Bob Huggins. I knew two things about Bob Huggins: that he had done an excellent job at Cincinnati and that he recruited athletic and tough players.

In early April of 2006, Tim told me Huggins had accepted our job. As word leaked out, our fan base went nuts: Bob Huggins was coming to town. He hired Frank Martin, Dalonte Hill, Brad Underwood, and a whole new staff.

The recruiting began for 2007 immediately. But there were some very good players coming back from the 2005-2006 team. They included Cartier Martin, David Hoskins, Clent Stewart, and Lance Harris. Martin made it into the NBA and Hoskins was a superb 6'5" inside player. Bill Walker, a 5-Star 6'6" power forward, came early from a high school in Cincinnati.[327]

With the same players who won only 15 games in 2005-06, Bob Huggins won 23 games and lost 12 in 2006-07. K-State had not won 23 games in eighteen years. Despite winning ten and losing six in Big 12 Conference play, we still missed the NCAA tournament. But many fans were already referring to Aggieville as "Huggieville."[328]

Bob Huggins and his wife, June, were happy at K-State. Tim and I believed that Bob would be with us for the duration. When I read that West Virginia's coach, John Beilein, was leaving for Michigan, I did have some angst. But Bob had a superb recruiting class lined up.

I soon learned that two old WVU "buddies" from his college days were flying to town. One was a powerful member of the school's Board of Regents and the other was an old friend from WVU. Billed as just close friends of "Huggie," they must have had authority from WVU's President and his AD. They told Bob that this was his last chance to coach at WVU. Tim Weiser, Bob Krause, and I met with Huggins for three hours at the president's house the night before.

BOB HUGGINS LEAVES FOR WVU AND HIS COMMENTS

The next morning, we heard the bad news. Coach Huggins gave in to the sentiments of his WVU friends. Huggs came over to see Tim Weiser and me in my office that morning. Weiser and I were dejected. It was one of my greatest disappointments in sports.

Still, I knew that Bob loved K-State. In May of 2012, Coach Huggins talked about his one year of coaching at K-State: "When anyone talks about the resurgence of K-State basketball, it needs to start with Tim Weiser and Jon Wefald. I have never worked for a better president or man than Jon Wefald. I would NEVER have left Kansas State if not for the opportunity to come home. It was my hardest decision so far. Jon Wefald taught me so much and I am a much better coach and person for the time I spent in Manhattan under his tutelage."[329]

In addition to winning 23 games with Jim Wooldridge's players, Huggins and his assistant coaches had an even more important success: they had recruited the nation's number 1 class for the year 2007-08. It was a class that put our basketball program back on the national map. I enjoyed helping Bob Huggins and Frank Martin recruit Michael Beasley, Bill Walker, Jacob Pullen, and Blake Young.

I remember hosting a dinner at the president's house early in October of 2006. Some of K-State's greatest basketball recruits were at the table—including Michael Beasley, Jacob Pullen, DeJuan Blair, D.J. Kennedy, and Fred Brown. Huggins got verbal commitments from Beasley, Pullen, and Brown. Bill Walker was still another 5-Star recruit.

Tim Weiser and I had to decide who should replace Bob Huggins. K-State had the nation's No. 1 recruiting class coming to town. In April of 2007, our leadership team faced a dilemma. Many of our fans and the media felt that we should launch a national search. After all, Frank Martin had never been a Division I head coach.

Tim Weiser, Bob Krause, and I met with Coach Martin twice to find out his interest to be our next head coach. We hired Frank. Although the decision was a calculated risk, it was an easy hire for me. The assistant coaches and staff all stayed. And Michael Beasley, Jacob Pullen, Bill Walker, and Jamar Samuels confirmed they were staying.

Wildcat fans could hardly wait for the next basketball season. Frank Martin's team struggled in November and December of 2007 with four losses to George Mason, Oregon, Notre Dame, and Xavier. After January 1, 2008, the Wildcats won six games in a row—including a decisive win on ESPN over an excellent KU team 84 to 75 on January 30, 2008. K-State had not beaten KU at home since 1983. It was K-State's biggest men's basketball win since 1990.

Frank's first team won 21 games and lost 12. Led by Michael Beasley, K-State finished third in the Big 12 with a record of ten wins and six losses. For the first time since 1996, K-State was selected for the NCAA Tournament. In the NCAA Midwest First/Second Round games in Omaha, Nebraska, the Wildcats beat a talented USC team 80 to 67. In the second round, Wisconsin beat K-State 72 to 55.[330]

For 2008-09, Jacob Pullen and Denis Clemente became the best guard tandem in years. This team had other good players in Jamar Samuels, Dominique Sutton, Darren Kent, and Fred Brown. K-State had a record of 22 wins and 12 losses. It finished in fourth place in the Big 12 with a record of nine and seven. After the NCAA Selection Committee failed to select KSU, the team went to the NIT tournament.[331]

There was optimism for the next season because Jacob Pullen, Denis Clemente, Jamar Samuels, and Dominique Sutton were returning. And there was more firepower on the way. In the spring of 2008, K-State signed two future stars from New York City, Curtis Kelly, who was a 6'9" power forward and a transfer from Connecticut, and Jordan Henriquez, a 6'11" freshman center.[332]

In the spring of 2008, I met Curtis and Jordan for the first time. I hosted a dinner for them. Scheduled to start at 7:00 p.m., Kelly and Henriquez showed up with six associates and hangers-on from New York City. Because our coaches could not be there right away, I entertained them until they came.

After an hour or so, I got up and gave them a spirited talk on the pluses of K-State. I stressed the quality of our academic programs; I told them never to miss class; I told them they would have to study several hours every day; and I told them they had to graduate.

The coaches came in one by one. It worked: within days, Curtis Kelly and Jordan Henriquez both signed. In the fall of 2008, I helped Frank Martin recruit Rodney McGruder and Wally Judge for the 2009-10 season. With these new players, our basketball program would be a major force in the Big 12 and nationally.[333]

On June 12, 2012, Brad Underwood, the former associate head coach at K-State and the associate head basketball coach at South Carolina at the time, told me about his time with our basketball program. In the spring of 2013, Brad was picked as the head coach at Stephen F. Austin University in Texas. After the 2016 NCAA Tournament, Brad was selected as the new basketball coach at Oklahoma State. Because Brad played under Jack Hartman, he knew how excellent the basketball program was from 1946 to 1990.

Shortly after Frank Martin and Brad Underwood had moved to South Carolina, Brad explained how we worked together while they were at K-State: "President Jon Wefald, 'The Closer' and 'Team Owner' as we called him later and still do at South Carolina, went beyond what any president did in involving himself in the process of recruiting. Every single recruit that visited K-State was going to have lunch or dinner with The Closer. His positive vibe helped us land the #1 recruiting class in America. Every recruit and his parents met Wefald. One game short of the Final Four in 2009-10, all of this was made possible by a president who played a pivotal role in building the program into a National Championship type program."[334]

During his years at K-State from 2007 to 2012, Coach Martin had the best record of wins and losses for his first five years as head coach as any coach in the school's basketball history—including Jack Gardner, Tex Winter, and Jack Hartman in their first five years.

There is no question about this: Coaches Bob Huggins and Frank Martin completely kick-started the school's men's basketball program. For the first time in sixteen years, K-State basketball was back on the national radar screen. Those two coaches did exactly the same thing for men's basketball from 2006 to 2012 that Bill Snyder did for our school's football program. Huggins and Martin restored the basketball glory years of KSU basketball after 2006.

In his five years, Frank Martin's Wildcats went to four NCCA tournaments and one NIT Tournament. In 2009-2010, the K-State men's basketball team advanced to the Elite Eight. During his five years, Coach Martin had some of the best players to ever wear the Purple and White—including Michael Beasley, Bill Walker, Jacob Pullen, Denis Clemente, Jamar Samuels, Curtis Kelly, Jordan Henriquez, Rodney McGruder, and Angel Rodriguez.[335]

Frank Martin will always be ranked as one of K-State's best

men's basketball coaches. According to an analysis by Bill Felber in the MANHATTAN MERCURY on March 4, 2012, Frank Martin's winning percentage in games decided by five points or less was the best of any of the other Big 12 coaches from 2007 to 2012. Coach Martin's winning percentage in games of less than five points was .564 in his five years.[336]

In K-State's Men's Basketball Guide for 2015-16, the media guide writers wrote this about Coach Martin: "The fiery Martin took the baton from Huggins and led the school to arguably its greatest stretch in its long and storied history. . .He is the first coach in school history to post five consecutive 20-win seasons and the first to guide the team to the postseason in each of his first five years."[337]

In a memo to me on June 12, 2012, Coach Frank Martin, who was now the head basketball coach at South Carolina, summed up our excellent partnership after he became K-State's basketball coach in the spring of 2007: "When you consider that Jon Wefald was responsible for hiring Bill Snyder, not once, but twice, and you couple the unbelievable success of football with the resurgence of basketball, you understand his commitment to excellence. Jon's outstanding recruiting for our men's basketball program can be summed up like this—there is no president anywhere in America who can recruit the very best players like he can. He made himself so available to assist me in recruiting that I could share stories that would last for a lifetime. Now at South Carolina, I completely believe that Jon Wefald rebuilt K-State from the brink both academically and athletically. He did this because he cared more than anyone about the university. Jon Wefald was, and is, our friend, our President, and our Team Owner."[338]

Because I practiced the management stragety of empowerment and delegation, there were hundreds of K-State leaders that made decisions every day. Thus, because I was not trying to micro-manage the entire school, I probably had much more time than the typical Power 5 Conference CEO to help out in some areas of importance. So I picked some areas in the university that needed help where I could make a difference—including the Debate Team, the Speech Squad, the Theatre Program, the Marching Band and four different sports.

I enjoyed recruiting student athletes. Of course, the well-being of our football, men's basketball, women's basketball, and volleyball teams were not only important for the school, but for our fans everywhere. In the years from the early 1990's to 2009, I hosted luncheons and dinners for well over 1,300 student athletes and their parents in all four sports. As the various newspaper accounts and the comments from a multitude of coaches suggest, I did impact quite favorably on a number of those recruits committing to K-State in those sports over the years.

I think you could say this: I doubt that there is any Power 5/BCS CEO in memory who successfully engaged student athletes like I did. Although I only spent 5% of my time recruiting and although I became a successful recruiter, I knew without question whether it was in 1995, 2005, or today that the most important factor for a winning team at K-State is this simple fact—it only happens if the head coach is an excellent coach and recruiter. Otherwise, a person like myself might as well have been spitting into the wind.

WINNING STOPS FOR COACH SNYDER IN 2004 AND 2005

For the first time since 1989, the KSU football team had two seasons in a row where our team lost more games than they won. Like Bill, I hated to lose. As he also often said, winning is difficult. K-State lost to Fresno State at home 45 to 21 on September 11, 2004. The Wildcats lost a close game to the Jayhawks in Lawrence 31 to 28. KSU finished the year with a record of only 4 wins and 7 losses. This was Coach Snyder's poorest year since 1989.[339]

In the last game of the season on November 20, 2004 against Iowa State, I remember walking down the stairs to the field with five minutes left in the game. The Wildcats lost to the Cyclones 35 to 23. As Bob Krause and I were walking down the stadium steps, a K-State fan saw me and yelled: "Hey, Wefald, get rid of Bill Snyder."

I was stunned. Luckily, I did not respond with a rude remark. But I did think that this "lady" had to be kidding. We had just come off a

BCS Fiesta Bowl game in Phoenix. Our football team had won 11 games in six out of seven years from 1997 to 2003. And this idiot was calling for Snyder to be fired. I guess she and some other fans had forgotten our years of losing football from 1935 to 1988.[340]

At Kansas State, a sense of insecurity seemed to lurk just below the surface during the first 75 years of the school's history. For many years after 1945, Kansas State fans developed a mind-set of being in second place and failing to catch up on so many fronts. I thought that K-Staters were mainly over that. I was wrong.

After the 2004 season was over, I met with Coach Snyder. He was seriously considering retirement from football. I told Bill that this was out of the question. He would call me back. He never did.

We were looking forward to the 2005 football season. The Wildcats beat Marshall University on the road in the second game 21 to 19. KSU beat KU at home 12 to 3 and Missouri at home 36 to 28. But the 2005 football team ended the year with five wins and six losses. After our homecoming loss to Colorado on October 29, 2005, Bill told me: "I think I will retire at the end of the season."

I suggested that we should meet with Tim Weiser and Bob Krause. A day or two later, we met at the president's house at 9:00 a.m. As the four of us were having a cup of coffee, Snyder said firmly but quietly: "You know why we are here. I want to retire at the end of the season." This time, Bill Snyder was categorical.

Like I did after the 2004 season, I should have told Bill retiring was out of the question. But he had made up his mind. Tim Weiser had to think about a fitting ceremony for Coach Bill Snyder after a brilliant football career. We decided to have a Bill Snyder Day after the last football game against Missouri.

Some fans believe today that Bill Snyder had changed his mind about retiring before the Missouri game. I wish he had called me and said: "I have changed my mind. I really want to keep coaching the Wildcats." That did not happen. The decision was made to name the stadium after Coach Snyder. Our players were fired up. The Wildcats beat a good Missouri team. An era had come to an end.

TIM WEISER'S SEARCH FOR A NEW COACH

Tim Weiser took charge of the search. He came up with a good list. Jim Leavitt, the head football coach at South Florida and the former defensive coordinator for K-State from 1990 to 1995, headed the list. Weiser hoped that TCU's head coach, Gary Patterson, might be interested. We also learned that Brett Bielema, who had been Snyder's defensive coordinator in 2002 and 2003, might want the job. Leavitt, Patterson, and Bielema all fit the bill.

In late November of 2005, Tim had lined up a Sunday trip to interview three candidates, Jim Leavitt in Tampa, Randy Shannon, Miami's defensive coordinator, in Miami, and Gary Patterson in Dallas. As we were boarding the plane to fly to Tampa, Florida, Weiser said Shannon had dropped out. There were two candidates to interview: Jim Leavitt and Gary Patterson.

Chuck Neinas, the former president of the College Football Association, was our consultant. Our group met with Jim Leavitt in a nearby Tampa hotel. The meeting lasted two hours. Every topic was covered. Even though Leavitt had built the South Florida program from scratch after 1996, he was very interested in the KSU job.

Unfortunately, Leavitt's team had one game left in the season. If they won that game, South Florida would win the Big East outright and go to a BCS bowl game. Few head coaches would leave their team with a BCS game on the line. Weiser told Coach Leavitt that he was willing to wait for about two weeks for a decision.

Then, Chuck Neinas reported that the TCU athletic director had called. Gary Patterson decided to remain at TCU. Bret Bielema became the head coach at Wisconsin. After waiting for two weeks, Tim Weiser notified Leavitt that we were moving on.

At the beginning of the search, Chuck Neinas had recommended we should look at two assistant coaches: Randy Shannon and Ron Prince, who was the offensive line coach at Virginia. With Shannon staying at Miami, Weiser asked Bob Krause and Jim Epps to fly with him to Charlottesville, Virginia to interview Ron Prince.

All three were impressed. In the interview, Ron Prince had a complete notebook on K-State football. He mentioned the coaches he would hire; he vowed to improve the recruiting of top-notch athletes; and he outlined what offensive and defensive schemes he would employ. All three also mentioned Prince's confidence.

When Weiser, Krause, and Epps came back, they were pumped up about Ron Prince. Bill Snyder and I met with them at the president's house the next day. By now, we had struck out on Jim Leavitt, Gary Patterson, and Brett Bielema. Tim asked Coach Snyder and me to join the three of them and interview Coach Prince in Topeka. In the two-hour interview, Prince was articulate and focused.

After meeting with Ron Prince, Snyder told us that Ron seemed to be a solid football coach. I often wished that Bill had bluntly told me that we should hire a successful head coach. Then, if we could not find a suitable head coach, we would ask Coach Snyder to return. Tim Weiser wanted to hire Coach Prince. I agreed.

COACH RON PRINCE'S ASSISTANT COACHES

When Ron Prince came to Manhattan, Kansas in late 2005, he started hiring assistant coaches from around the country, including two future head coaches. Raheem Morris was selected as K-State's defensive coordinator. After one year, Morris became a cornerback coach for the Tampa Bay Buccaneers.

James Franklin was hired as the offensive coordinator and he did an excellent job for two years. Coach Franklin became a successful head football coach at Vanderbilt. He is now the head coach at Penn State.

There were four assistant coaches at K-State for just one year: Tim Horton, James Jones, Pat Washington, and Raheem Morris. Two assistant coaches were at K-State for only two years, James Franklin and Matt Wallerstedt. Three of his new coaches, Mo Latimore, Tim McCarty, and Tim Tebesar were at Kansas State for three years.

The rest of the assistant coaches in 2007 and 2008 included Dave Brock, Frank Leonard, and Ricky Rahne; Greg Burns for the 2007 season; and three new coaches for the 2008 season, Cornell Jackson, Jeff Rogers, and Warren Ruggiero.

That summer, Ron Prince toured the state talking to various Cat-backer events. A terrific speaker, Ron projected confidence. Many fans felt that Prince exhibited considerable football knowledge. Ron also convinced Josh Freeman, a 6'6" 250-pound quarterback at Grandview High School in Missouri, to change his commitment from Nebraska. Many K-Staters believed their school had hired a winner.

THE UPS AND DOWNS IN KSU FOOTBALL FROM 2006-2008

The 2006 football season got off to a nice start with three straight wins. But the Wildcats lost four of their next five games. In the next two weeks, K-State beat Iowa State and Colorado. Wildcat fans were ecstatic when K-State beat Texas 45 to 42 on November 11, 2006. Most fans would say that 2006 was a pretty good year because K-State was invited to play Rutgers in Houston's Texas Bowl. KSU lost the game 37 to 10.[341]

For the 2007 season, there was quiet optimism. The season started with a loss against a Top 20 team, Auburn. After winning the next three games in a row, a big win came when K-State beat an excellent Texas team in Austin by a score of 41 to 21 on September 29. This was Prince's best win in his three years. Our biggest boosters were now enamored with Ron Prince.

The next week K-State lost to a solid Kansas team 30 to 24. But the most heartbreaking loss came on October 20, 2007 in Stillwater when K-State lost to Oklahoma State on a last-second field goal 41 to 39. Kansas State looked like a sure winner right up to the last minute. This loss likely turned out to be the negative tipping point for Ron Prince's football program.[342]

After a loss to Iowa State in Ames by a score of 31 to 20 on November 3, 2007, K-State traveled to Lincoln the next week. Looking like the New England Patriots, Nebraska whipped K-State 73 to 31. For many fans, this loss reminded them of the old days of losing football in the 1970's and 1980's.

The last two games were equally grim. Missouri beat K-State at home 49 to 32 on November 17, 2007. In an away game, Fresno

State ran roughshod over Kansas State all day long. We lost 45 to 29. The 2007 season could not have ended more badly.[343]

After Kansas State had beaten Texas for the second year in a row on September 29, 2007, Tim Weiser met with Coach Prince the next day. Tim made a verbal offer to Prince for a new contract. He told Ron that he was willing to increase his salary by $500,000 to a total salary of over $1.1 million a year, including added incentives, for the next five years. Weiser absolutely would not guarantee $5 million for the years remaining on Ron's contract if he were fired.

Unfortunately, Ron Prince and his agent, Neil Cornrich, rejected Weiser's offer for a new five-year contract. Weiser called me on Monday about his verbal offer. I thought his offer for a good salary increase was eminently fair. Evidently, Ron Prince and his hard-nosed agent, Neil Cornrich, thought otherwise.

This duo likely thought the Wildcat football team could win enough games during the rest of the 2007 season to change Weiser's mind about guaranteeing Ron's contract. But by the end of the 2007 season, Tim believed Coach Prince could not be successful.

In the summer of 2008, I still had some tiny optimism. Ron Prince had won 12 games in his first two years. The last coach to win that many games in his first two years was Coach Z. G. Clevenger. He won 12 games in 1916 and 1917. From 1945 to 1989, none of our football coaches had won 12 games in their first two years. It even took Bill Snyder three years to win 13 games. [344]

Even though Ron Prince had won 12 games in his first two years and triumphed over Texas in 2006 and 2007, the 2007 season ended on a downward trajectory. After losing badly the last four games, our fans were hardly optimistic about 2008. The department heard from many fans that summer. Some fans wanted Prince fired. Most felt he should have one more year, but with no guarantees.

By the end of the 2007 season, Tim agreed Ron Prince should have one more year. This meant Prince would coach in his third year on the old contract. Tim Weiser's view of Ron Prince at the end of the 2007 season was similar to what he had said about Jim Wooldridge in 2005—meaning that neither coach was the right coach for our school. I also started feeling exactly the same way.[345]

MY HUGE MISTAKE IN LETTING TIM WEISER LEAVE KSU

After I retired as president in late June of 2009, I often found my mind wandering back to December of 2007 and January of 2008. I think back to those two months because I should have retained Tim Weiser as our athletic director.

In his seven years, Tim and I disagreed on only a few issues. The first issue came about in 2005 when I felt that Jim Wooldridge should get a sixth year. Tim wanted to fire him. Weiser was right. Wooldridge was not the right coach. After the 2007 season, I thought we should cancel the 2008 football game with Fresno State. I was wrong on that issue too.

The truth is that Tim Weiser was an excellent athletic director. He believed in hiring the best coaches and backing those coaches. He believed in the concept of fiduciary responsibility. He had a balanced budget during his tenure. In fact, Tim had set up a reserve account for future exigencies. He was respected and well liked by our coaches. Moreover, Tim Weiser was extraordinarily skillful in working with the media.

Tim had told me many times how stressful the job was. I am sure that many AD's in all of the major conferences would say exactly the same thing. After Dan Beebe was selected as the new Big 12 Commissioner on September 5, 2007, I knew that Beebe and Weiser had been close friends for years. And I knew Dan hoped that Tim would become the next Deputy Commissioner of the Big 12.

I should have stopped that conversation in its tracks. But I did not. The only way that Tim Weiser could ever consider that position was if our administration worked out some kind of buyout. Because Tim was on a ten-year contract, I knew that it would be very expensive—even if we looked only at 20 per cent of his multi-year contract. It would cost as much as $1.9 million. Still, Weiser was unsure if he should join the Big 12 or stay on as K-State's athletic director.

I was the decider. I cannot blame this on anyone else. This happened on my watch. Maybe I thought after 22 successful years at K-State that I could permit this kind of outrageous expenditure. Equally stupid, maybe I thought that I could get along without Tim.

By letting Weiser go to the Big 12 with this big payment in tow, I made a huge mistake. I will always regret letting him leave K-State. In looking back on my entire career, this was absolutely the worst personnel decision I ever made. For months after I retired, I could not get this decision out of my mind.

Tim Weiser would have taken a hard line on a new contract for Ron Prince in the summer of 2008. He would have asked Prince to coach in his third year on his "old" 2005 contract. For years, I always listened to people; I always tried to do the right thing; and I always knew I was never the smartest guy in the room. In this case, I was completely wrong.

On February 21, 2008, Tim Weiser announced he was accepting the position of Deputy Commissioner of the Big 12 conference. He has remained a good friend. I talk to Tim Weiser often. I know that Tim loves being the Big 12 Deputy Commissioner. After he left, I appointed Jim Epps the interim athletic director.

In the season of 2007-08, Suzie Fritz's volleyball team finished third in the Big 12 conference with a record of 23 wins and nine losses, advanced to the second round of the NCAA tournament, and finished 16th in the final national rankings. Deb Patterson's women's basketball team won the Big 12 Championship in 2008 with a record of 13 wins and three losses. Under Frank Martin, the men's basketball team finished fourth in the Big 12 conference. The Wildcats achieved a record of 21 wins and 12 losses, beat KU in Manhattan 84 to 75 on January 30, 2008, and bested USC in Omaha, Nebraska 80 to 67 in the first round of the NCAA tournament.

I ANNOUNCED MY RETIREMENT IN MAY OF 2008

After 22 years as president, I announced my retirement on May 12, 2008. I would be at Kansas State for one more academic year. I was ready to move on. I was eager to do something else and spend more time with my family.

On June 6, 2008, I appointed Bob Krause as athletic director. As a lame duck, I did not feel that it would be appropriate to have a national search for a new athletic director. The new president would want to appoint his own athletic director. Since 1988, Bob had been the interim athletic director three times. He always did an excellent job.

I first met him when I became president of Southwest State University in Marshall, Minnesota in 1977. I sensed right away Bob Krause was keenly intelligent and a problem-solver. He had a high learning curve. When I became the Chancellor of Minnesota's seven state universities in 1982, I hired him as the Vice-Chancellor of Student Affairs. He did a terrific job. From 1986 to 2008, Krause was an excellent Vice-President for Institutional Advancement. I decided that he would be a capable athletic director.

TOO MANY ASSISTANT COACHES COMING AND GOING

The biggest decision for the department was getting a new contract for Coach Ron Prince before the start of the 2008 season. Although K-State had lost its last four games in 2007, our fans worried more about the turnover of assistant coaches. Four coaches were gone at the end of year one, three of them involuntarily. Two more coaches left after year two. There were three new assistant coaches for the 2008 season. It was a football merry-go-round.

By 2008, it was becoming obvious that Ron Prince had no interest in connecting with either Snyder's former players or our fans. In fact, whether it was former players, lifelong Wildcat fans, high school football coaches, or major boosters, most of them felt no bond at all with the football program and its head coach.

THE QUESTION OF EXTENDING RON PRINCE'S CONTRACT IN 2008

Jim Epps reminded me of a meeting that took place in my office on Monday afternoon, March 24, 2008 with him, Bob Krause, and me. It was held to discuss the status of Coach Prince's contract for the 2008 season. Epps explained what we decided: "I definitely remember that you asked Bob Krause to reaffirm the new contract extension for Coach Prince would be for one year only and there would be a salary increase from $750,000 to $1.2 million a year. Bob agreed with those terms and conditions."

On August 7, 2008, Coach Prince signed a new contract through the 2012 season. The deal was retroactive to January 1, 2008 and ran through December 31, 2012. It replaced the original contract signed in December of 2005. This new contract provided for a total guaranteed package of $1.2 million. I thought it was fair.

THE DIFFICULTIES OF THE 2008 SEASON

The 2008 season would begin in three weeks. Starting the season with two wins, K-State lost the next week on the road to an average Louisville team. On October 4, Texas Tech overwhelmed K-State. After beating Texas A&M, the Wildcats lost another game on the road to a struggling Colorado team. A week later, Oklahoma beat K-State handily at home. In Lawrence on November 1, 2008, KU clobbered K-State 52 to 21. Our football team was going south.[346]

After the KU game, I felt the head football coach, the assistant coaches, and players alike had lost their confidence and any concept of teamwork. Our fans, the media, and many of us were hearing of tensions among the assistant coaches, between the assistant coaches and the head coach, and between the players and their coaches. By 2008, Coach Prince had hired sixteen different assistant coaches.

On December 9, 2008, Jon Garten, a sports columnist for the Kansas State COLLEGIAN, wrote about Coach Prince's three seasons: "There were a lot of reasons for the collapse of the Ron Prince era, but the biggest might have been his lack of quality assistant coaches. It's possible that five of Prince's nine assistant coaches will have to take lesser jobs. This fact explains why K-State struggled so much this season. Snyder built K-State football with great assistants."[347]

THE NEED TO HIRE A NEW FOOTBALL COACH

The KU game was a watershed event for me. Our football team had not looked like this since the 1980's. I did not see any light at the end of the tunnel. Early on the Monday morning of November 3, 2008, Bob Krause, Jim Epps, and I met with Coach Prince. After thanking him for his dedication to the KSU football team, we told Ron we would be looking for a new coach at the end of the season.

After the season ended, Coach Prince received a $1.2 million buy-out and an additional $150,000 as part of a longevity bonus. With three games left to play, Missouri dominated K-State on November 8 and Nebraska easily beat Kansas State on November 15. K-State beat Iowa State at home 38 to 30 in Ron's final game. When I think back to all of our athletic teams from 1986 to 2009, the 2008 football season was the most devastating.

BILL SNYDER WAS MY CHOICE

The first person I considered as a replacement was our former head coach, Bill Snyder. I was not sure he would be interested. From 2006 to 2008, Bill and I had gone to many road games together. I enjoyed sitting next to him in the visiting AD's suite. Snyder never criticized Coach Prince's game management. Indeed, he was the same as a fan as he was a coach: calm, always calm.

After the season was over, Bob Krause and I went through a list of names for the job. But we met with Bill Snyder as soon as the 2008 season ended. This time Bill wanted time to consult with his family. Several times during this process, I dearly wished that he had consulted with his family like that at the end of the 2005 season—and then, stayed on to rebuild the K-State football program.

Despite his reputation as one of America's best football coaches, a multitude of K-State fans did not want us to bring Bill Snyder back. Many now claimed that he was too old; that the game had passed him by; and that his teams had losing records in 2004 and 2005.

My memory of Bill Snyder's record was simple: he had won 11 games in six of seven years from 1997 to 2003. Therefore, at the press conference in December of 2008, I stated: "I hope there is no one here who doubts that Coach Snyder will turn our football program around once again."

Kansas State football history had been extraordinarily bleak from 1935 to 1989. Bill Snyder had set the bar very high from 1989 to 2005. Anyone who followed Coach Snyder would have been under intense pressure. Because K-State had won so many games from 1993 to 2003, many of our fans had forgotten how difficult it is to field winning football teams at any number of schools.

Many of our fans forgot that many major universities had suffered from losing football programs for years and even decades. It is easy to put together a list of some BCS/Power 5 schools that found out how difficult it was to find a coach who was the right coach.

Indiana, Kentucky, Minnesota, and Notre Dame, for example, come to mind. Compared to K-State, all four of these schools have a much larger pool of outstanding football players in their regions. All four have excellent athletic facilites. All four can pay their head coaches whatever it takes to hire them. Yet these four schools—and many more—have seen how difficult it is to hire the right football coach.

Today, Indiana fans probably wish that they only had one short period in the past twenty years where their football team struggled. The truth is that from 1947 to 2010, Indiana has had 12 football coaches in a row with losing records. From 1962 to 2010, Kentucky has had nine coaches in a row with losing records.

From 1972 to 2010, Minnesota hired and fired seven coaches. Five of the seven had losing records. One of seven won half of his games. Only one of the seven had a winning record: Glen Mason, KU's former head coach. The University of Minnesota Golden Gophers won six National Championships from 1934 to 1960. Believe it or not, Minnesota has not even won a Big 10 title since 1967.[348]

Even Notre Dame, the most iconic football program in America, found it difficult to hire the right coach after Lou Holtz left in 1996.

With coaches like Knute Rockne, Frank Leahy, Ara Parseghian, and Dan Devine, Fighting Irish fans believe that every one of their new coaches should win every year.

Notre Dame has the traditions, the resources, and the national prestige to find exactly the right coach every time. Yet after Lou Holtz left in 1996, the Fighting Irish hired and fired three coaches in a row from 1997 to 2010.

If a school like Notre Dame can go for 13 years in a row without finding another Frank Leahy or Ara Parseghian, maybe BCS football fans throughout America should be a little more gracious when their alma mater fails to find the right coach.[349]

THE GRANT THORNTON AUDIT IN 2008-2009

In late September of 2008, the President and CEO of the Kansas Board of Regents, Reggie Robinson, called me to say the Board of Regents would be asking the Grant Thornton, LLP accounting firm to do an audit of specific funds at Kansas State. Grant Thornton called the audit "an exit analysis of certain non-State funded accounts administered and/or controlled by President Jon Wefald of Kansas State University or his direct subordinates."

On October 21, 2008, Grant Thornton wrote the following: "The key objective of this engagement was to evaluate whether financial transactions involving these employees within the specified accounts for the period 2003 to the present were for legitimate business purposes and were appropriately documented and approved."[350]

President Robinson called me to explain the purpose of the audit. He explained what the Board of Regents had in mind: First, Chancellor Bob Hemenway and I were the first CEO's to be covered by this new policy. Second, he told both of us when an exit analysis was concluded it would remain confidential. This meant that initially only the President of the Board of Regents and selected Regents would read the exit analysis. Third, when completed, the exit analysis would be shown to their successors at K-State and KU so that they could accept any of its recommendations.

The final report of Grant Thornton, entitled "Confidential Exit Analysis Related to the Retirement of Dr. Jon Wefald President of Kansas State University," was sent to Reggie Robinson on April 27, 2009. Several weeks before the final report was sent to the Board of Regents office, Robinson had received a rough draft of the exit analysis.

On a Friday afternoon, President Robinson called me to say he had quickly read the rough draft of the exit analysis. He was the only person in the Board of Regents office I ever talked with about the audit. I never saw the audit until it was publicly released. Robinson's initial view was that the exit analysis did not contain any illegalities. He believed that the issues cited in the audit were all solvable. Reggie told me that he would carefully read the audit.

On the following Monday, he called me for a second time. After reminding me that he was an attorney, Robinson said he had completely studied the Thornton audit. He repeated what he had told me two days earlier. There were no illegalities. Moreover, he stated all of the problems outlined in the exit analysis would be solved quickly by the new administration.

Robinson did highlight the major criticism in the audit—the lack of documentation for 13 selected disbursements to former coaches like Bill Snyder, Jim Wooldridge and, our former AD, Tim Weiser, totaling $845,000. Reggie told me again the new administration would quickly find where those monies went and how they were disbursed. The audit also outlined that I had delegated too much authority to Bob Krause over the years.

THE RELEASE OF THE "SECOND" PRINCE CONTRACT

The Thornton exit analysis remained confidential for the next thirty days. With the exception of an open records request from the MANHATTAN MERCURY, no other paper or media in the state had inquired about the Thornton exit analysis.

It was only after the release of a second secret contract between Bob Krause, our athletic director, and Coach Ron Prince that the audit became controversial. The media now demanded to see the audit. The

Board of Regents made the right decision. They released the audit.

Unknown to me or anyone else at K-State, on August 7, 2008, when the new contract between K-State and Ron Prince was announced, Bob Krause had signed a second separate and secret contract with Coach Prince for an additional $3.2 million. It had been negotiated between Neil Cornrich, Prince's agent, and Bob Krause. This contract would be paid out in 2015, 2016, and 2020.

One of the Kansas State attorneys had been going through e-mails on a completely separate contractual dispute filed by a former assistant coach for Ron Prince, Tim Tibesar. As the school attorney was going through e-mails pertaining to the Tibesar case, he came upon a number of confidential emails between Neil Cornrich and Bob Krause involving the undisclosed contract.[351]

I will always remember the morning when I was told about the secret emails. I was heartsick. It became the longest day of my life. It hurt even more because the athletic director, Bob Krause, had been my best friend and ally for over thirty years.

I was only a month away from retirement. I called Bob right away. He came to my office immediately. We went upstairs to meet with Richard Seaton, the university attorney, Chuck Reagan, and Jim Epps. I asked Bob many times how this could have happened.

One hour later, I had not heard one good answer. I could not sit down during the entire meeting. I never dreamed something like this could happen on my watch. I had never been in a meeting like this ever. My disquietude over this contract persisted for months.

After a university attorney had discovered this unknown contract in the second week of May 2009, it took several days to ascertain exactly what took place on August 7, 2008. On May 20, 2009, Kansas State and its athletic corporation filed suit to have the "secret contract" between Ron Prince and Bob Krause declared invalid.

Bob Krause had negotiated the agreement in the late summer of 2008 with Prince's attorney, Neil Cornich, an Ohio sports agent. The agreement would require K-State to pay a total of $3.2 million in three deferred payments to a Ron Prince corporation.

Jim Epps, the associate AD, announced: "On May 11, 2009, I

learned of a secret deferred compensation agreement that Bob Krause apparently negotiated with Ron Prince's attorney. This deal was constructed as a further supplement to the buyout provision contained in Prince's contract. I do not know why Bob concealed this agreement from everyone until it was discovered last week."[352]

On August 10, 2009, attorneys for Ron Prince filed a counterclaim against Kansas State athletics seeking $3 million in punitive damages. On September 11, 2010, lawyers for Kansas State and Ron Prince met for a hearing in hopes of a summary judgment from the Riley County District Court Judge, David Stutzman. The hearing lasted for two hours. Judge Stutzman rendered no decision.

The judge declared that he had to review more documents regarding the case before making a ruling. According to an article by Cole Manbeck in the MANHATTAN MERCURY on September 12, 2010, the attorneys for Kansas State pointed "to several distinct issues that they believed to be in their favor in the previous day's hearing: Jon Wefald, the university president at the time, never knew about the MOU (Memo of Understanding) and never signed off on it, thus making the MOU invalid."[353]

The attorneys for Ron Prince disagreed: "It's a moot point, stating the MOU was negotiated on behalf of the Intercollegiate Athletics Council, a private corporation separate from K-State." Cole Manbeck quoted Prince's attorneys: "If we were trying to bind K-State to the agreement, I could understand why the K-State president (Wefald) would want to know about it. . .But it's not his (Wefald's) contract; it's not his (Wefald's) corporation (IAC); it's not his (Wefald's) money; it's the IAC's (Intercollegiate Athletic Council) money."

The major arguments of Ron Prince's attorneys amounted to the following: they either viewed Bob Krause as the co-president of Kansas State University or that he was the "president" of the athletic department. There is no example of any other major Division I athletic director ever signing two contracts—one for public consumption and the other one that was strictly private.[354]

Kansas State now faced an extraordinary legal tangle. Even if Bob Krause was the IAC president in August of 2008, no other athletic director had ever argued the title of IAC president was of any major consequence. Everyone had viewed the position as ceremonial.

Kansas State and its athletic corporation filed suit on May 20, 2009 to declare the second Prince contract null and void. I had hoped that Bob would have stated that he did not have the authority to sign this contract; that he would publicly explain his reasons for signing this contract; and that he would apologize.

On May 6, 2011, the attorneys for Kansas State announced that a settlement had been reached between Ron Prince and K-State athletics. Prince and his attorney had been asking for the full payment of $3.2 million. The university agreed to pay one lump sum of $1.65 million to Prince's company. Prince had earlier received $1.2 million from the agreed to public contract of August 7, 2008.[355]

I can only speculate on the reasons why Bob signed this second contract. First, he might have believed that Coach Prince would win seven or eight games in the fall of 2008—and, then, renegotiate a new five-year contract. Second, he might have developed a point of view that he had the authority to run the department without any interference from anybody, including me. Third, I have no idea.

Bob Krause had ignored the standard protocol found at any Division I university that only the president could authorize a major contract to any head football or men's basketball coach—especially one of historic proportions.

The contract we all signed on August 7, 2008 was more than fair and reasonable. On the same day of May 20, 2009 that our school filed suit to declare the secret agreement invalid, I had to dismiss a long time and close friend, Bob Krause.

A POSTSCRIPT

Bob Krause was a dear friend and colleague for 32 years. Sadly, Bob died on December 16, 2015. He had worked for me for five years at Southwest State University in Marshall, Minnesota, four years in the Minnesota State University System in St. Paul, and twenty-three years at K-State from 1986 to 2009. In all of these positions, Bob

Krause was an exceptional leader. He was the ultimate problem-solver. He was a visionary. He could quickly size up almost any problem or situation. And he always worked superbly well with students.

Bob's work at Kansas State was outstanding. He helped turn around K-State's enrollment. He became one of Bill Snyder's best supporters. He was the major fiscal planner for our new football and athletic facilities. He was a key leader for our new BRI building and for our new KSU campuses in Salina and in Olathe. He played a very important role in the DHS selection of Kansas State for NBAF. In my career and in my life, I will always consider Bob Krause as one of my best friends.

STILL, THE 2ND CONTRACT HAPPENED ON MY WATCH

As I thought about the secret contract, I realized it happened on my watch. I had to take responsibility too. When the second contract was made public, I apologized to everyone at the university and to our supporters around the country. I should have been more aggressive with the leaders of the athletic department and the AD during the entire summer of 2008.

Despite the meeting of Jim Epps, Bob Krause, and me on March 24, 2008, when we agreed that any new contract for Coach Prince for 2008 would be for one year only and include a salary increase of $500,000, I should have been asking questions that entire summer. I did not do that. But I did recall President Harry Truman's sign on his White House desk: "The Buck Stops Here."

If you are president of a university, a corporation, or the nation, you have to take the blame for the bad decisions if you want to have credit for the good decisions. I knew that our best American presidents apologized for their mistakes.

But there were many Presidents and business leaders who could never apologize for their big mistakes. Indeed, the list of people in politics, business, and sports who were/are incapable of an apology for anything is quite long actually. A short list includes Richard Nixon, Lyndon B. Johnson, Steve Jobs, Jamie Diamond, Donald Sterling, Paula Dean, Martha Stewart, Lance Armstrong, Pete Rose, Roger Clemens,

Bill Clinton, Hillary Clinton, Barack Obama, and Donald Trump.

Two recent excellent presidents did apologize for their decisions. Even though the Bay of Pigs invasion of Cuba by Cuban exiles had been planned by the former administration of President Eisenhower in 1959 and 1960, President Kennedy supported the plan in April of 1961. It turned into a disaster. But President Kennedy said: "I assume full responsibility because this happened on my watch."

In 1985, two major officials in President Ronald Reagan's Office of National Security, John Poindexter and Lieutenant Colonel Oliver North, pleaded guilty to selling arms to Iran and giving the funds from those sales to the Nicaraguan Contras. Both actions violated congressional legislation.

After the Iran Contra scandal became public in 1987, Reagan declared: "Let me say I take full responsibility for my actions and for those of my administration. As angry as I may be in some who served me, I am still the one who must answer to the American people for this behavior."

I had hired Bob Krause as our athletic director on June 6, 2008. Later that year, I sensed that the job of athletic director was not a good fit for either Bob or the department. We talked about this several times in early 2009 and he resigned from his position as athletic director on January 27, 2009 to be effective on March 31, 2009. On April 1, 2009, I appointed Bob Krause as the Director of Development for the K-State Olathe Innovation Campus. I had to let him go from that position on May 20, 2009.

THE IMPORTANCE OF KSU'S TRANSITION AUDIT REPORT

On November 19, 2009, the new president of Kansas State University, Kirk Schulz, presented to the Kansas Board of Regents a report entitled: TRANSITION AUDIT FINAL REPORT. On June 29, 2009, President Schulz held a campus-wide forum to hear faculty, staff, and student concerns with the issues raised in the audit. Schulz announced the establishment of a peer committee that was tasked with analyzing the issues listed in the audit.

A number of faculty, staff, and student leaders were appointed to the Audit Oversight Committee. They included the following: the Chair of the Audit Committee, Brian Spooner, the Director of the Division of Biology; Melody LeHew, the Faculty Senate President; Fred Fairchild, a former President of the Faculty Senate; Carolyn Elliott, the Classified Senate President; Dalton Henry, the President of the Student Senate, Lori Goetsch, the Dean of the Libraries, and a number of others. These faculty, staff, and student leaders spent over four months in the summer and fall of 2009 studying and analyzing all aspects of the Final Report.[356]

The Kansas State University TRANSITION AUDIT FINAL REPORT focused initially on the 13 missing transactions totaling $845,000 that had been highlighted in the Grant Thornton LLP Confidential Exit Audit Analysis on April 27, 2009.

The 13 missing transactions totaling $845,000 were identified early in the school's investigation of those funds. In the KSU TRANSITION AUDIT FINAL REPORT, it indicated that the 13 items had been thoroughly examined and that there was "complete reconciliation to the payees."

This was a pivotal finding. This meant that the 13 selected cash disbursements totalling $845,000 were quickly located and that the disbursements in question for Bill Snyder, Tim Weiser, Jim Wooldridge, and Bob Krause went to the appropriate employees as intended.[357]

The Kansas State University TRANSITION AUDIT FINAL REPORT of November 19, 2009 provided four summary recommendations:

"First, it is apparent to us that Jon Wefald invested too much power in Bob Krause and provided inadequate oversight and supervision of him. Additionally, Dr. Wefald did not place adequate checks and balances on financial controls, allowing Mr. Krause far too much influence over a variety of University-related funds. Mr. Krause treated these funds as one pool of money, which created a variety of accounting and governance issues."

"Second, we have concerns regarding the scholarship deficit that accrued over several years. We were unable to assign specific blame for this oversight. But we believe that this deficit resulted from a lack of communication between the University administration and the Foundation."

"Third, we have general concerns regarding the University's relationship with NISTAC, because NISTAC's overly complex structure clouds its benefits to the University. The benefits from NISTAC need to be better defined and communicated to the University and to the public, so they can evaluate NISTAC's overall utility."

"Finally, we are encouraged by the current administration's approach to financial and decisional transparency. This is most apparent in Athletics, where the new corporate structure encourages strong oversight by University administrators and the new Athletic Director has adopted a new code of transparency and fiscal accountability."[358]

I agree with and completely accept the four Summary Final Recommendations of the Kansas State University TRANSITION AUDIT FINAL REPORT of November 19, 2009.

In my years as president, I implemented a policy of delegation and empowerment. The meaning of this strategy was simple—meaning that when our leadership team hired a vice-president, an associate vice-president, a dean, a department head, or an athletic director, they always had considerable authority to make decisions. Even though we had a consistent policy of delegating authority, this was never an absolute.

A policy of empowerment can only work if everyone operates as a team. Still, the CEO ultimately has to be in charge. The president of any institution must make sure that everything is done correctly and according to the policies and rules of the Kansas Board of Regents.

In any major organization, mistakes are inevitable. In my years, vice-presidents, deans, athletic directors, and department heads made many decisions to offer contracts to new staff and faculty members.

If something like the second contract for Coach Prince had happened in 1995 or 2006, I would have made sure that this would never be repeated. I would have implemented the appropriate rules. Because this contract was only discovered a month before I retired, I had to leave the solution of this problem to the next administration.

OUR LEADERSHIP TEAM LEFT BEHIND SUPERB HEAD COACHES

After 23 years, we left behind the best head coaches in the history of Kansas State sports. That included Coach Bill Snyder. He was the most successful football coach in the history of K-State and one of the greatest Division I head football coaches in America. He turned the football program around for the second time after 2009.

Three years after his return, the Wildcats won ten games in 2011 and earned a place in the Cotton Bowl. In 2012, the Snyder-coached football team won 11 games, won the Big 12 Championship, and played in the BCS Fiesta Bowl. And, fittingly, our eminent and legendary head football coach was selected to be in the College Football Hall of Fame on December 8, 2015.

From 2007 to 2012, Frank Martin became one of the best men's basketball coaches in the history of K-State basketball by going to the NCAA tournament in four out of five years. Importantly, Frank Martin won more games in his first five years than Jack Gardner, Tex Winter, and Jack Hartman. As the authors of the KSU 2015-16 Media Guide for Men's Basketball concluded: Frank Martin "led the school to arguably its greatest stretch in its long and storied history."

Deb Patterson became the best women's basketball coach in the school's history. From 2002 to 2009, Deb's teams advanced to six NCAA Tournaments, won two Big 12 Championships in 2004 and 2008, and won the WNIT Championship in 2006.

From 2001 to 2009, Suzie Fritz's volleyball team was selected for the NCAA Tournament in seven of the next eight years—including winning the 2003 Big 12 Championship. Coach Fritz has won more games and advanced to more NCAA tournaments than any volleyball coach in Kansas State history.

The baseball team, under Brad Hill's excellent coaching, was selected to three NCAA Regional tournaments in 2009, 2010, 2011, and won the Big 12 title in 2013. Cliff Rovelto has been a great track and field head coach at K-State since 1992. He continued to have elite and nationally competitive track and field teams after 2009.

All of K-State's head coaches continued to have winning teams after 2009 in the Big 12 Conference. They kept having success against the University of Kansas. Indeed, the LAWRENCE JOURNAL WORLD sports columnist, Tom Keegan, wrote a column on July 15, 2011 about all of the games played between KU and KSU during the school year 2010-11. The headline was "KSU 13, KANSAS 1, REALLY!" Across the board, our coaches were successful.

THE VITAL IMPORTANCE OF BEING IN THE BIG 12 AFTER 2009

Our leadership team had made sure after 1986 that K-State would never be dropped from the Big 8 Conference. I was totally determined to make sure that Kansas State University would not slip into a mid-major conference. I would not let the football program disappear into the night. Instead, we transformed the football program into a nationally elite program. All of this led directly to Kansas State becoming a valued member of the Big 12 in 1994.

From 1990 to 1994, I was one of several Big 8 CEO's who played a pivotal role in putting together the new Big 12 Conference. The Big 12 Conference has been an extraordinary success story for Kansas State University. It will be for years to come.

From 1987 to 2009, our leadership team completely rebuilt the football, basketball, baseball, volleyball, and track and field facilities. On July 1, 2009, Kansas State University had excellent and nationally competitive athletic facilities. There was no question about this: The future for the athletic teams of Kansas State University was bright, very bright indeed.

Chapter 9

From 2000 To 2009: A Plethora Of Successes

In the decade of the 1990's, Kansas State's strategic priorities were based on university-wide initiatives. The entire university needed to be turned around first. Our leadership team had to turn the enrollment around, sharply improve private giving, build a first-class library, dramatically improve the university's research and graduate programs, initiate a major effort in information technology, and expand our efforts in diversity.

Between 1998 and 2009, Provost Jim Coffman and Duane Nellis, his successor in 2004, requested the deans and department heads to identify the programs that were already very good and what measures were needed to upgrade them into national excellence. No school can be good at everything. We were now asking our departments and colleges to set several academic program priorities.

THE GOAL OF BECOMING A TOP TEN LAND GRANT UNIVERSITY

By 1999 and 2000, our major goal was to elevate K-State into one of the nation's Top Ten land grant universities. John Johnson, a professor of Library Science and a Faculty Senate leader, had been investigating for several years exactly where K-State ranked among all land grant schools in America.

He focused on the "American Research University Data Center" website collection located at the University of Florida. After looking at measures rating universities such as research dollars, federal research, academy members, faculty awards, national merit scholars, endowments, and annual giving, Johnson came up with a brilliant idea: namely, to compare K-State to other land grant universities without medical schools.[359]

I never cared who came up with a great idea. If the idea was good for KSU, my motto was: let's do it. John Johnson reminded us the best medical schools had as much or more federal research funding as the main campus. Michigan State, Minnesota, and Wisconsin were all land grant schools. But all three had superb medical schools.

In April of 2004, Johnson analyzed all of the relevant data and determined that K-State was ranked 17th of all the land grant universities without medical schools. Now we had to get better.[360]

THE TARGETED EXCELLENCE PROGRAM

Initiated by Provost Jim Coffman in 2003 and implemented by our new provost after June of 2004, Duane Nellis, we launched our "Targeted Excellence" program. This new university program would fund selected and key interdisciplinary research projects at about $2 million a year for three years.

The goal was to find niches where the university already had strengths, to give those programs targeted funding increases, and to upgrade those academic programs into national prominence.

In September of 2003, our first Targeted Excellence program was announced for pre-proposals—54 of them were received for consideration. The recommended proposals for funding were made by a panel of on-campus research faculty and off-campus scholars. For the first year proposals, $1.25 million was set aside for funding. The total amount allocated over five years would be $5.38 million.

The panel looked for wide-ranging and interdisciplinary research teams. For the first round, the final research proposals chosen included Biomaterials by Design; a Center of Nanostructure Studies with Ultrafast Lasers; Enhancing Military History and Security Studies; a K-State Initiative in Genome Biology; and Food Safety and Animal Health: Protecting America's Health and Agriculture.[361]

KEYNOTING OUR FOOD SAFETY AND ANIMAL HEALTH PROGRAM

Kansas State had built up a strong research faculty in programs protecting and sustaining America's food supply over thirty years. In

1999, our leadership team decided that our No. 1 university-wide research priority would be food safety and animal health.

We soon assembled a national class scientific team made up of over 130 superb researchers from the Colleges of Veterinary Medicine, Agriculture, Arts and Sciences, Human Ecology, and Engineering and 12 of their top academic departments.[362]

This interdisciplinary team of researchers combined their scientific expertise to focus both on intentional and unintentional threats to the nation's food supply. This team of 130 scientists and researchers soon put K-State right in the middle of a national agenda to protect both human health and animal health.

When our food safety and animal program became the school's No. 1 priority, I knew that Kansas State University would become the leading university in America in this important arena.

Humans and animals alike are threatened throughout the world by numerous transgenic organisms—including Anthrax, West Nile Virus, Asian Bird Flu, Ebola, Marburg, Nipah, Rabies, Lassa, SARS, and Mad Cow Disease. In a POPULAR SCIENCE article in October of 2012, David Quammen writes: "About 60 per cent of human infectious diseases are zoonoses, meaning animal infections that spill into people. They result from infection by one of six types of pathogens—viruses, bacteria, fungi, protists, prions, and worms." This means that most of the world's worst pandemic diseases from 1945 to the present were spread from animals to people.[363]

In March of 1999, Ron Trewyn and Jim Guikema prepared a major white paper entitled: THE HOMELAND DEFENSE FOOD SAFETY, SECURITY, AND EMERGENCY PREPAREDNESS PROGRAM. This document listed the major research areas for farm animals and field crops. It underscored the fact that agriculture was the most vital industry in America. At the very same time, several Congressional leaders were warning Americans of agro-terromism threats.[364]

Senator Pat Roberts of Kansas, for example, had long argued that America's food supply was crucial to our national security. In 1999, Roberts was the Chairman of the U.S. Senate Subcommittee on

Emerging Threats and Capabilities. He invited our top animal health scholars to testify before his subcommittee on October 27, 1999.

Our delegation included Ralph Richardson, the Dean of Veterinary Medicine, James Marsden, a superb animal scientist, Jerry Jaax, a top expert on animal diseases, Ron Trewyn, and me. This U.S. Senate testimony was a tipping point for our animal health program.[365]

THE EMERGENCE OF OUR BIOSECURITY RESEARCH INSTITUTE

Meanwhile, our state legislative leaders were talking more about enhancing the research capabilities of Kansas, Kansas State, and Wichita State. In the summer of 2001, those leaders included Kent Glasscock, the Speaker of the House, Kenny Wilk, the Chair of the House Appropriations Committee, Dave Kerr, the President of the State Senate, and Steve Morris, the Chair of the Senate Finance Committee.

Representative Wilk and Senator Morris held hearings that summer throughout the state on these special university research projects. They included future buildings for the three largest universities: a life sciences facility for the KU Medical School; a food safety and animal health building for Kansas State; and an aviation research facility for Wichita State.

In early January of 2002, Senators Dave Kerr and Steve Morris, and Representatives Kent Glasscock and Kenny Wilk spearheaded a plan to have the Kansas Legislature travel to K-State for a meeting to focus on the importance of these new research facilities. On January 17, 2002, 110 state legislators made the trip to K-State for this meeting of state legislators. It might be the only time in the history of Kansas when the state legislature met outside of Topeka.

After Senator Roberts' major address, KU's Michael Welch made a compelling case for the Life Sciences Innovation Center at the KU Medical Center; Wichita State's Don Beggs outlined the case for the Aviation Engineering Complex at WSU; and I argued the case for a KSU Food Safety and Animal Health Research Facility.

Kenny Wilk, the Chair of House Appropriations, called the meeting "truly magical and defining." This historic and bipartisan legislative meeting set the stage for the legislature to approve $120 million in funds for the three new research buildings.[366]

The Chair of the Board of Regents, Clay Blair, became a key leader among the regents for the three new research buildings. Although Blair was only a regent from 1999 to 2002, he was selected twice to be the chair. Clay had a brilliant knack for developing excellent partnerships with top leaders in the legislature. He helped convince the key Senate and House leaders to back this important legislation.

The 2002 legislature approved $120 million in funds for the three state universities to construct major research buildings. The bill created a University Research and Development Enhancement Corporation. After his term as a regent, Blair was selected to chair the URDEC. His mission was to oversee the construction of the projects and to help control their costs.[367]

After the legislature passed legislation in the spring of 2002 for the new buildings, Tom Rawson estimated that the Biosecurity Research Institute (BRI) building would cost $54 million. To pay for the BRI, the state agreed to issue 30-year bonds at a cost of roughly $2.4 million a year. The state would pick up the bond payments for the first five years of the bond payments and K-State would pay the bond payments for the last 25 years.

Key members of the president's staff were worried about the difficulty of paying out $2.4 million a year for the final 25 years of the bonds. That gave our team pause. All of us worried whether we could afford $2.4 million a year and where the monies would come from. Ron Trewyn argued that these yearly costs would leave little room for reinvestment in K-State's research infrastructure and new research proposals.[368]

THE PIVOTAL DECISION TO BUILD THE BRI

As the new chair of the Kansas Research and Development

Enhancement Corporation (KRDEC), Clay Blair would supervise the construction of the new research buildings. In the fall of 2002, Clay called to ask me if K-State was in or out on the funding for our new BRI building. He reported that KU was totally committed to funding their new Life Sciences building. But he said WSU was doubtful they would move forward on their new Aviation building.

In his call, Clay was blunt: "I need Kansas State to make a definitive decision on whether your school will or will not proceed with the new building!" At our staff meeting the next day, I got right to Clay's question. We had to make the decision now.

Jim Coffman, Tom Rawson, and Ron Trewyn all leaned against the new project for the same reasons: one, the steep costs of paying out $2.4 million a year for 25 years for the bond payments; two, the monies would come from our yearly research overhead funds (SRO); and third, the SRO funds needed for investment in new research infrastructure would be sharply reduced.

Decision day was here. We had to settle right now whether this new BRI building should be built. My attitude was simple. It was now or never. Yes, it would be a calculated risk. But I knew that most great leaders in history took big calculated risks.

I recalled Julius Caesar's decision to risk crossing the Rubicon River in 49 B.C. After conquering most of Europe from 58 B.C. to 50 B.C. with eight legions, the Roman Senate saw Caesar as a threat and left him with one legion of 5,000 soldiers. Top Roman leaders wanted Caesar to retire in Spain. But Caesar took that one legion to the Rubicon River—which divided Rome from the rest of the Empire.

Julius Caesar shouted to his troops: "If we do not cross the Rubicon, we will be sorry. If we do cross the Rubicon, the whole world will be sorry." They crossed. Caesar became the first Emperor of Rome in 49 B.C. The Roman Empire lasted for 400 more years.

If we said no to the BRI, I knew we would live to regret it. If we took the bet to construct a new state-of-the-art BRI building, I believed K-State would become the No. 1 school in America in animal health. Jawaharlal Nehru once said: "Life is a game of cards. The hand that is dealt you represents determinism; the way you play it is free will." We decided to move forward.

On Friday, October 24, 2003, K-State broke ground for the new $54 million BRI. A good crowd assembled, including Senator Roberts, Governor Sebelius, the Regents' Chair, Janice DeBauge, and the URDEC Chair, Clay Blair. Ron Trewyn declared that the new BRI would allow our scientists to do research on infectious diseases that threaten the nation's livestock industry and study meat processing methods to bring safer meats to consumers.[369]

THE IMPORTANCE OF BUILDING THE NEW BRI

On October 27, 2006, the Biosecurity Research Institute was dedicated—which we named Pat Roberts Hall. How vital was the construction of the BRI for the future of Kansas State University?

Without the BRI, the Department of Homeland Security would never have selected K-State for the National Bio and Agro Defense Facility (NBAF). Without the BRI, K-State would have had little or no chance for a new animal health campus in Olathe.

In reflecting back to whether or not K-State should move forward with building the BRI, Clay Blair told me on October 14, 2012: "When I got into the public sector as a regent in 1998, I noticed how timid so many of our so-called state leaders were and how so many lacked vision or initiative. But, when it came to the BRI, you were the center of the K-State piece; you had the most risk and the most to gain if you would just step up. Guess what, you did step up and few will know. But that's what happened."[370]

BY 2005-06, KANSAS CITY IS PROMOTING ANIMAL HEALTH

Often, timing is everything. In 2005 and 2006, the Greater Kansas City Chamber of Commerce, the Kansas City Area Development Council (KCADC), and the Kansas City Area Life Sciences Institute, Inc., combined to launch an Animal Health Initiative. It united the region's corporations, universities, governments, and civic leaders in both Missouri and Kansas.

In 2006, KCADC hired Brakke Consulting to quantify the area's animal health industry. Their analysts found that the region from Manhattan, Kansas to Columbia, Missouri had the world's largest concentration of animal health industry assets.[371]

Brakke's final report projected that a number of major animal health companies would locate somewhere in this region. Today, there are now 200 companies and 20,000 people working in the larger Kansas City animal health industry complex. These companies accounted for more than one-third of the global sales of the $19 billion animal health industry. From 2006 to 2010, 24 animal health businesses were recruited to the Animal Health Corridor.[372]

K-State was firmly on Kansas City's radar screen now. Our school's animal health programs were gaining traction in the metropolitan area. With the dedication of the new $54 million BRI facility in 2006, key leaders in the Kansas City corridor understood how vital K-State could be for the region's animal health corridor.[373]

MIGHT THERE BE A K-STATE CAMPUS IN JOHNSON COUNTY?

For decades, K-State alums in the Kansas City region hoped that we would have a campus one day in Johnson County. But this dream seemed futile—mainly because the Kansas Board of Regents in the mid-1970's had divided the state up into so-called Geographic Service Areas. The three geographic regions were as follows: KU and Pittsburg State would control eastern Kansas; Emporia State and Wichita State would command south central Kansas; and KSU and Fort Hays State would lead in western Kansas.[374]

This division of the state in the 1970's meant one thing for Kansas State: KU would have veto power in Johnson County. By definition, this key county was at once the most populated and wealthiest county. In each of these geographic areas, the CEO's would have veto authority to keep other universities out of their region.

This meant that the Chancellor of KU could thwart any K-State academic program or campus that our school might like in Johnson County. In the early 1990's, Provost Coffman asked his counterpart at KU if we could offer several academic programs in Johnson County. The response was always no. There seemed to be no chance for K-State to have a campus in Johnson County in my lifetime.

Indeed, it might take a miracle. Enter the Mayor of Olathe, Kansas—Michael Copeland. He believed that Olathe needed a major college campus similar to the KU Edwards campus in Overland Park. On March 8, 2005, Mayor Copeland set up a breakfast meeting at a Kansas City Plaza Hotel with Clay Blair, now the Chairman of the Kansas Bioscience Authority (KBA), Bob Krause, and me.[375]

THE KEY ROLE OF MICHAEL COPELAND AND CLAY BLAIR

At the breakfast, Mayor Copeland told us that he convinced the Olathe City Council in 1995 to utilize the city's existing land of 100 acres near K-10 Highway for future economic opportunities. Both Copeland and Blair proposed that Olathe, Kansas State, and the KBA should work together on a new three-way partnership—with the city of Olathe donating the 100 acres to the KBA and K-State.

I told Mayor Copeland and Clay Blair that they were missing a key fact. I outlined how the Board of Regents had divided the state up into three regions in the 1970's—meaning that the KU Chancellor had total veto authority over K-State coming into Johnson County. In short, this meant Kansas State would need the imprimatur of the KU Chancellor Bob Hemenway to come in. This was hardly a given.[376]

THE KEY ROLE OF REGENT DICK BOND

Enter Dick Bond of Overland Park, Kansas. Dick was a superb Republican state senator from Johnson County. From 1997 to 2000, he was the President of the Kansas State Senate. In 2002, Governor Bill Graves appointed Dick Bond as a member of the Board of

Regents. He served until 2007. He was the chair from 2004 to 2005. Dick was one of the most influential KU graduates anywhere in Kansas. He was a splendid regent and the quickest wit in the West.

After a monthly regents meeting in late 2005, I was preparing to drive back to Manhattan for the thousandth time. Bond beckoned me. He asked if KSU would be willing to help KU get a key bill passed in the 2007 legislative session—which would allow Johnson County to have the "legislative authority to levy a tax for higher education facilities and programs." If authorized by the legislature and passed by the county's voters, the tax monies would provide new funding for the KU Edwards Campus and the KU Med Center.

Dick was politely asking Sue Peterson and me to help KU pass this legislation in the 2007 session. Dick said, if that happened, we could then request similar language for K-State either in Manhattan or Salina. On the way home, I had a "hallelujah" moment. I yelled at Bob Krause: "This is the moment we have been waiting for."[377]

After a day or so, I called Dick Bond back. With a bit of Norman Vincent Peale and a touch of Machiavelli, I threw out a plan. I told Dick that K-State would assist KU in getting the appropriate bill passed in the 2007 session. Then, I threw Dick a curve ball.

I told Dick that KU alone might not be able to convince the voters of Johnson County in 2008 to pass their tax levy. Pausing for a deep breath, I asked Bond to imagine a team of 45,000 Jayhawkers and 25,000 Wildcats in Johnson County working in tandem to forge a historic partnership that would get this tax package passed.[378]

As I was praying, Regent Bond said he liked my idea. Then, it dawned on me: K-State might just fulfill an old dream of having a new campus in Johnson County. Dick, once again, was trying to help KU and K-State at the same time. I knew Bob Hemenway was the decider. But I knew that Dick Bond was a major KU player as well.

Indeed, as it turned out, Bond was a master political strategist. In a few days, he called back. I was stunned. Dick had already asked Bob Regnier and Bill Hall to drive over and meet with Bob Hemenway in Lawrence. Regnier was a K-Stater and the CEO of the Blue Valley State Bank. Hall was the President of the Hall Foundation.

Their mission was simple—to ask Bob Hemenway to back K-State coming into Johnson County.[379]

DICK BOND GETS CHANCELLOR BOB HEMENWAY ON BOARD

Their pitch to Chancellor Hemenway was cloaked in the historic tradition of enlightened self-interest—namely, that K-State and its thousands of Wildcats would tip the scales in favor of a county tax plan that would benefit everyone: the KU Med Center, the KU Edwards campus, and the new K-State, Olathe Campus. Dick could not have picked two better movers and shakers to do this job than Bob Regnier and Bill Hall.

Dick called me with the great news. The Chancellor had given his blessing for this new KU and KSU partnership. Bob wanted to call the new partnership the Johnson County Education and Research Triangle. That it was called.[380]

Nelson Galle of Manhattan, Kansas became the next Chair of the Board of Regents on July 1, 2006. Nelson Galle was a superb leader in business and education. Everyone viewed him as fair and knowledgeable. Galle, a KSU graduate, and Bond, a KU graduate, worked as a team on a variety of subjects. These two pals persuaded their Regent colleagues to back this new KU/KSU partnership.

In the 2007 session, Senator Barbara Allen, the Chairman of the Senate Taxation Committee and aided by KU and KSU, got the Triangle tax legislation passed. The bill passed a full year ahead of time.

Bob Hemenway and I immediately called on Annabeth Surbaugh, the Chair of the Johnson County Commission. We asked her to put the sales tax plan on the November 2008 ballot. Her fellow Johnson County commissioners did exactly that. The proposed one-eighth cent sales tax had to be approved by a majority vote.[381]

Bill Hall agreed to raise the money to conduct the fall Triangle campaign in 2008. Bill and his excellent team raised over $300,000. Fred Logan, an influential Kansas City attorney, agreed to be the campaign chairman. The campaign's executive committee included

Mary Birch, Bob Regnier, Bill Hall, Dick Bond, Fred Logan, Bob Hemenway, Bob Clark, David Adkins, Laura McKnight, and me.

The Triangle organization hired the former president of the Overland Park Chamber of Commerce, Mary Birch, as the executive director. She provided excellent leadership. The campaign had hundreds of volunteers who did post card mailings and put up hundreds of yard signs. I went to ten meetings. Everyone knew that K-State would play a key role in the upcoming county elections.[382]

THE JOHNSON COUNTY SALES TAX PASSES EASILY

The Triangle tax of one-eighth cent sales tax passed in the November, 2008 general election by a substantial margin: 57 per cent to 43 per cent. Importantly, this sales tax was passed without any sunset amendment.

I doubt that a similar county tax increase would have any chance of passing today in Johnson County or anywhere else. It passed because KU and K-State alums worked together like we had all gone to the same school.

We proved again that bipartisan politics always works well in either Kansas or America. This county tax provided $5 million per year to each of the three university entities in perpetuity: the KU Edwards campus, the KU Cancer Research Center, and the K-State, Olathe Campus. Bill Hall estimated that this meant each school had the floating equivalent of an endowment of over $300 million.

Dick Bond declared publicly that the passing of the Triangle tax measure "is one of a kind in the nation where a county passes a tax to support state university programs within that county."[383] Let me put it this way—today it would be virtually impossible to find one county in America where its citizens would pass a tax to support the academic programs of two statewide funded public universities.

Mayor Copeland stated that his city council would approve an agreement with KSU and the KBA. On a 92-acre plot next to Olathe Northwest High School, K-State's new campus would be located in the new Olathe business park. In the next several years, Kansas State, Olathe constructed a beautiful new 108,000-square-foot building that cost $28 million.[384]

In 2012, the leaders of Kansas State, Olathe outlined the wide-ranging academic programs the new school would have in animal health and food safety. The initial academic programs would include graduate-level Master's and Ph.D programs for students in the bio-sciences, biotechnology, and animal health and food safety.[385]

In 2008, Dan Richardson became the new Chief Executive Officer of our new campus in Olathe. Recruited by Bob Krause, Dan had perfect qualifications. A graduate of the KSU College of Veterinary Medicine, he was the Vice-President for Hill's Pet Nutrition for years. Krause had spent several years working closely with Mayor Mike Copeland, the Olathe City Council, and Clay Blair to solve a variety of problems facing our new Olathe campus.[386]

HOW K-STATE GOT A NEW CAMPUS IN OLATHE, KANSAS

For over a generation, K-State alums wondered why our school was not more involved in Johnson County. This new campus happened because we never gave up. We waited for the right opportunity. We took calculated risks. We participated in county and state politics. When the door opened a little bit, we found a way to walk through it. We did what good leaders have always done.

Two superb Johnson County leaders, Clay Blair and Dick Bond, played decisive roles in our success. Both were Republicans. But they were not political partners. Their paths hardly ever crossed. Our K-State team had to be very strategic. We had to operate on two different political tracks. One track dealt directly with the two Olathe leaders, Clay Blair and Mayor Copeland. The other track dealt with Regent Dick Bond and KU's Chancellor, Bob Hemenway.

In my 23 years as K-State's president, this was the most complicated political puzzle I faced. For one thing, the KU Chancellor had to say yes before we could have a new Johnson County campus. That never seemed likely. For another thing, if I could not persuade Dick

Bond that KSU could make the difference in passing a sales tax increase, our chances for a new campus would be zero.

If Mayor Copeland decided that the political and economic odds for his city were too steep, the dream of a new campus vanishes. But two friends joined forces for our new campus in Olathe: Michael Copeland and Clay Blair. As a major supporter of the project, Clay helped convince the mayor to offer city land to KSU for the campus. In a July 15, 2006 LAWRENCE JOURNAL WORLD column, Dolph Simons wrote: "The gift of land is the result of a team effort. However, the prime leader in the project was Clay Blair."[387]

Over many years, it seems that many Kansas State leaders often missed opportunities. Sometimes, they might have viewed the opportunity as impossible. Other times, they might have been unwilling to take calculated risks. With our new campus in Olathe, Mayor Michael Copeland and Regent Dick Bond realized we were both players and risk-takers.

Mayor Copeland talked about my role in a letter on July 15, 2011: "On those rare occasions when serendipity and vision meld, great things happen. And, Jon, no one deserves more credit for having that vision than you." But to have a fanatical Jayhawk like Dick Bond write something nice about a K-Stater is special. In a letter on September of 2011, Dick wrote: "Jon Wefald played a critical role in the the passage of the Johnson County Triangle Tax. Without Jon and Kansas State, I don't believe the issue would have prevailed."[388]

COULD K-STATE EVER HAVE A CHANCE TO LAND NBAF?

Whether it was 2000 or 2004, no one ever believed that K-State would have a shot at a new national animal health facility that would parallel the Center for Disease Control in Atlanta. Few of us had ever heard of Plum Island, including me. It was an 840-acre island several miles from Long Island, New York. In 1954, the USDA acquired Plum Island from the U.S. Army for animal health research. The USDA's mission was to respond to foot and mouth disease outbreaks in the United States, Mexico, and Canada in 1954.[389]

The Plum Island facility had developed diagnostics for suspected cases of foot and mouth disease and produced vaccines for FMD, classic swine fever, and the vesicular stomatitus virus. In June of 2003, a presidential directive transferred the Plum Island complex from the USDA to Homeland Security. DHS officials were soon complaining that the Plum Island facility was antiquated.[390]

In 2005, the Department of Homeland Security decided to build a new state-of-the-art B-Level 4 facility. It would be called the National Bio and Agro Defense Facility (NBAF). The NBAF Facility would be about 600,000 square feet. It would focus on human, zoonotic, and foreign animal diseases—including foot and mouth disease, African swine fever, Rift Valley fever, Japanese encephalitis, Nipah virus, and the Hendra virus.

In March of 2006, the DHS asked research universities and its communities to submit an Expression of Interest. There were 29 submissions from around the nation.[391] We filed two submissions: one for K-State and Manhattan, and one for Leavenworth, Kansas. In February of 2007, 17 sites were down-selected by the DHS. A review team of seven USDA and DHS decision-makers would visit every site. The DHS Undersecretary, Jay Cohen, would lead this review team. He would visit each site personally.[392]

THE VITAL ROLE OF THE BRI IN LANDING NBAF

The USDA/DHS team wanted to visit the Leavenworth site in the morning and the K-State site in the afternoon on July 17, 2007. Ron Trewyn and I sensed that the team was hardly enthused about our site. They might have viewed K-State initially as an inferior land-grant school and Manhattan as a small town in Kansas.

But we believed that our NBAF team could change their impressions. The BRI was our ace in the hole. The first order of business was to have the DHS/USDA review team to tour our BRI facility.[393]

The BRI blew them away. It was a game-changer. They saw that K-State had the best BL-3 animal health facility in the nation. I made an opening presentation. Senator Pat Roberts delivered a stirring talk. Ron Trewyn gave a riveting talk on the workings of the BRI. Sometimes one "tour" is worth a thousand white papers. Suddenly, the Review Team was in no hurry to leave. They now wanted to tour our entire campus, the downtown mall, and the city.

The momentum had shifted. At the end of their visit, Senator Roberts, Bob Krause, and I met Undersecretary Jay Cohen in front of the new BRI. After chatting for a few minutes, Jay casually asked me: "President Wefald, do I understand you right, that if we picked K-State, you would turn over the entire state-owned BRI building to the DHS?" My response was: "Yes." As the review team was driving away, Pat Roberts said: "You know what? We have a pretty darn good chance to win this."

THE IMPORTANCE OF A STRATEGY OF BIPARTISANSHIP!

Although the DHS/USDA visit to KSU was vital for our chances, it was the process used throughout the selection process that was decisive. It is called bipartisanship. Our proposal had no chance unless we operated as a seamless team of Republicans and Democrats—a team that included a Democratic Governor, two Republican U.S. Senators, the entire Kansas Congressional delegation, the Republican Kansas Speaker of the House, the Republican President of the Senate, and the two Democratic minority leaders in each house.

This special bipartisanship was embodied at its best when a Democratic Governor, Kathleen Sebelius, appointed a Republican U.S. Senator, Pat Roberts, to be the Chair of the Governor's Task Force on NBAF. We were off to a good start.

In looking back at our strategy for winning this national prize, I have often wondered why all state and national politicians do not strive for bipartisanship. From the get-go, we were the underdogs. The University of Georgia and Athens, Mississippi State and Flora, North Carolina State and Butner represented serious opposition.

But K-State's biggest challenge came from the University of Texas in San Antonio and the Texas Governor, Rick Perry. Texas never considered losing this fight. The stakes were monumental. With NBAF projected to cost $1.3 billion and employing up to 350 people, the economic impact for the winning state would exceed $1.5 billion and create up to 1,500 construction jobs.[394]

Our bipartisanship tactics went back to our January 17, 2002 meeting when 110 state legislators traveled to Manhattan to discuss the three new research buildings for KU, KSU, and WSU. It became evident in 2007 when the state legislature voted unanimously for $105 million for a future NBAF facility at K-State. How often is the legislature unanimous on anything? The KBA committed $35 million. The city committed $5 million for new infrastructure.[395]

These funding decisions were not reported in the press. The other four finalists were playing exactly the same fiddle. All four had the financial funds to win the NBAF sweepstakes.

But Governor Perry, UT in San Antonio, and the city of San Antonio did not take K-State seriously. For us, it was like David and Goliath. You can guess who David was. Could Kansas and K-State beat Texas and Governor Perry? Well, Texas also had President Bush.

Officials in San Antonio started hearing rumors of what Kansas and K-State were up to in 2007. By that time, it might have been too late. We were a seamless team. When any set of public leaders operate as a unified nonpartisan team, upsets can happen.

THE HISTORIC MEETING CALLED BY SENATOR PAT ROBERTS

Senator Pat Roberts called a meeting of the leaders from the Governor's Task Force on NBAF in his Senate conference room for February 26, 2008. That morning, Sue Peterson and I flew out of Manhattan before 6:00 a.m. Stopping in Topeka to pick up the House Speaker, Melvin Neufeld, and the Minority Senate Leader, Anthony Hensley, the four of us got there on time at 10:00 a.m.

The list of leaders was impressive, inclusive, and bipartisan. It included Senators Pat Roberts and Sam Brownback; the entire congressional delegation; Governor Kathleen Sebelius; Lt. Governor, Mark Parkinson; the Kansas House Speaker, Melvin Neufeld; the Kansas Senate President, Steve Morris; the House Minority leader, Dennis McKinney; the Senate Minority leader, Anthony Hensley; the KBA President, Tom Thornton; the USDA Secretary, Dan Glickman; the former Governor of Kansas, John Carlin; Sue Peterson; and me.

Pat chaired the meeting. He opened it up with a declarative statement: "At this meeting in Washington D.C. on February 26, 2008, we have gathered together the largest, the most historic, and the most bipartisan meeting of key federal and state leaders of Kansas in the history of the state." Everyone nodded.

When our team met after lunch with Jay Cohen, the DHS Undersecretary, we sat around his conference table. In introducing ourselves, Cohen was stunned because he had never been at any major meeting in his conference room where all of a state's Republican and Democratic political heavy hitters were present. I doubt the other four finalists ever set up a similar meeting.

K-STATE WAS SELECTED BY THE DHS FOR NBAF

By July of 2007, there were five finalists. The DHS/USDA review team analyzed the Environmental Impact Studies of all five finalists. On December 12, 2008, the Final EIS was published. The DHS/USDA review team, the Department of Homeland Security, and Admiral Jay Cohen, unanimously selected Kansas State for NBAF. On Monday, December 1, 2008, I was officially notified that K-State had been selected to be the new home of NBAF. A press conference was called for Thursday, December 4, 2008.[396]

On Thursday morning, political leaders from Washington D.C. and Topeka, Kansas started gathering together in our BRI auditorium. The two U.S. Senators, several U.S. House members, the Governor, the Lt. Governor, the President of the State Senate, the Speaker of the State House of Representatives, the President of the KBA, and many others attended this press conference.

Everyone explained how important NBAF would be for the

state's economy. After all, it would become the animal health center for America and the world. A powerful comment came from the House Speaker, Melvin Neufeld. This farmer legislator declared: "With the selection of K-State for NBAF, this is the best news for the future economy of Kansas since the first railroads crossed the entire state of Kansas in the 1870's."

The Republican Senator Pat Roberts and the Democratic Governor Kathleen Sebelius concurred that Kansas could become the leading state in America in animal health. Lt. Governor Mark Parkinson focused on our strategy of bipartisanship: "This victory shows what we can accomplish when we set partisan politics aside and work together as Kansans." I predicted that NBAF would become for animal health in America what the Center for Disease Control had become for human health since 1945.[397]

KSU'S SELECTION FOR NBAF IS HISTORIC

The DHS selection of K-State for NBAF is arguably the most important event in our school's history. As our school entered the 21st century, no K-Stater would have believed that nine years later we would have a $54 million national Biosecurity Research Institute; land a special new Kansas State, Olathe Campus in Johnson County; and be selected by the DHS for the nation's animal health equivalent of the CDC in Atlanta, Georgia. This $1.3 billion NBAF facility will become the largest and most expensive public building constructed in the history of Kansas.

These significant and historic events took place because our KSU leadership team started setting priorities in the 1990's for all of our academic departments, colleges, and the entire university. If we had not made food safety and animal health our number one priority in 1999, Kansas State would have been unsuccessful in getting the new campus in Johnson County and unsuccessful in landing NBAF.

Equally important, if our colleges and departments were expected to set one or two strategic priorities after 2000, it was mandatory for the entire university to have a number one goal.

OUR GOAL OF BECOMING A TOP TEN LAND GRANT UNIVERSITY WITHOUT A MEDICAL SCHOOL

With each passing month and year, the majority of K-State's faculty backed our goal of becoming a Top Ten land grant university without medical schools. They liked this strategy because it was a stretch goal. But it was a realistic and obtainable goal as well. Between 2000 and 2009, most of our colleges and departments made good progress in elevating a number of their programs into a Top Ten land grant program without medical schools in the nation.

By 2008-09, Kansas State had over 35 academic departments and academic programs ranked in the Top Ten of either all land-grant universities in the nation or all land-grant universities without medical schools. In 2006, the Center for Measuring University Performance moved from Florida to Arizona State. The ASU Center employs the same measures to rate public universities—including total research dollars, federal research, faculty awards, number of doctoral students, post-docs, national merit scholars, endowments, and annual giving.[398]

In 2004, Kansas State was listed as 17th of all land-grant universities without medical schools. By 2008-09, Kansas State was ranked 11th of all land grants without medical schools.

Provost Duane Nellis talked to the Arizona State Center in 2006. He asked them to add two key pieces of data to its rankings: namely, to incorporate into their rankings the incredible success that Kansas State's students had in winning the nation's five most prestigious student scholarships over two decades; and include in their rankings the number of Kansas State's faculty winning the Carnegie (CASE) U.S. Professors of the Year and the Carnegie (CASE) State Professors of the Year.

Every prominent public and private university in America had students and faculty applying for these awards. They were both easily verifiable.

Like the number crunchers for U.S. NEWS AND WORLD REPORT, the Arizona State data collectors were indifferent to K-

State's academic successes for students and faculty. If the ASU Center for Measuring Performance had added those two value-added criteria, K-State would have moved up to at least seventh or eighth of all land grants without medical schools. If Michigan or UCLA had recommended these two new criteria, the ASU data collectors might have listened.[399]

By the spring of 2009, K-State's colleges and departments had enchanced their academic excellence. In virtually all of our academic departments, faculty members were either doing exceptional basic and applied research or writing important monographs, books, and scholarly articles in important national publications.

KANSAS STATE'S RESEARCH GRANTS SOARED FROM 1986 TO 2009

From 1986 to 2009, K-State's research funding had increased from $19 million to $134 million. In 1987, K-State was ranked about 105th of all public research universities in the nation for competitive grants. By 2009, with competitive grants totaling $134 million, the Arizona State Research Center now ranked Kansas State 75th in the nation for competitive grants for public research universities.

This means that our administration had improved our competitive grants by at least 25 places—from about 105th in 1990 to 75th in 2009 for all public universities. K-State had become a nationally ranked public research university in America by 2009.[400]

A NEW ACADEMIC PROGRAM APPEARS: LEADERSHIP STUDIES

By the late 1990's, a new academic program appeared. It was called Leadership Studies. Two campus faculty and staff leaders in 1997, Robert J. Shoop and Susan Scott, initiated a study of an academic field of study that had been absent from Kansas State's history—Leadership Studies. By 2002-03, leadership studies had become one of the hottest new campus programs.[401]

On March 3, 1997, the Board of Regents approved an 18-hour interdisciplinary minor in leadership studies at K-State. The first course was entitled Introduction to Leadership Concepts. Shoop and Scott taught the course. They were academic pioneers. Without them, this new program would not exist at K-State today.[402]

Bob and Susan argued leaders were not born. Rather, they believed that leadership could be learned. I agreed with their thesis. Saint Francis of Assisi stated the views of Shoop and Scott quite simply: "Start by doing what's necessary, then what's possible, and suddenly you are doing the impossible."

In 1997, two courses in Leadership Studies were taught. By 2001, the new minor was offering 14 courses or sections with 108 students enrolled. By 2009, the Leadership Studies program had mushroomed to 48 courses or sections with an enrollment of 2,700 students. Few academic programs at K-State have skyrocketed in importance like this one did.[403]

The program lacked a building to house the faculty, staff, and the students. Enter Warren and Mary Lynn Staley. I first met the Staleys in the 1990's. As a 1965 Kansas State graduate, Warren had a BS in electrical engineering and a MBA from Cornell University. Warren started his career at Cargill in 1969.[404]

Neal St. Anthony wrote an article about Warren Staley in the MINNEAPOLIS TRIBUNE on June 6, 2008. Wherever Cargill assigned Warren Staley a job anywhere in the world after 1969, he met the challenge. In 1998, he became the President and Chief Operating Officer. In 2000, he was chosen to be the Chairman of the Cargill Board. From 1999 to his retirement in 2007, Staley proved to be one of Cargill's most brilliant business leaders.[405]

Mary Lynn graduated from Kansas State in 1965 with a bachelor's degree in elementary education. At K-State, she was a member of Delta Delta Delta sorority, the Chimes honorary society, and student government. She was consistently involved with leadership positions in the Greater Twin Cities United Way and the Board of Governors of Eleven Who Care. Both Staleys saw the importance of developing leaders who had high ethical standards.[406]

On Thursday night, October 30, 2003, Ruth Ann and I hosted a dinner for the Staleys at the president's house. While I had lunch with Warren on Friday, Susan Scott asked Mary Lynn to meet with her and some of her best Leaderhsip Studies students. Susan believes this meeting might have provided the "spark" for Warren and Mary Lynn Staley to consider providing the lead gift for a future Leadership Studies Building. We all remained hopeful.[407]

On November 5, 2005, Ruth Ann and I hosted a lunch for the Staleys at the president's house. Bob Shoop, Mike Holen, Susan Scott, Gary Hellebust, and Mitzi Richards attended. I asked the Staleys if they might consider making the lead gift for a new Leadership Studies building. Several weeks later, they called Gary Hellebust to say that they would like to make the lead gift. Gary called me with the good news. I called Susan Scott. We were all thrilled.[408]

In early 2008, the Staleys and the Foundation believed they had sufficient private gifts to proceed. The groundbreaking for the new building was on April 18, 2008. It was a wonderful celebration. The stage was set for a new Leadership Studies building.

After a superb career, Susan Scott stepped down as the Director of the School of Leadership Studies in 2009. Mary Hale Tolar, a Rhodes scholar, was selected as the interim director. In the fall of 2009, Mary was a great choice to be the school's next director.

The construction of the new building began in 2009. I doubt if any new proposed building in the history of Kansas State ever had more input from a multitude of dedicated individuals than the Leadership Studies building. The process was fully democratic. Maybe that is one reason why the new building turned out to be quite perfect.[409]

At the dedication ceremony on April 16, 2010, the entire Staley family was joined by a number of administrators, faculty, and students. It was a joyous occasion. Constructed with Kansas limestone, the new building was breathtaking in its prize-winning beauty, space, exterior and interior architecture. It was 35,500 square feet and it cost over $11 million. This Leadership Studies Building took its place as one of the most beautiful buildings constructed in the history of Kansas State.[410]

THE NEW BUILDINGS AND MAJOR RENOVATIONS: 1986-2009

From 1986 to 2009, our administration had constructed four of the most impressive buildings in the history of Kansas State. The Hale Library, the Beach Museum of Art, the Alumni building, and the Leadership Studies building are that special and historic. On July 4, 1997, Walt Braun, the editorial page editor for the MANHATTAN MERCURY, called the new Hale Library an "architectural masterpiece." The Beach Museum of Art, the Alumni Building, and the Leadership Studies buildings are close behind.[411]

OUR KSU TEAM BUILT 35 NEW BUILDINGS IN 23 YEARS

Over 23 years, our leadership team constructed 35 new buildings. From 1986 to 2009, the number of new buildings and major renovations of existing buildings at Kansas State represented a total of 5,943,295 million square feet (GSF).

A. Abe Fattaey, the Director of Facilities Planning and University Architect, outlined the meaning of these statistics on May 14, 2013: "In 23 years, your administration added 2,329,600 square feet of new buildings and had major renovations of existing buildings totaling 3,613,695 square feet for a total of 5,943,295 GSF. K-State's total square footage for all buildings in 2009 was 9,207,145 GSF."[412]

THIS MEANS WE CONSTRUCTED TWO-THIRDS OF THE ENTIRE CAMPUS IN NEW BUILDINGS AND MAJOR RENOVATIONS

When you look at the total square footage of the entire KSU campus in 2009, Fattaey reports that the construction of new buildings and major renovations over our 23 years represented 64.55% of existing buildings. Tom Rawson explains the upshot of all our new construction this way on April 14, 2014: "By impacting a total of 5.9 million square feet of space, this means that about two-thirds of the total campus space was either constructed or renovated during the Wefald administration."[413]

Abe Fattaey analyzed what all of these buildings and renovations would cost today: "Looking at the total buildings project costs for the new College of Business Building and the new College of Engineering building in 2014 at a value of $400 per square foot is estimated to be a close average to use. Thus, given the total square footage of the new buildings constructed on campus from 1986 to 2009 ($2,300,000 x $400), the costs for these new buildings in 2014 dollars would be about $920,000,000."

On renovations, Fattaey writes: "To build the major renovation and remodeling projects on campus an average value of $275 per square foot is estimated to be a reasonable price for today's building costs. Using the $275 per square foot for major renovation and remodeling projects on the campus projects from 1986 to 2009, these projects today would cost at least $990 million."[414]

THESE PROJECTS TODAY WOULD COST ABOUT $2 BILLION

Abe Fattaey sums up the building figures this way: "Using the above estimation of today's cost of new buildings and major renovation for projects completed on campus from 1986 to 2009 would be close to $2 billion."

The above figures and costs during my 23 years do not include the 2002 Alumni Building at a cost of $12.9 million totaling 52,000 GSF or the 2009 new animal health building on the Kansas State, Olathe Campus at a cost of $28 million totaling 108,000 GSF.[415]

In addition to the Hale Library, the Beach Museum of Art, the Alumni Building, and the Leadership Studies building, Victoria L'Ecuyer, K-State's Space Coordinator for Campus Planning, reported on the many other excellent new buildings constructed from 1986 to 2009. They include: Dole Hall; Biochemistry building; Rathbone Hall for Engineering; Fiedler Hall Wing for Engineering; two major additions to Throckmorton Hall; Parking Garage; Chalmers Hall

Ackert Addition; Center for Child Development; Chester Peters Recreational Complex; Galacia Human Ecology building; and Hoeflin Stone House.

Victoria L'Ecuyer also listed the other major buildings constructed from 1986 to 2009. They include: Bramlage Coliseum, Indoor Practice Facility, several major additions to the Bill Snyder Football Stadium (which we count as one building); Women's Rowing Facility; International Grains building; Bioprocessing and Industry Value Added Program building; Hal Ross Flour Mill; Pat Roberts Hall; the first phase of the new Jardine Apartments Redevelopment (counted as one building but it is 14 new buildings); KSU Salina Aero Center; KSU Salina College Center; KSU Salina Harbin Hall; KSU Salina Student Life Center; and a number of other important buildings.[416]

THE JARDINE APARTMENTS REDEVELOPMENT

Early in the 1990's, the K-State Department of Housing and Dining Services devised a plan—"The Jardine Apartments Redevelopment: Creating the Magic." Chuck Werring, the outstanding assistant vice president of the housing and dining services, had been a fan of all Disney properties.

Chuck started visiting Disney World and Disneyland as a college student. He analyzed their operations. Chuck saw the magic. He witnessed the quality, the beauty, and the cleanliness of the Disney buildings and grounds. He saw how the Disney spirit could be applied to the plans for the project.[417]

The first phase included 14 new buildings. The second phase of 14 additional buildings will be finished by 2017. This new $102 million Jardine Apartments plan became one of the largest publicly funded projects in the history of Kansas. If you have never visited the handsome and extraordinary Jardine Apartments project, the next time you visit the campus you should tour our magic kingdom.[418]

THE CONSTRUCTION OF THE COLBERT HILLS GOLF COURSE

In the spring of 1994, Jim Colbert and Bob Krause envisioned a new university world-class golf course located in the beautiful Flint Hills on the west side of Manhattan. Both saw the need for a K-State golf course. Both were visionaries and leaders.

Jim Colbert was always an outstanding athlete. In high school, he was a multi-purpose athlete, playing football, basketball, and golf. At K-State, Jim focused on golf. He was a star on the Golf Team for four years. As a senior, he was second in the NCAA golf championships.

Turning pro in 1965, Colbert was a champion eight times on the PGA Tour. He won two PGA tournaments in 1983. Later, he won 20 tournaments on the Senior Champions Tour. Jim became one of the best golfers in the history of Kansas. He was selected to the K-State Sports Hall of Fame and the Kansas Golf Hall of Fame.[419]

From the beginning of the project in 1994 to its completion, Jim and Bob were partners. They found the perfect 300 acres of land in the nearby beautiful Flint Hills of Kansas. The course would extend 7,400 yards from the back tees. It would also include a clubhouse, a state-of-the-art driving range, and a Par three teaching course.[420]

Under the umbrella of the K-State Golf Course Management and Research Foundation (KSUGCMRF), a multitude of generous golf-playing alums pitched in. Some of the finest K-Staters I have ever met stepped up to the plate—including Howard Sherwood, Bernie Butler, John Graham, Dick Thiessen, Mark Truitt, Joe Downey, Nelson Galle, R.D. Hubbard, and Paul Stephenson. The PGA Tour Golf Course Properties and Golf Course Superintendent Association of America played key roles in the success of Colbert Hills. Jim Colbert and Jeff Brauer were the co-architects.[421]

Ernie Barrett was the key fundraiser. Bob and Marcia Hagans provided a major gift of $1 million on May 1, 2000 and later another $300,000 for the Bar and Grill in the new clubhouse. In 2002, Jay and Jinny Crofoot from Lubbock, Texas provided $1.2 million for the course. Jim and Marcia Colbert made the lead gift of over $1 million to Colbert Hills. Howard Sherwood and Jim Tadtman, donated $1.2 million in cash and gifts-in-kind.[422]

In 1999, the KSU Foundation Executive Committee made an excellent initial commitment of $100,000 followed up with $30,000 a year for a ten-year total commitment of $400,000. In 2005, the KSU Foundation committee made a second commitment of $50,000 a year for a seven-year total of $350,000.

In the history of Colbert Hills, there have been about 150 significant donors. An amazing 82 of them have contributed over $100,000 each. There has never been any project or building in KSU's history that has had 82 donors gifting $100,000 each. All of these gifts were crucial for the Colbert Hills golf course.[423]

Now the new course needed an outstanding clubhouse. It would need to be one that befitted the majestic Flint Hills golf course. The clubhouse was dedicated in May of 2010. For Jim Colbert and a score of dedicated Colbertarians, this was a dream come true. The new, sparkling clubhouse was built for $5.4 million with a total of 13,500 square feet. It was splendid.

Many people stepped up to the plate for this clubhouse. The Grand Mere Development Company made an excellent lead gift. Jack and Joann Goldstein donated $300,000 for the Founders Room. Fred and Virginia Merrill donated $300,000. Bob and Betty Tointon contributed $200,000. Bob Campbell of Wichita provided a gift of $200,000 for the handsome entrance.[424]

Through the Coonrod Family Foundation, the Coonrod Associates Construction Company provided $300,000 for the Pro Shop in the new building. Scott Wolfington and the Coonrod Construction Company did a great job in building the new clubhouse.

Thousands of golfers were ebullient over the new course and clubhouse. Jim Colbert and Bob Krause are pleased and proud of Colbert Hills. There are thousands of K-State golfers who are equally pleased and proud of the course they call Colbert Hills.[425]

THE RECRUITING OF INTERNATIONAL STUDENTS: CHINA

Kansas State has been recruiting international students since the 1960's. By the 1980's, the number of these students was about 800. By the 1990's, it leveled off at about 1,000 students. Frankly, I had largely ignored the importance of having students from throughout the world. By 2005, I knew that had to change.[426]

I remember reading Thomas Friedman's book THE WORLD IS FLAT in the spring of 2005. It got my attention. Friedman argued that the world had flattened when the increasing availability of personal computers converged with the world deployment of fiber-optic micro cables. His thesis is revolutionary: the evolving world globalization meant every nation had equal opportunity.

Increasingly, nations like China and India had become world centers of trade, banking, and manufacturing. In less than a generation, China and India had created huge and wealthy middle-classes and upper middle classes. China led the way. By 2005, many of their citizens had become millionaires and billionaires.

In early December of 2005, I invited two staff members in the Office of International Programs to a meeting of the president's staff—Kristine Young, the assistant provost for international programs, and Jim Lewis, the director of international admissions and recruiting. I argued that K-State's scattergun approach of recruiting students from everywhere was not working. Starting tomorrow, I announced that our International Programs staff should target a few countries—China, India, South Korea, and Saudi Arabia.

But we all agreed—namely, that China would be by far our No. 1 target. In 2005, China had a middle class and upper middle class of over 350 million people. We did not need a consultant. I knew we had the right people at our "local" level that could do the job. I never liked consultants and their bureaucrats. Over the years, we always had people up and down the line who would stand up and lead.

I looked right at Jim Lewis who had been at KSU for years. I told him to get cracking on the Chinese market. Jim had never been asked to lead. He not only stood up, he became a superb leader. We never had a thick bureaucracy or employed a top-down approach—meaning that Jim Lewis had to be at once the leader and the worker on the ground. He did that and far more.

Jim Lewis got right to work. On August 23, 2006, he emailed me about contacting a business leader who was working in the Beijing office of the Kansas Commerce Department. He was Chinese and his name was Karl Zhao. Jim reported that he was the first university recruiter to personally visit with Karl. Although I never met Zhao, he became a game-changer for our International Programs.[427]

Karl Zhao's versatility was stunning. He told Jim Lewis exactly how K-State could build a successful recruiting office in China: "Because of the one-child policy, parents play a big role in deciding about higher education for their child. They want value, quality, and a degree from a credible university. Parents and students need a contact in China, with materials in Chinese for them to read. The Chinese government runs two-thirds of the businesses in China. You need to know the Chinese system, speak Chinese, and be able to work the government to effectively recruit in China."

In Lewis' first meeting with Karl Zhao in Beijing, they drew up a perfect plan detailing precisely how K-State could set up a recruiting office in the Chinese capital and how it could be a place for advising parents and students on some of the advantages in attending KSU.[428]

By October of 2006, our China Office was organized. K-State might have been the first American university to have a fully supported office in China. Lewis asked Zhao who would be the best leader to hire as our first office director. Karl gave us the name of a great candidate: Jack Xia.

Then, Lewis convinced our administration that Xia would be the ideal first director for our Beijing office. After meeting Jack in Manhattan, we all agreed and offered him a contract. It was a typical business contract that allowed his Beijing office to receive a modest percentage of every student's tuition recruited to K-State.[429]

Xia flew back to Beijing shortly to set up a K-State office. He hired another full-time person. Today, Jack has two additional part-time employees. The office soon became a place where students and their parents could get free information about K-State and our academic programs in Chinese. Xia developed a Chinese language website and brochures in Chinese were prepared. Jack Xia and Jim Lewis soon organized an agent network all over the country.[430]

The decision we made in December of 2005 at our staff meeting has paid huge dividends for K-State now and for years to come. In the fall of 2003, we had zero Chinese undergraduates. In the fall of 2005, there were 8. In the fall of 2006, there were still only 24.

But the numbers soon skyrocketed. The number of Chinese undergraduates increased to 265 in the fall of 2008, to 534 in the fall of 2009, and to 628 by the fall of 2010. By the fall of 2009, you could not go anywhere on campus without running into Chinese students coming and going. By the fall of 2012, Kansas State had enrolled 800 Chinese undergraduates.[431]

When we put the spotlight on China in our December 2005 staff meeting, hardly anyone thought that we could recruit 800 Chinese high school graduates to K-State six years later. Many people made this happen. But the true MVP of the "KSU China Miracle" is Jim Lewis. He made it happen and he will always be a hero of mine.

By 2008, K-State also had 204 students from India, 103 from Saudi Arabia, and 69 from South Korea. The total number of International students increased from about 1,000 in 2005 to 1,717 in the fall of 2009. By 2012, Kansas State had over 2,000 international students.

For K-State, the increase in the number of Chinese students and other international students after 2006 meant an additional $11 million in Kansas State's base budget by 2012. With the recent budget cuts, the additional millions helps Kansas State's budget a great deal. The decision we made in December of 2005 will pay off for years to come.[432]

OUR VALUABLE PARTNERSHIP WITH FT. RILEY

For years, our administration bemoaned the lack of a viable partnership between Ft. Riley and Kansas State. I kept hoping that somebody would give us a blueprint on how to forge a solid partnership. It never happened. Although we always had some staff members working Ft. Riley, the progress remained marginal. We simply missed opportunity after opportunity.

Positive changes started to happen when Jim Coffman, Bob Krause, and I hired Art DeGroat to be the Department Head of Military Science in 2000. Art was a (Ret) U.S. Army Lieutenant Colonel. He quickly restored our Army and Air Force ROTC programs to national distinction. In the next six years, both programs gained in enrollment and quality. Art also assisted us by supporting our military programs at both Ft. Riley and at Ft. Leavenworth.

In 2006, we created a Director of Military Affairs position. Bob Krause and I decided to hire Art DeGroat. In addition to 22 years in the U.S. Army, Art had a BS from Seton Hall, a Master's Degree from K-State, and a Masters of Military Arts and Sciences from the General Staff College at Ft. Leavenworth. Art was soon spending hours at Ft. Riley. He was basically living there.

In a memo to me on December 11, 2011, DeGroat explained how important it was that we created this new Military Affairs position in 2006. Many Ft. Riley soldiers and family members became K-Staters by taking classes, achieving degrees, and going to our games.

In 2006, K-State had 96 military students and 150 ROTC cadets. By the fall of 2009, K-State had 984 military students and 210 ROTC students for a total of 1194 military students. Our school had ramped up its historic partnership with Ft. Riley in 2006. The soldiers, their families, and K-State itself have all benefited.

THE LANDON LECTURES

From 1986 to 2009, many events helped put Kansas State on the national stage. One of the most important was the Landon Lectures series. Started in 1966 by Governor Alf Landon and President James McCain, Kansas State launched a lecture series that would attract a legion of prominent national and international leaders. In the Landon speakers, I used the same mission statement for each one: "The goal of the Landon Lectures is to bring the most prominent public figures to discuss the pressing issues of the day."[433]

Chuck Reagan was the chair of the Landon Lecture Series during my 23 years. He was brilliant. In 2010, he wrote an excellent book entitled POLITICAL POWER AND PUBLIC INFLUENCE: THE LANDON LECTURES, 1984 TO 2010. Chuck talked about the monthly lunches that Alf Landon and James McCain had at a Topeka café in the 1960's: "Both men lamented the fact that major political figures rarely came to Kansas and even more rarely to a university campus. They decided to see if they could correct this. Alf would invite influential political friends and President McCain would host them and pay their expenses."[434]

Anyone at K-State who has ever worked on attracting impressive Landon speakers knows it is a colossal challenge. Kansas is a long way from Washington D.C. It is a small, rural state. It has few TV sets. In fact, it is a state that most political leaders love to fly over.

From 1986 to 2009, Chuck Reagan and I worked with political leaders like U. S. Senators Nancy Landon Kassebaum, Bob Dole, Pat Roberts, Sam Brownback, and Governors like Bill Graves and Kathleen Sebelius. If you worked closely with them, the results were amazing. Ed Seaton, the publisher of the MANHATTAN MERCURY and the Chairman of the Landon Patrons, helped convince a number of Latin American Presidents to give Landon Lectures.

Chuck Reagan and I ran the ground game. We never hired outside help. You have to do things yourself. Otherwise, nothing happens. Often, we spent months to attract America's top policy-makers. It was almost impossible to convince a sitting President to come. It was hard to get a sitting Secretary of State or Secretary of Defense. It was challenging to get a FBI Director or a CIA Director.

I wrote many letters over the years. Chuck did too. Both of us made a ton of calls. The letters from me to a Secretary of Defense, the Director of the FBI, or a popular U.S. Senator were necessary. We wanted the readers to see the sterling quality of the previous Landon speakers. Both of us called their schedulers. We might make 15 to 20 calls on certain Landons. Chuck flew to Washington D.C. many times. Often without an appointment, he walked into their offices. In short, Chuck and I often employed a full-court press.

For potential Landon speakers like President George W. Bush, former President Bill Clinton, and the former USSR President, Mikhail Gorbachev, a specific game plan was drawn up for each one. First, we made contact with our state's political leaders. Second, an appropriate letter was hand-delivered to each speaker. Third, Chuck would fly to Washington D.C. and visit directly with the scheduler. Fourth, I frequently called either the scheduler or the key politician.

With President George W. Bush, we agreed to wait until after the 2004 Presidential election. Meanwhile, Senator Roberts had become the Chair of the Senate Intelligence Committee. With this job, he met in the White House every two weeks with an elite group called the "Gang of Eight." It included key leaders in both houses and the Chairs of the two Intelligence Committees. I talked with Pat once a month and I always asked him how we were doing in landing 43.

For the next two years, Roberts said to everyone in the White House—including President Bush and Vice-President Cheney: "Look, President Bush has to give a Landon Lecture. And we will not give up until he agrees." One day Pat was walking down a White House hallway for his "Gang of Eight" meeting. He saw Dick Cheney. Before Pat could even say hello, Cheney said, "Senator, I know, I know what you are going to say. You want the President to come to K-State. Well, he is coming soon." It happened on January 23, 2006.

From 1986 to 2009, our university had 81 Landon speakers. From 1966 to 1986, there were 72 Landons. Our lecture series attracted a virtually unmatched list of prominent American and world leaders. Maybe Harvard or Yale had a better list. Few, if any, major public universities ever had a more distinguished lecture series. Over my 23 years, our Landon Lecture Series had three Presidents of the United States, six foreign Presidents, four Secretaries of Defense, one Secretary of State, the Director of the FBI, and the Director of the CIA.[435]

As I look back on our 81 Landon Lectures, I cannot remember a bad one. All of them were good. Many were sensational. Anytime you have a sitting president or a former one, it is special. Presidents Jimmy Carter, George W. Bush, and Bill Clinton all did an exceptional job. Four Secretaries of Defense came—including William Perry in March of 1995, William Cohen in September of 1997, Don Rumsfeld in November of 2006, and Robert Gates in November of 2007.

We were fortunate to attract two of America's finest U.S. Army Generals in a generation, General Colin L. Powell in November of 1989 and General David Petraeus in April of 2009. In April of 1996, the former Secretary of State, Henry Kissinger, delivered a lecture; in April of 2004, the Director of the FBI, Robert Mueller, gave one; in April of 2004; the Director of the CIA, General Michael Hayden, was here to give a Landon Lecture in April of 2008.[436]

K-State was lucky to get several foreign Presidents to fly to Manhattan to give a Landon Lecture. They included the former President of Poland, General Wojciech Jaruzelski, in March of 1996; the former President of Mexico, Ernesto Zedillo, in May of 2001; the former President of the Soviet Union, Mikhail Gorbachev, in January of 2006; the former President of Poland, Lech Walesa, in April of 2006; and the former President of Mexico, Vicente Fox, in September of 2008.[437]

In her forward to Chuck Reagan's book, our former outstanding U.S. Senator and daughter of Governor Alf Landon, Nancy Landon Kassebaum Baker, summed up the success of the Landons: "The guiding goal for the selection of speakers is maintaining the level of prominence one has on the public issues of the day. This has been one of the strengths of the lecture series, the reach of which goes far beyond the campus in Manhattan, Kansas. Secretary of Defense Robert Gates said that he was in a mountainous area of Afghanistan following his Landon Lecture. He was greeted by a village leader who said, 'I watched your speech at Kansas State on CNN.'"[438]

THE JUNE 11, 2008 TORNADO THAT DAMAGES THE CAMPUS

I announced my retirement on May 8, 2008. Everyone hopes for a good last year. Although I had always worried about a tornado hitting our campus, I hardly expected a direct hit on our campus during my last year. At the time, we had one of the most beautiful and clean campuses in America.

On June 11, 2008, all that changed. The National Weather Service had predicted a cold front would move in from the west later that day. By the early evening, the NWS in Topeka had upgraded a rainstorm warning into a tornado watch. Ed Rice, who was our Associate Vice-President for Facilities from 1987 to 2009, wrote: "A tornado watch in Kansas during this time of year is common. At 10:00 p.m., a tornado warning was put into effect until 10:30 p.m. At 10:48, the tornado was spotted ten miles southwest of Manhattan."[439]

An F-4 tornado howling at 200 miles an hour hit about five blocks west of Ed Rice's house on Amherst Avenue. It followed Amherst to the east where it destroyed 40 homes and damaged many others. Moving in a northeasterly direction, it crossed Seth Child Road and destroyed a True Value Hardware store and a mini-storage facility.

The tornado, then, slammed into the southwest corner of the campus at 11:00 p.m. It was now an F-2 tornado with winds of 120 to 150 miles per hour. It left the northeast corner of Kansas State at 11:03 p.m. In three minutes, the tornado had heavily damaged four buildings and seriously damaged 40 others.[440]

Ed Rice wrote: "The tornado had left a forty-five degree swath of destruction about a quarter-mile wide straight through one-third of our main campus." The destruction was enormous. Roofs were torn up. Thousands of windows were blown out. Many mature trees were blown over. Pieces of insulation were splattered on virtually every building on the main campus.[441]

There were 30 facility workers on duty when the tornado struck. Starting that night, hundreds of facility employees worked with a sense of urgency. Our staff started calling contractors and subcontractors right away for emergency duty. Rice was pleased with his call to the Director of State Purchasing. As Ed said: "The Director gave us permission due to the emergency to directly contact suppliers and contractors. This allowed us to save time and get good prices."

Three general contractors were hired immediately for our most damaged buildings—Fiedler, Cardwell, Bushnell, and Weber Hall.[442]

After the Director of State Purchasing gave K-State the 'green light' to hire contractors and subcontractors, we categorically told Ed Rice and his staff to take charge. And take charge they did. The key decisions would be made at the "local level." Basically, we gave Ed and his staff complete authority to rebuild our campus.

From day one, the goal was to get the campus repaired by the time school started in late August. Overnight, Ed's staff had hired a score of contractors and subcontractors. Many of them were already on campus and making necessary repairs. The skill of the contractor's managers and employees was beyond reproach. They approached the repair and renovation of our buildings like they were working on their own homes. Many worked six days a week.

Our own facilities staff of electricians, plumbers, painters, roofers, carpenters, and equipment workers did an exemplary job. It was a team effort. All of them deserve an A+ for their dedicated and outstanding work. I often think today how much progress could be made if business and government worked together as a team.

Ed Rice complimented our entire facilities staff. But he mentioned especially the work of K-State's two project managers, Mark Loberg and Kevin Minnihan. Assigned to work with FEMA, the insurance adjusters, the contractors, and our maintenance workers, Rice said: "Mark and Kevin pulled off the greatest project management achievement in Kansas history."

Mark and Kevin became perfect examples of ordinary working employees who become extraordinary. Overnight, these two unknown guys became great leaders. They were unknown to me. Over and over again in my years at K-State, I saw faculty and staff members who did great things when called upon to lead.

Tom Rawson, the Vice-President for Administration, Bruce Shubert, his Associate Vice-President, Ed Heptig, the Director of Maintenance, and Ed Rice also deserve extraordinary credit for their work during the summer of 2008.[443]

From June 11 to the first week of September, the Kansas State facilities workers put in 17,765 hours of labor to clean up the damage. They replaced 3,577 windows and removed 281 mature trees and 5,500 yards of building debris. In riding my bike one night to the parking lot north of the Claflin dormitories, I was shocked to see several mountains of trash and debris. The total cost for repairing buildings and removing debris was $10.7 million.[444]

Our facilities staff embraced the values that all Kansans prize—an incredible work ethic, unbridled dedication, common sense of the highest order, and a commitment to excellence. They did not have to ask me for approval of their decisions. I trusted K-State faculty, staff, and students for 22 years. I was not going to change now.

Instead, I doubled down on my leadership model of delegation of authority and trusting people to make the right decisions. If we had asked FEMA to take the lead on the rebuilding of our campus, it might have taken a year. Instead, the job was done in about 65 days.

I did come up with one pretty good clean-up idea. I might have been one of few people on campus who saw that pieces of insulation had been blasted firmly on many of our buildings. Our limestone buildings provided a perfect home for the "insulation spitballs." With winds up to 157 miles per hour, the F-2 tornado literally blasted the "spitwads" onto our uneven limestone walls.

In mid-June, I asked the Travelers Insurance Company if they would power-wash all of the affected buildings. Two company adjusters came to our campus. In touring the campus, I asked the adjusters to see if they could scratch the spitballs off the limestone walls. They could not.

The next week they gave us the permission to hire two power-washing companies in the region. There were only two such companies within 250 miles: the Belfor Restoration Company in Kansas City and the Mid-Continental Restoration Company in Ft. Scott, Kansas. Both were hired.[445]

In the next month, these two companies power-washed 60 buildings on the main campus. Over 20 of our main buildings, including Anderson Hall, the Hale Library, Eisenhower Hall, the Student Union, Ahearn, the Alumni building and 14 other buildings would have all four sides power-washed. For the other 40 buildings, they would only have to power-wash two or three sides of each one. The two CEO's told me K-State was the first university to have all of their buildings power-washed. By September 1, 2008, our buildings were the cleanest they had ever been in history.

Kansas State was a campus torn asunder on the Thursday morning of June 12, 2008. Our main campus had a swath of destruction about a quarter of a mile wide. The school had never seen this kind of devastation. We wanted the campus restored by August 20, 2008. It was. When our students returned for the fall semester, many said: "I read about the big tornado that tore up the school. Where did it go, anyway?"

To celebrate the renewal of Kansas State University, I hosted an Ice Cream Social for Wednesday, August 27, 2008. Hundreds of faculty, students, staff, and the K-State Marching Band were all there. The ice cream cones tasted better than ever on a sunny afternoon. K-Staters celebrated on the afternoon of August 27. After 65 days, our campus was once again one of the cleanest and most beautiful campuses anywhere in America.

CONCLUSION

In 1986, our administration faced a number of intractable problems. The challenges included: K-State had the worst library in the Big 8. It was the only school without an art museum in the Big 8. It had largely ignored the importance of basic research from 1945 to 1986. It was essentially an undergraduate teaching instituition from 1900 to 1990. Its private giving was behind Wichita State. Its Information Technology program was at ground zero. It had the worst football program in the Big 8 and the nation. Most of these challenges took about a decade to unravel.

In the summer of 1986, we had several short-term challenges. They included putting together a new administrative team and turning the enrollment around. Both of these problems were solved in several years. From 1981 to 1986, the university's enrollment had dropped from 19,000 students to about 16,500. Several of the school's leaders in 1985 had predicted that K-State's enrollment would decline to about 12,000 students. Most alums were not only worried about that trend, they sensed their school was in decline.

In our first several years, we assembled an excellent team of administrators. Jim Coffman, Tom Rawson, Bob Krause, Tim Donoghue, Chuck Reagan, Pat Bosco, Sue Peterson, and Ron Trewyn were all first-rate. We had put together a team of problem-solving, dedicated, and never-give-up leaders. None of them ever saw our challenges as unsolvable or impossible. I never heard one of them say: "It can't be done."

On December 22, 2015, Dolph Simons, the Editor of the LAWRENCE JOURNAL WORLD, wrote exactly that about our leadership team. The Wefald Team "was a powerful group in every respect, one that should serve as a model for other universities. Some schools have it; others don't. It requires hard work, vision, and true leadership, but the dividends of such commitment are rewarding for all parties. Consider what took place at Kansas State."

After I hired Pat Bosco as our Director of Recruiting, I saw the enrollment decline as solvable. Pat and I would never permit the school's enrollment to fall to 11,000 or 12,000 students. Rather, we believed that K-State's enrollment would be over 20,000 students within five years. With 597 new students in 1987, 1,242 in 1988, 709 in 1989, and 1,027 in 1990, Kansas State University's enrollment soared from 16,500 students to over 20,000 students in four years.

Still, the problems our administration faced in the late 1980's were virtually endless. The library, for example, was in horrible shape. It was the only library in the Big 8 that was not a member of the Association of Research Libraries (ARL). For two generations, Kansas State leaders never got it right on the library. From the building of the Farrell Library in 1927 to the two new additions in 1954 and 1969, the adage of "half is good enough" prevailed.

Provost Jim Coffman and I still believe that fixing our library problem was the most intractable issue we faced in 23 years, including the mediocre football program. It was people on the ground like Dean Brice Holbrock and our Student Senate leaders who led us to the construction of a national class library.

After a decade of dedication, risk-taking, great student leadership, the work of Jim Coffman and Brice Hobrock—and a little luck, the dream of a beautiful, high-tech research library was realized with the dedication of the Hale Library on October 5, 1997.

In 1986, K-State was the only university in the Big 8 without an art museum. An amazing group of K-State volunteers led by Ruth Ann Wefald laid the foundation. She found two angels in Hays, Kansas to provide the lead gifts for a new art museum: Ross and Marianna Beach. After a decade of hard work and a multitude of volunteers working seamlessly together, an elegant Marianna Kistler Beach Museum of Art was dedicated on October 13, 1996.

During my 23 years as president, a total of 35 new buildings were constructed at Kansas State. These new buildings represent a total Gross Square Footage of 2,329,600 million (GSF). The major renovations of existing buildings represent a square footage of more than 3,613,695 million GSF for a combined total of 5,943,295 million GSF. In 2009, Kansas State's total square footage for the entire campus was 9.2 million GSF.

All of this means that our administration literally built 64.55% of the university's new buildings and major renovations of the total existing campus space from 1986 to 2009. The grand total spent on new buildings and major building renovations over those years is estimated to cost about $2 billion in 2014 dollars.

Our leadership team worked hand-in-glove with the Foundation leaders to increase private fund-raising from $5 million in 1986 to $100 million in 2009. In private giving, KSU had caught up to KU by 2009. In 1986, few K-Staters anywhere would ever have believed that their alma mater could raise $100 million a year anytime soon. Indeed, with our Changing Lives Campaign from 2000 to 2007, we raised well over $500 million.

From 1986 to 2009, our research funding was increased from $20 million to $134 million. With $134 million in extramural funding in

2009, KSU in Manhattan had more competitive grants than KU in Lawrence for the first time in history.

In 1986, KSU was ranked about 105th of the nation's public research universities in competitive grants. With our total research funding in 2009, the Arizona State University Center for Measuring University Performance moved our school up by at least 25 spots. Thus, by 2009, the ASU Center now ranked K-State 75th of the Top 200 public universities in competitive grants.

K-State had 129 students win nationally prestigious scholarships like the Rhodes, Marshalls, Trumans, Goldwaters, and Udalls from 1986 to 2009. This means that KSU was No. 1 out of all 500 public universities in winning these five elite scholarships over 23 years—including pre-eminent public universities like Michigan, Wisconsin, UCLA, North Carolina, and Texas.

The CASE/Carnegie Foundation selects only one National Professor of the Year every year. K-State professors were selected for that award in 1996, 2007, and 2008. K-State is the only land grant school to win that award three times. From 1990 to 2009, 7 KSU faculty members won the state Professor of the Year awards.

By 2001, Kansas State's food safety and animal health programs had become the best in the world. The building of the Biosecurity Research Institute in 2006, the creation of the new KSU Olathe campus in 2008, and the selection of K-State by the DHS in 2008 to be the home of NBAF represent arguably the greatest academic successes in the history of Kansas State University.

For the first time, K-State had a major campus in the state's most affluent and populated county: Johnson County. The $1.3 billion NBAF complex will become the animal health equivalent for America that the Center for Disease Control (CDC) in Atlanta has been for human health since World War II.

K-State leaders—like Jim Coffman, Ron Trewyn, Sue Peterson, Jim Guikema, Paul Lowe, and Bob Krause—along with a multitude of state and federal political leaders—like Governor Kathleen Sebelius, Lt. Governor Mark Parkinson, and our two U.S. Senators, Pat Roberts and Sam Brownback, and state legislative leaders like Senator Steve Morris and Representative Melvin Neufeld and the two minority leaders, Senator Anthony Hensley, and Representative Dennis McKinney—made NBAF happen. Because of our bipartisan strategy, the DHS selected K-State unanimously for NBAF.

From the beginning, however, from 1999 to 2008, it was Senator Pat Roberts who was the leader, visionary, and strategic leader who led our bipartisan team to winning NBAF. Pat Roberts has reminded me several times over the years of a meeting the two of us had at the President's house in late 2005 about NBAF when I told him, "Pat, we can do this." Senator Roberts agreed and we spent the next three years making it happen.

On January 11, 2014, the U.S. Senate finally put the final $404 million in the 2015 national budget for NBAF. The next day, Pat called to remind me of our long partnership on NBAF: "Jon, the K-State selection for NBAF would not have happened without your administration making the decision in 1999 that the school's No. 1 priority would be animal health—and I just wanted you to know that."

In 1986 and 1987, several members of the Board of Regents openly complained that K-State leaders had looked mainly to the western part of Kansas from the 1950's to the 1980's. Yet, in 2008, the two major daily papers to the east, the TOPEKA CAPITAL JOURNAL and the KANSAS CITY STAR, recognized that we had been quite successful in the eastern part of Kansas over 22 years.

After I announced my retirement on May 12, 2008, both papers wrote that we had gotten a great deal accomplished. The TOPEKA CAPITAL JOURNAL posted a nice editorial on May 21, 2008: "When Jon Wefald cleans out the president's office in Anderson Hall he will have left his mark on virtually every aspect of the university. . . Kansas State University may not see his like again anytime soon."

On May 15, 2008, the KANSAS CITY STAR penned the following editorial: "Kansas State University President Jon Wefald is gifted with the common touch and uncommon vision. Without a trace of pretension, the folksy leader turned a sleepy land grant university into an academic, athletic, and economic powerhouse. Kansas is much the better for it. . .Wefald will leave the state's young people with a first-rate college choice in Manhattan."

On July 14, 2014, Dolph Simons, the publisher and chief editor of the LAWRENCE JOURNAL WORLD, proclaimed: "Few American university presidents or chancellors have made such a difference in their institutions as did Jon Wefald in his 23 years as president of Kansas State University. . .A huge transformation took place under Wefald's leadership. . .Wefald turned the school around."

Brad Everett, a city commissioner from 2001 to 2006, explained the differences between Manhattan before 1986 and after 2009 in a memo on May 25, 2014. Brad's family moved to Manhattan in 1957. His family lived on the corner of College Avenue and Hobbs Drive with a pasture right across the street. He graduated from Kansas State in 1987. Today, he is the General Manager of the Hilton Garden Inn and the Manhattan Conference Center.

Looking back to Manhattan before 1986, Brad remembered that the city basically stopped at Hudson Avenue on the west side of town: "After 1986, everything changed with Jon Wefald's arrival. He transformed our modest town into a lively, well-known, and prospering community. I was soon seeing by the early 1990's a multitude of new housing developments and new shopping centers. The growth in the west part of Manhattan was stunning. The student body grew; the city limits expanded; and the previously sub-par Kansas State football program became an elite program. Through his hard work and vision, Jon Wefald has taken Manhattan, Kansas from the smaller Flint Hills to the proverbial mountaintop."[446]

On Wednesday, June 18, 2014, I was thrilled to get a call from President Kirk Schulz that he was going to recommend naming a new state-of-the-art $77 million, 129,000-square-feet residence hall Wefald Hall in 2016. Kirk called it a transformational hall.

I was pleased to see some nice quotes the next day about the naming from several members of the Board of Regents. Regent Ed McKechnie, for example, was quoted in the MANHATTAN MERCURY: "This is a transformational hall, which is pretty neat, for a transformational guy."

The Chairman of the Regents, Fred Logan, also made some nice comments about my 23 years: "I think if you looked at higher education in Kansas he was, it's fair to say, a historic figure. He was an historic president."[447]

When I arrived at K-State in 1986, most educational analysts believed that KU was light-years ahead of our school in so many areas, including research funding, private giving, new buildings, and athletic success. By 2009, no one was saying that anymore.

In 23 years, we had accomplished at least as much academically, administratively, and athletically as any administration in the history of the school. By 2009, Kansas State University had become one of the best land grant schools in America. The upshot of our 23 years is quite simple: From 1986 to 2009, our administration completely transformed Kansas State University.

Footnotes

[1] Column, MARSHALL INDEPENDENT and reprinted, MANHATTAN MERCURY, May 11, 2007

[2] Malcolm Gladwell, THE OUTLIERS: THE STORY OF SUCCESS (Little, Brown and Company, 2008), 40.

[3] James C. Carey, KANSAS STATE UNIVERSITY: THE QUEST FOR IDENTITY (Lawrence, Kansas, The Regents Press of Kansas, 1977), 40.

[4] J.D. Walters, HISTORY OF KANSAS STATE AGRICULTURAL COLLEGE (Manhattan, Kansas, The Printing Department of the Kansas State Agricultural College, 1909), 47.

[5] Carey, KANSAS STATE UNIVERSITY: THE QUEST FOR IDENTITY, 43-46.

[6] Carey, THE QUEST FOR IDENTITY, 43-46.

[7] Julius Willard, HISTORY OF KANSAS STATE COLLEGE OF AGRICULTURE AND APPLIED SCIENCE (Kansas State College Press, Manhattan, Kansas, 1940), 35-47.

[8] Carey, THE QUEST FOR IDENTITY, 98.

[9] Carey, THE QUEST FOR IDENTITY, 98

[10] Willard, HISTORY OF KANSAS STATE COLLEGE, 150

[11] Carey, THE QUEST FOR IDENTITY, 101-107

[12] Clifford S. Griffin, THE UNIVERSITY OF KANSAS: A HISTORY (Lawrence, Kansas: The University Press of Kansas, 1974), 336-340

[13] Griffin, THE UNIVERSITY OF KANSAS, 411-413

[14] Carey, THE QUEST FOR IDENTITY, 141

[15] Carey, THE QUEST FOR IDENTITY, 155

[16] Stephen Ambrose and Richard H. Immerman, MILTON S. EISENHOWER: EDUCATIONAL STATESMAN (Baltimore: The John Hopkins Press, 2009) 79-80

[17] Carey, THE QUEST FOR IDENTITY, 179

[18] Carey, THE QUEST FOR IDENTITY, 185-205.

[19] Carey, THE QUEST FOR IDENTITY, 185-205, 267-278.

[20] Griffin, THE UNIVERSITY OF KANSAS, 2

[21] Carey, THE QUEST FOR IDENTITY, 277

[22] Presentation by President Duane Acker, "A Report on Kansas State University, May, 1986," 5

[23] Duane Acker, TWO AT A TIME (New York, iUniverse, 2010) 260-265

[24] Presentation by Duane Acker, "From a University President: the Next Step, May 1, 1986," 5

[25] Editorial, MANHATTAN MERCURY, July 23, 1985.

[26] Editorial, WICHITA EAGLE, August 6, 1985.

[27] Editorial, MANHATTAN MERCURY, August 6, 1985

[28] John Dunbar, OPPORTUNITY KNOCKED AND I LISTENED (Manhattan, Kansas, Sunflower University Press, 2002) 237.

[29] Column, MANHATTAN MERCURY, April 18, 1985.

[30] (Pat Bosco, October 7, 2010, email message to author.)

[31] (Pat Bosco, October 7, 2010, email message to author). State of the University Presentation, September 12, 1989.

[32] (Pat Bosco, October 7, 2010, email message to author).

[33] (Tom Rawson, October 21, 2010, email message to author)

[34] (Tom Rawson, October 21, 2010, email message to author).

[35] State of the University Presentation, September, 12, 1989.

[36] State of the University Presentation, September 12, 1989.

[37] State of the University Presentation, September 11, 1990.

[38] State of the University Presentation, September 11, 1990

[39] State of the University Presentation, September 11, 1990

[40] State of the University Presentation, September 11, 1990 and (Tom Rawson, October 21, 2010, email to author)

[41] (Ruth Dyer, May 24, 2013, email message to author)

[42] (Tom Rawson, October 21, 2010, email message to author)

[43] (Tom Rawson, October 21, 2010, email message to author)

[44] Kansas State University Press Release, September 11, 1990.

45 Column in MANHATTAN MERCURY, November 11, 1990.

[46] Column in MANHATTAN MERCURY, November 11, 1990 and Kansas State News Services Press Release, September 11, 1990.

[47] Column, UNIVERSITY DAILY KANSAN, November 2, 1990.

[48] Column in MANHATTAN MERCURY, November 2, 1990.

[49] Column in MANHATTAN MERCURY, November 5, 1990.

[50] (Randy Martin, April 19, 2011, email message to author)

[51] (Dan Bolen, October 13, 2011, email message to author)

[52] Daniel Goleman, EMOTIONAL INTELLIGENCE (New York, Bantam Books, 1995) 4.

[53] Elizabeth Haas Edersheim, THE DEFINITIVE DRUCKER (New York, McGraw-Hill, 2007), 12-15.

[54] James J. Duderstadt, A UNIVERSITY FOR THE 21ST CENTURY (Ann Arbor, Michigan, The University of Michigan Press, 2000).

[55] Charles Reagan, THE LANDON LECTURES, 1984-2010 (Manhattan, Kansas, Ag Press Publishing, 2011), 57-58.

[56] Daniel Schulman, SONS OF WICHITA (Grand Central Publishing, 2014) 240-255.

[57] Schulman, SONS OF WICHITA, 240-255.

[58] THE GOALS OF THE K-STATE PRESIDENT FOR 2001-02 SENT TO THE KANSAS BOARD OF REGENTS, August, 2001.

[59] THE GOALS OF THE K-STATE PRESIDENT FOR 2001-02 SENT TO THE KANSAS BOARD OF REGENTS, August, 2001.

[60] Ed Rice, NOTES COMPILED ON THE EVENTS OF JUNE 11, 2008.

[61] (Elizabeth Unger, March 3, 2011, email message to author)

[62] (Mel Chastain, September 27, 2006, email message to author)

[63] (Yar Ebadi, February 9, 2011, email message to author)

[64] (Michael Holen, July 1, 2011, email message to author)

[65] (Dennis Law, June 4, 2011, email message to author)

[66] (Terry King, October 21, 2011, email message to author)

[67] (Fred Fairchild, July 8, 2010, email message to author)

[68] (Fred Fairchild, July 8, 2010, email message to author)

[69] Letter to the editor, MANHATTAN MERCURY, March 4, 1996.

[70] Robert J. Shoop, A UNIVERSITY RENAISSANCE: JON WEFALD'S PRESIDENCY AT KANSAS STATE (Manhattan, Kansas. AgPress Publishing, 2001) 84.

[71] Shoop, UNIVERSITY RENAISSANCE, 181-182.

[72] Column, K-STATE COLLEGIAN, October 6, 1996.

[73] Column, K-STATE COLLEGIAN, September 10, 1996.

[74] Richard Current, T. Harry Williams, and Frank Freidel, AMERICAN HISTORY: A SURVEY, (New York, Alfred A. Knopp, 1963), 514 and 637.

[75] Wheat Genetics Resource Center, accessed March 16, 2014.

[76] Wheat Genetics Resource Center, accessed March 16, 2014.

[77] Ron Trewyn, VALUE-ADDED: THE IMPACT OF TEACHING AND RESEARCH AT KANSAS STATE UNIVERSITY, 1998.

[78] (Jim Coffman, December 23, 2011, email message to author)

[79] (Jim Coffman, December 23, 2011, email message to author & Harald Prins, December 21, 2011, email message to author)

[80] (Harald Prins, December 21, 2011 & December 22, 2011, email messages to author)

[81] (Harald Prins, December 21, 2011 & December 22, 2011, email messages to author)

[82] (Lew Cocke, January 1, 2012, email message to author & Dean Zollman, January 5, 2012, email message to author & Physics Department Website Facts, December 287, 2011)

[83] (The Kansas State University Division Website, December 27, 2011 & A History of the Division of Biology by Brian Spooner, December 29, 2011, email message to author)

[84] (Brian Spooner, January 11, 2012, email message to author)

[85] (Brian Spooner, January 11, 2012, email message to author)

[86] The Arizona State University Center for Measuring University Performance, The Top 200 Institutions—Total Research Expenditures (2009 Control Rank)

[87] Jon Wefald, State of the University Address, September 11, 1990.

[88] (Paul Lowe, July 19, 2011, email message to author)

[89] (Paul Lowe, July 19, 2011, email message to author)

[90] Kansas State News Services, Press Release on Ron Trewyn's appointment as Associate Vice-Provost for Research, September 2, 1994.

[91] (Paul Lowe, July 19, 2011, email message to author)

[92] Paul Lowe, July 19, 2011, email message to author)

93 (Paul Lowe, January 4, 2012, email message to author)

94 (Paul Lowe, July 19, 2011, email message to author)

95 The Arizona State University Center for Measuring University Performance, The Top 200 Institutions—Total Research Expenditures (2009 Control Rank)

96 (Paul Lowe, July 19, 2011, email message to author)

97 (Beth Unger, May 11, 2010, email message to author)

98 (Beth Unger, May 11, 2010, email message to author)

99 (Beth Unger, May 11, 2010, email message to author)

100 (Beth Unger, May 11, 2010, email message to author)

101 (Beth Unger, May 23, 2011, email message to author)

102 (Beth Unger, May 23, 2011, email message to author)

103 (Beth Unger, May 11, 2010, email message to author)

104 (Beth Unger, May 11, 2010, email message to author)

105 (Beth Unger, May 11, 2010, email message to author)

106 Kansas State News Services, Press Release, November 25, 1997.

107 Kansas State News Services, Press Release, May 2, 1989.

108 Kansas State News Services, Press Release, June, 7, 1990.

109 Kansas State News Services, Press Releases, September 8, 1992 and September 30, 1993.

110 (Myra Gordon, August 3, 2011, email message to author)

111 (Myra Gordon, August 3, 2011, email message to author)

112 (Myra Gordon, August 3, 2011, email message to author)

113 ANNUAL REPORT OF THE KANSAS STATE UNIVERSITY FOUNDATION ANNUAL REPORT 2004: 1944 to 2004, 2-4.

[114] FOUNDATION ANNUAL REPORT 2004, 7-8.

[115] ANNUAL REPORT 2004, 7-11.

[116] Griffin, The University of Kansas: A History, 441-442, 524-526

[117] FOUNDATION REPORT 2004, 9-10.

[118] FOUNDATION REPORT 2004, 10-11

[119] Shoop, UNIVERSITY RENAISSANCE, 176-178.

[120] (KSU Foundation's Communication Department, October 2, 2009, email message to author)

[121] (Communication Department, October 2, 2009, email message to author)

[122] (Julie Lea, Foundation Communications, August 11, 2011, email message to author)

[123] (Foundation Communications, October 2, 2009, email to author)

[124] (Tim Lindemuth, December 13, 2010, email message to author)

[125] (Tim Lindemuth, December 13, 2010, email message to author)

[126] (Tim Lindemuth, December 13, 2010, email message to author and Amy Button Renz, September 29, 2011, email to author)

[127] (Lynn Beier, August 15, 2011, email message to author)

[128] (Tim Lindemuth, December 13, 2010, email message to author)

[129] (Amy Renz, September 29, 2011, email message to author and Tim Lindemuth, December 13, 2010, email message to author)

[130] (Brice Hobrock, October 28, 2010, email message to author)

[131] Brice Hobrock, A Brief History of the Kansas State Library (unpublished paper, April 22, 2010), 1-3.

[132] Hobrock, A Brief History of the Kansas State Library, 2-4.

[133] Hobrock, A Brief History of the Kansas State Library, 1-2.

[134] Giffin, THE UNIVERSITY OF KANSAS, 78-80.

[135] Brice Hobrock, A Brief History of the Kansas State Library, 2nd Edition (Unpublished, October 28, 2010) 1-2

[136] Hobrock, A Short History of the Kansas State Library, April 22, 2010, 2-3.

[137] Hobrock, A Short History, 3.

[138] Hobrock, A Brief History, 4.

[139] State of the University Presentations, 1989, 1990, 1995, and Hobrock, A Brief History, 4-5.

[140] Hobrock, A Brief History of the Library, 2nd Edition, 2-4.

[141] Hobrock, A Brief History, 3-5.

[142] Hobrock, A Brief History, 4-5.

[143] Hobrock, A Brief History, 4-5.

[144] Hobrock, A Brief History, 5.

[145] Hobrock, A Brief History, 5-6.

[146] Hobrock, A Brief History, 5-6

[147] Hobrock, A Brief History, 7.

[148] Hobrock, A Brief History, 5-6

[149] Hobrock, A Brief History, 6-7.

[150] Hobrock, A Brief History, 6-7.

[151] Hobrock, A Brief History, 2nd Edition, 4-5.

[152] Hobrock, A Brief History, 2nd Edition, 5-6.

[153] Hobrock, A Brief History, 2nd Edition, 6-7.

[154] Ann Thackrey Berry and Russell Thackrey, A BRIEF HISTORY OF THE FRIENDS OF ART (Montgomery Publications, 1995), 1-3.

[155] (Jessica Reichman, November 19, 2010, email message to author)

[156] Kansas State News Services Press Release, March 7, 1990

[157] Wefald, Ruth Ann. 2010. Interview by author. Manhattan. October 2.

[158] Wefald, Ruth Ann. 2010. Interview by author. Manhattan. October 2.

[159] Kansas State News Services Press Release, September 13, 1993.

[160] Wefald, Ruth Ann. 2010. Interview with author.

[161] (Lorne Render, January 4, 2016, email message to author)

[162] Nelson Britt's Resume. February, 14, 1992.

[163] (Jessica Reichman, November 19, 2010, email message to author).

[164] (Lorne Render, May 10, 2010, email message to author).

[165] (Lorne Render, May 10, 2010, email message to author).

[166] Kansas State News Services Press Release, October 2, 1996.

[167] (Beth Unger, October 29, 2010, email message to author)

[168] Kansas State News Services Press Release, October 2, 1996.

[169] (Lorne Render, May 10, 2010, email message to author)

[170] (Lorne Render, May, 10, 2010, email message to author)

[171] (Lorne Render, May 10, 2010, email message to author)

[172] (Lorne Render, May 10, 2010, email message to author)

[173] (Lorne Render, May 10, 2010, email message to author)

[174] (Linda Duke, January 8, 2016, email message to author)

[175] Column in MANHATTAN MERCURY, October 31, 1966.

[176] (Joe Aistrup, December 19, 2011, email message to author)

[177] (Tom Rawson, December 19, 2011, email message to author)

[178] (Karin Westman, February 6, 2012, email message to author)

[179] (Karin Westman, February 6, 2012, email message to author)

[180] (Karin Westman, February 6, 2012, email message to author)

[181] (Steve White, December 13, 2011, email message to author)

[182] (Robert Corum, December 27, 2011, email message to author)

[183] (Robert Corum, December 27, 2011, email message to author)

[184] (Richard Marston, December 28, 2011, email message to author)

[185] (Richard Marston, December 28, 2011, email message to author)

[186] (Angela Powers, February 20, 2012, email message to author)

[187] Marcelo Sabates, February 27, 2012, email message to author)

[188] Marcelo Sabates, February 27, 2012, email message to author)

[189] (Joe Aistrup, January 16, 2012, email message to author)

[190] (Dale Herspring, February 1, 2012, email message to author)

[191] (Sue Zschoche, February 17, 2012, email message to author)

[192] (Sue Zschoche, February 17, 2012, email message to author)

[193] (David Stone, January 17, 2012, email message to author)

[194] (Charles Reagan, January 25, 2012, email message to author)

[195] (Charles Reagan, January 25, 2012, email message to author)

[196] (David Stone, January 17, 2012, email message to author)

[197] (Dana Hastings, November 11, 2011, email message to author)

[198] (Marci Maullar, May 10, email message to author)

[199] (Charlie Griffin, May 25, 2010, email message to author)

[200] (Frank Tracz, November 10, 2010, email message to author)

[201] (Frank Tracz, August 5, 2011, email message to author)

[202] (Frank Tracz, November 11, 2011, email message to author)

[203] (Charlie Griffin, May 25, 2010, email message to author)

[204] (Charlie Griffin, May 25, 2010, email message to author)

[205] (Justin Green, April 4, 2011, email message to author)

[206] (Jim Hohenbary, February 2, 2012, email message to author)

[207] (Jim Hohenbary, February 2, 2012, email message to author)

[208] (Jim Hohenbary, February 2, 2012, email message to author)

[209] (Cheryl May, November 1, 2011, email message to author)

[210] (Jim Hohenbary, February 2, 2012, email message to author)

[211] (Jim Hohenbary, February 2, 2012, email message to author)

[212] (Jim Hohenbary, February 2, 2012, email message to author)

[213] (Jim Hohenbary, February 2, 2012, email message to author)

[214] (Cheryl May, November 1, 2011, email message to author)

[215] (Cheryl May, November 1, 2011, email message to author)

[216] (Cheryl May, November 1, 2011, email message to author)

[217] (Mark Taussig, February 10, 2012, email message to author)

[218] (Mark Taussig, February 10, 2012, email message to author)

[219] (Mark Taussig, February 10, 2012, email message to author)

[220] (Mark Taussig, February 10, 2012, email message to author)

221 (Tom Warner, January 22, 2012, email message to author)

222 (Tom Warner, January 22, 2012, email message to author)

223 (Tom Warner, February 5, 2012, email message to author)

224 (Tom Warner, January 22, 2012, email message to author)

225 (Tom Warner, January 22, 2012, email message to author)

226 (Kiffnie Holt, February 5, 2012, email message to author)

227 (Dennis Kuhlman, October 20, 2011, email message to author)

228 (Dennis Kuhlman, October 20, 2010, email message to author)

229 (Dennis Kuhlman, December 22, 2011, email message to author)

230 (Charles Reagan, January 30, 2012, email message to author)

231 Jim Coffman, KANSAS STATE'S PROPOSAL TO THE REGENTS REGARDING THE MERGER OF THE KANSAS COLLEGE OF TECHNOLOGY WITH KANSAS STATE UNIVERSITY, 1-4.

232 (Dennis Kuhlman, October 20, 2011, email message to author)

233 (Dennis Kuhlman, October 20, 2011, email message to author)

234 (Charles Reagan, January 30, 2012, email message to author)

235 (Charles Reagan, January 30, 2012, email message to author)

236 (Dennis Kuhlman, October 20, 2011, email message to author)

237 (Dennis Kuhlman, October 20, 2011, email message to author)

238 Column, SPORTS ILLUSTRATED, September 4, 1989.

239 Column, SPORTS ILLUSTRATED, September 4, 1989.

240 K-STATE 2011-12 MEN'S BASKETBALL MEDIA GUIDE.

241 Column, SPORTS ILLUSTRATED, September 4, 1989.

[242] Kevin Haskins, KANSAS STATE UNIVERSITY FOOTBALL VAULT: THE HISTORY OF THE WILDCATS (Whitman Publishing Company, Atlanta, Georgia, 2009), 67-68.

[243] Tim Fitzgerald, WILDCAT GRIDIRON GUIDE: PAST AND PRESENT STORIES ABOUT K-STATE FOOTBALL (Spirit Street Publishing, Manhattan, Kansas, 2001), 56-66.

[244] Fitzgerald, WILDCAT GRIDIRON GUIDE, 56-66.

[245] Mark Janssen, BILL SNYDER: THEY SAID IT COULDN'T BE DONE (Worzalla Publishing, Steven Points, Wisconsin, 2006), 43-44.

[246] George Lynn Cross, THE OU FOOTBALL TRADITION: PRESIDENTS CAN'T PUNT (University of Oklahoma Press, Norman, Oklahoma, 1977), 3-131

[247] "Gaylord Family Oklahoma Memorial Stadium," WIKIPEDIA. Accessed January 10, 2011, http//en.wikipedia.org/wiki.html.

[248] Cross, PRESIDENTS CAN'T PUNT, 36-149 and Jim Fletcher, GUIDE TO SOONER FOOTBALL (Regnery Publishing, Inc., Washington D.C., 2008) 87-90.

[249] Rob Doster, editor, GAMEDAY: NEBRASKA FOOTBALL, (Triumph Books, Chicago, Illinois, 2006), 63-78.

[250] Tfedderson2, 2010, "Obituary—Clifford M. Hardin." Accessed April 1, 2014. http://scarletunl.edu/7p=8007. Doster, NEBRAKSA FOOTBALL, 6-9.

[251] KANSAS STATE WILDCATS YEARBOOK: 1993.

[252] Fitzgerald, WILDCAT GRIDIRON GUIDE,

[253] Column, SPORTS ILLUSTRATED, September 4, 1989

[254] David Smale, THE HISTORY OF KANSAS STATE FOOTBALL (Lenexa, Kansas, Quality Sports Publication, 1994) 30-31 and Janssen, BILL SNYDER, 47-48

[255] Fitzgerald, WILDCAT GRIDIRON GUIDE,

[256] Janssen, BILL SNYDER, 48-52

[257] Column, SPORTS ILLUSTRATED, September 4, 1989.

[258] Janssen, BILL SNYDER, 52-53.

[259] 1993 KANSAS STATE UNIVERSITY FOOTBALL MEDIA GUIDE, Column, SPORTS ILLUSTRATED, August 31, 1992, Janssen, BILL SNYDER, 61-68, Smale, THE STORY OF KANSAS STATE FOOTBALL, 12

[260] 1993 KANSAS STATE UNIVERSITY FOOTBALL MEDIA GUIDE, 1994 KANSAS STATE UNIVERSITY FOOTBALL MEDIA GUIDE, Column, SPORTS ILLUSTRATED, August 31, 1992.

[261] 2002 KANSAS STATE FOOTBALL MEDIA GUIDE, 2003 KANSAS STATE MEDIA GUIDE, 2004 KANSAS STAE FOOTBALL MEDIA GUIDE, 2010 KANSAS STATE FOOTBALL MEDIA GUIDE, Janssen, BILL SNYDER, 61-68.

[262] 2003 KANSAS STATE FOOTBALL MEDIA GUIDE, 2004 KANSAS STATE FOOTBALL MEDIA GUIDE, 2010 KANSAS STATE FOOTBALL MEDIA GUIDE

[263] Column in SPORTS ILLUSTRATED, August 31, 1992.

[264] Stan Weber, TALES FROM THE KANSAS STATE SIDELINE (Champaign, Illinois, Sports Publishing L.L.C, 2005), 28-49.

[265] Column, MANHATTAN MERCURY, June 28, 1993.

[266] Janssen, BILL SNYDER, 111.

[267] Janssen, BILL SNYDER, 108.

[268] Column, MANHATTAN MERCURY, September 21, 2011.

[269] Column, HOUSTON POST, September 20, 1992.

[270] Column, CHICAGO TRIBUNE, December 16, 1993.

[271] Jeffrey J. Selingoo and Jack Stripling, "Nebraska's Ouster opens a Painful Debate Within the AAU, THE CHRONICLE OF HIGHER EDUCATION, May 2, 2011.

[272] Column, NEW YORK TIMES, May 2, 2011 and Column, BLEACHER REPORT, May 7, 2011.

[273] Column, LAWRENCE JOURNAL WORLD, JUNE 12, 2010; Column, TOPEKA CAPITAL JOURNAL, June 6, 2010; Column, KANSAS CITY STAR, June 11, 2010.

[274] Column, KANSAS CITY STAR, June 11, 2010.

[275] Column, KANSAS CITY STAR, September 7, 2011; Chris Day, NEWSPRESS, September 3, 2011. Accessed September 4, 2011. http:11www.stwnewspress.com/osusports/x1095935786.

[276] Column, DAILY TEXAN, September 21, 2011; Jenni Carlson, "The Oklahoma Plan is so crazy it just might work," September 20, 2011. Accessed September 22, 2011. http://newsok.com.; WIKIPEDIA 2014. "The Big 12 Conference." Accessed April 6, 2014. http://en.wikipedia.org/wik/Big 12 Conference.

[277] Wikipedia 2014. "The Big 12 Conference." Accessed April 6, 2014. http://en.wikipedia.org/wik/Big 12 Conference.

[278] 2010 K-STATE FOOTBALL MEDIA GUIDE.

[279] 2010 K-STATE FOOTBALL MEDIA GUIDE.

[280] 2010 K-STATE FOOTBALL MEDIA GUIDE.

[281] 2010 K-STATE FOOTBALL MEDIA GUIDE.

[282] Fitzgerald, WILDCAT GRIDIRON GUIDE, 198-206.

[283] 2010 K-STATE FOOTBALL MEDIA GUIDE.

[284] Column, USA TODAY, November 26, 2012.

[285] Column, USA TODAY, December 12, 2013.

[286] Column, KANSAS CITY STAR, November 7, 2011.

[287] Column, CHRONICLE OF HIGHER EDUCATION, December 11, 2011.

[288] 2003 AND 2004 KANSAS STATE FOOTBALL MEDIA GUIDE.

[289] 2010 KANSAS STATE FOOTBALL MEDIA GUIDE.

[290] 2004 KANSAS STATE FOOTBALL MEDIA GUIDE.

[291] Janssen, BILL SNYDER, 195.

[292] Janssen, BILL SNYDER, 199

[293] Janssen, BILL SNYDER, 199.

[294] Janssen, BILL SNYDER, 201-204.

[295] Column, MANHATTAN MERCURY, December 19, 1993.

[296] Column, MANHATTAN MERCURY, December 19, 1993.

[297] Column, MANHATTAN MERCURY, DECEMBER 19, 1993 and Column in MANHATTAN MERCURY, September 24, 2000

[298] Column, MINNEAPOLIS TRIBUNE, July 15, 2010.

[299] (John Kadlec, March 27, 2012, email message to author)

[300] Shoop, UNIVERSITY RENAISSANCE, 59.

[301] Shoop, 192-193.

[302] (Bob Stoops, April 25, 2012, email message to author)

[303] (Bret Bielema, April 10, 2013, email message to author)

[304] (Mark Mangino, May 8, 2012, email message to author)

[305] (Phil Bennett, April 18, 2012, email message to author)

[306] (Ron A. Hudson, April 28, 2012, email message to author)

[307] (Mike Leach, January 13, 2014, email message to author)

[308] Letter to Editor, MANHATTAN MERCURY, November 8, 2012.

[309] 2011 K-STATE VOLLEYBALL MEDIA ALMANAC.

[310] 2011 K-STATE VOLLEYBALL MEDIA ALMANAC.

[311] (Jim McLaughlin, April 24, 2012, email message to author)

[312] (Jim McLaughlin, April 24, 2012, email message to author)

[313] 2011 K-STATE VOLLEYBALL MEDIA GUIDE.

[314] (Suzie Fritz, May 5, 2012, email message to author)

[315] 2011-12 K-STATE WOMEN'S BASKETBALL MEDIA GUIDE.

[316] 2011-12 K-STATE WOMEN'S BASKETBALL MEDIA GUIDE.

[317] Shoop, UNIVERSITY RENAISSANCE, 193.

[318] (Deb Patterson, May 4, 2012, email message to author)

[319] (Kamie Ethridge, May 4, 2012, email message to author)

[320] 2011-12 K-STATE WOMEN'S BASKETBALL MEDIA GUIDE.

[321] (Deb Patterson, May 4, 2012, email message to author)

[322] 2011-12 K-STATE MEN'S BASKETBALL MEDIA GUIDE.

[323] 2011-12 K-STATE MEN'S BASKETBALL MEDIA GUIDE.

[324] (Charles Baker, April 15, 2012, email message to author)

[325] 2011-2012 KANSAS STATE MEN'S BASKETBALL MEDIA GUIDE.

[326] WIKIPEDIA, 2012. "Auburn's Men's Basketball," Accessed, May 18, 2012. http://en.wikipedia.org/wiki,Auburn; WIKIPEDIA, 2012. "Northwestern Wildcat Men's Basketball." Accessed, May 18, 2012. http:en.wikipedia.org/wiki, Northwestern; WIKIPEDIA, 2012, "Oregon State Beavers Men's Basketball," Accessed May 18, 2012. http://en.wikipedia.org/wiki/Oregon State.

[327] 2011-12 K-STATE MEN'S BASKETBALL MEDIA GUIDE.

[328] 2011-12 K-STATE MEN'S BASKETBALL MEDIA GUIDE.

[329] (Bob Huggins, May 12, 2012, email message to author)

[330] 2011-12 KANSAS STATE MEN'S BASKETBALL MEDIA GUIDE.

[331] 2011-12 KANSAS STATE MEN'S BASKETBALL MEDIA GUIDE.

[332] 2011-12 KANSAS STATE MEN'S BASKETBALL MEDIA GUIDE.

[333] 2011-12 KANSAS STATE MEN'S BASKETBALL MEDIA GUIDE.

[334] (Brad Underwood, June 7, 2012, email message to author)

[335] 2011-12 KANSAS STATE MEN'S BASKETBALL MEDIA GUIDE

[336] Column, MANHATTAN MERCURY, March 4, 2012

[337] 2015-16 KANSAS STATE MEN'S BASKETBALL GUIDE, 177

[338] (Frank Martin, June 14, 2012, email message to author)

[339] 2007 KANSAS STATE FOOTBALL MEDIA GUIDE.

[340] 2007 KANSAS STATE FOOTBALL MEDIA GUIDE.

[341] 2010 KANSAS STATE FOOTBALL MEDIA GUIDE.

[342] 2010 KANSAS STATE FOOTBALL MEDIA GUIDE.

[343] 2010 KANSAS STATE FOOTBALL MEDIA GUIDE.

[344] 2010 KANSAS STATE FOOTBALL MEDIA GUIDE.

[345] 2010 KANSAS STATE FOOTBALL MEDIA GUIDE.

[346] 2010 KANSAS STATE FOOTBALL MEDIA GUIDE.

[347] Column, KANSAS STATE COLLEGIAN, December 9, 2008.

[348] INDIANA FOOTBALL HISTORY DATABASE. Accessed August 26, 2012. http://www.nationalchamps.net/NCAA/database. Htm. KENTUCKY FOOTALL HISTORY DATEBASE. Accessed March 16, 2012. Hhtp://www.nationalchamps.net/NCAA/database/Kentucky. Htm. WIKIPEDIA. 2012. "Minnesota Golden Gophers Football." Accessed February 20, 2012. http://en.wikipedia.org/wiki/Minnesota Gophers. Htm.

[349] NOTRE DAME FOOTBALL HISTORY DATABASE. Accessed March 19, 2012. http://www.national champs.net/NCAA/database/notre dame database. Htm.

[350] KANSAS BOARD OF REGENTS CONFIDENTIAL EXIT ANALYSIS. Prepared by Grant Thornton LLP, April 27, 2009.

[351] Column. MANHATTAN MERCURY, September 9, 2010. Accessed September 12, 2010. http://themercury.pressmart.net/MM/MM/2010/09/12/ArticleHtmls. WIKIPEDIA 2012. "Prince Buyout." Accessed May 5, 2012. http://en.wikipedia.org/wiki/

[352] WIKIPEDIA 2012. "Prince Buyout." Accessed May 5, 2012. Hhtp://en.wikipedia.org/wiki/

[353] Column, MANHATTAN MERCURY, September 12, 2010. http://the mercury. Pressmart.net/MM/MM/2010/09/12/ArticleHtmis.

[354] Column, MANHATTAN MERCURY, September 12, 2010. http://the mercury.Pressmart.net/MM/MM/2010/09/12/ArticleHtmis.

[355] WIKIPEDIA 2012. "Prince Buyout." Accessed May 5, 2012. http://en.wikipedia.org/wiki/

[356] Kirk Schulz, TRANSITION AUDIT FINAL REPORT presented to the Kansas Board of Regents, November 19, 2009.

[357] Kirk Schulz, TRANSITION AUDIT FINAL REPORT presented to the Kansas Board of Regents, November 19, 2009

[358] Kirk Schulz, TRANSITION AUDIT FINAL REPORT presented to the Kansas Board of Regents, November 19, 2009

[359] 19th ANNUAL STATE OF THE UNIVERSITY ADDRESS, September 24, 2004.

[360] 19th ANNUAL STATE OF THE UNIVERSITY ADDRESS, September 24, 2004.

[361] 19th ANNUAL STATE OF THE UNIVERSITY ADDRESS, September 24, 2004. 20th ANNUAL STATE OF THE UNIVERSITY ADDRESS, September 2, 2005.

[362] 19th ANNUAL STATE OF THE UNIVERSITY ADDRESS, September 24, 2004. 20th ANNUAL STATE OF THE UNIVERSITY, September 2, 2005. Jon Wefald, REPORT TO THE KANSAS BOARD OF REGENTS: 2005-06 GOALS, May 19, 2005.

[363] David Quammen, "Out of the Wild," POPULAR SCIENCE, October, 1962.

[364] Ron Trewyn and Jim Guikema, THE HOMELAND DEFENSE FOOD SAFETY, SECURITY, AND EMERGENCY PREPAREDNESS PROGRAM, March, 1999.

[365] Kansas State News Services Press Release, October 27, 1999.

[366] Jon Wefald, Prepared Notes on the Legislative Meeting at K-State, and the 2002 Legislative Session, May 1, 2002.

[367] Jon Wefald, Prepared Notes on the Legislative Meeting at K-State and the 2002 Legislative Session, May 1, 2002.

[368] Bruce Shubert, October 9, 2012, email message to author.

[369] K-State Press Services New Release, Friday, October 24, 2003.

[370] Clay Blair, October 14, 2012, email to author.

[371] Gail Eyestone, October 12, 2012, email to author.

[372] Gail Eyestone, October 12, 2012, email to author.

[373] K-State Press Services Press Release, October, 2006.

[374] KANSAS BOARD OF REGENTS: POLICY AND PROCEDURES MANUAL, LEGAL AUTHORITY, APPENDIX B (Rev.06-16-11)

[375] Letter from Mayor Michael Copeland to Jon Wefald, July 15, 2011.

[376] Copeland to Wefald, July 15, 2011.

[377] Letter from Dick Bond to Jon Wefald, September 8, 2011.

[378] Bond to Wefald, September 8, 2011.

[379] Bond to Wefald, September 8, 2011.

[380] Bond to Wefald, September 8, 2011.

[381] Bond to Wefald, September 8, 2011.

[382] Bond to Wefald, September 8, 2011.

[383] Bond to Wefald, September 8, 2011.

[384] Copeland to Jon Wefald, July 15, 2011.

[385] TALKING POINTS: KANSAS STATE UNIVERSITY, OLATHE. Accessed October 16, 2012. http://webmail. K-State.edu/service/homehtml.

[386] TALKING POINTS, Accessed October 16, 2012.

[387] Column, LAWRENCE JOURNAL WORLD, July 15, 2006.

[388] Copeland to Wefald, July 15, 2011. Bond to Wefald, September 8, 2011.

[389] WIKIPEDIA 2014. "Plum Island Animal Disease Center." Accessed April 19, 2014. http://en.wikipedia.org/wik/Plum_Island_Animal_Disease_Center.

[390] WIKIPEDIA 2014, "Plum Island Animal Disease Center."

[391] Jim Guikema, October 31, 2012, email to author, WIKIPEDIA 2014, "National Bio and Agro-Defense Facility. Accessed April 19, 2014. http://en.wikipedia.org/wiki/National_Bio_and_Agro_Defense_Facility.

[392] Guikema, October 31, 2012, email message to author. WIKIPEDIA 2014, "National Bio and Agro Defense Facility. Accessed April 19, 2014.

[393] Guikema, October 31, 2012, email message to author.

[394] Guikema, October 31, 2012, email message to author. WIKIPEDIA 2014, "National Bio and Agro Defense Facility, Accessed April 19, 2014.

[395] Column, KANSAS CITY STAR, April 11, 2013. Guikema, October 31, 2012, email message to author.

[396] Guikema, October 31, 2012, email message to author. WIKIPEDIA 2014, "National Bio and Agro-Defense Facility."

[397] K-STATER, ""National Bio and Agro-Defense Facility to be built in Manhattan: WE GOT IT," Spring, 2009.

[398] Jon Wefald, STATE OF THE UNIVERSITY ADDRESS, September 14, 2007; Jon Wefald, STATE OF THE UNIVERSITY ADDRESS, September 12, 2008; Jon Wefald and Duane Nellis, STATUS REPORT ON PRIORITY SETTING IN THE COLLEGES AND DEPARTMENTS: RANKINGS OF TOP DEPARTMENTS AND PROGRAMS; Jon Wefald's REPORT TO THE KANSAS BOARD OF REGENTS, 2008-09 GOALS.

[399] Jon Wefald, 23rd ANNUAL STATE OF THE UNIVERSITY ADDRESS, September 12, 2008; Jon Wefald, REPORT TO THE KANSAS BOARD OF REGENTS, 2008-09 GOALS; Jon Wefald and Duane Nellis, STATUS REPORT ON PRIORITY SETTING IN THE COLLEGES AND DEPARTMENTS: RANKINGS OF TOP DEPARTMENTS AND PROGRAMS.

[400] The Arizona State University Center for Measuring University Performance, The Top 200 Research Institutions, (2009).

[401] Robert J. Shoop, "Journey in Leadership," EDUCATIONAL CONSIDERATIONS, Vol. 37. No. 1, Fall, 2009, 2-3.

[402] Shoop, EDUCATIONAL CONSIDERATIONS, 2-3.

[403] Shoop, EDUCATIONAL CONSIDERATIONS, 2-3.

[404] Column, MINNEAPOLIS MORNING TRIBUNE, June 8, 2008.

[405] Column, MINNEAPOLIS TRIBUNE, June 6, 2008.

[406] Column, MINNEAPOLIS TRIBUNE, June 6, 2008. Joe Kimball. MINNPOST. March 16, 2012. http://www.minnpost.com/mary_staley_elected-habitat-humanity-international_board.

[407] Jon Wefald, Prepared Notes on Warren and Mary Lynn Staley: 2003-09.

[408] Wefald, Prepared Notes: 2003-09.

[409] Wefald, Prepared Notes: 2003-09.

[410] SCHOOL OF LEADERSHIP STUDIES: OUR BUILDING. Accessed November 14, 2012. http://www.k-state.edu/leadership/building/photos.html.

[411] Editorial, MANHATTAN MERCURY, July 4, 1997.

[412] (A. Abe Fattaey, May 22, 2013, email message to author)

[413] (Tom Rawson, April 21, 2014, email message to author)

[414] (Abe Fattaey, December 12, 2014, email message to author)

[415] (Victoria L. Ecuyer, January 23, 2012, email message to author) (Tom Rawson, January 30, 2013, email message to author)

[416] (Victoria L. Ecuyer, January 23, 2012, email message to author)

[417] Letter from Chuck Werring to Jon Wefald, April 26, 2010.

[418] Letter from Chuck Werring, April 26, 2010.

[419] Wikipedia 2012, "Jim Colbert." Accessed November 11, 2012. http://en,wikipedia.org/wiki/Jim_Colbert.

[420] COLBERT HILLS: A CHAMPION'S VISION, May 1, 2000.

[421] (Bernie Haney, December 5, 2012, email message to author)

[422] (Bernie Haney, December 5, 2012, email message to author)

[423] (Bernie Haney, December 5, 2012, email message to author)

424 (Bernie Haney, December 5, 2012, email message to author)

425 (Bernie Haney, December 5, 2012, email message to author)

426 Letter from Christine Young to Jon Wefald, April 2, 2010.

427 (Jim Lewis, August 23, 2006, email message to author)

428 (Jim Lewis, August 23, 2006, email message to author)

429 (Jim Lewis, November 26, 2012, email message to author)

430 (Jim Lewis, November 26, 2012, email message to author)

431 (Jim Lewis, November 26, 2012, email message to author)

432 (Jim Lewis, November 26, 2012, email message to author)

433 Charles Reagan, POLITICAL POWER AND PUBLIC INFLUENCE: THE LANDON LECTURES, 1984, 2010, xi-xii.

434 Reagan, LANDON LECTURES, xi-xii.

435 Reagan, LANDON LECTURES, 164-69.

436 Reagan, LANDON LECTURES, 164-69.

437 Reagan, LANDON LECTURES, 164-69.

438 Reagan, LANDON LECTURES, iv.

439 Ed Rice, NOTES COMPILED ON THE EVENTS OF JUNE 11, 2008.

440 Rice, NOTES COMPILED.

441 Rice, NOTES COMPILED.

442 Rice, NOTES COMPILED.

443 Rice, NOTES COMPILED.

444 Rice, NOTES COMPILED.

445 Rice, NOTES COMPILED.

[446] (Brad Everett, May 25, 2014, email message to author)

[447] Column in MANHATTAN MERCURY, Wednesday, June 18, 2014

Index

–A–

–B–

–C–

–H–

–I–

–J–

–K–

–Q–

–R–

–S–

–X–

–Y–

–Z–